WHAT
MAKES US
CATHOLIC

WHAT
MAKES US
CATHOLIC

EIGHT GIFTS FOR LIFE

THOMAS H. GROOME

HarperSanFrancisco
A Division of HarperCollins*Publishers*

HarperCollins books may be purchased for educational, business, or sales pro-
motional use. For information please write: Special Markets Department,
HarperCollins Publishers, Inc., 10 East 53rd Street, New York, NY 10022.

HarperCollins Web site: http://www.harpercollins.com

HarperCollins®, ✦®, and HarperSanFrancisco™ are trademarks of
HarperCollins Publishers, Inc.

FIRST EDITION
Designed by Joseph Rutt

Library of Congress Cataloging-in-Publication Data
Groome, Thomas H.
What makes us Catholic : eight gifts for life / Thomas H. Groome.
p. cm.
Includes bibliographical references and index.
ISBN 0-06-063398-0 (cloth : alk. paper) — ISBN 0-06-063399-9 (pbk. : alk. paper)
1. Catholic Church—Doctrines. 2. Spirituality—Catholic Church. I. Title.

BX1751.3 .G76 2001
282—dc21   2001039770

02 03 04 05 06 ❖/QM 10 9 8 7 6 5 4 3 2

For Theodore Thomas Griffith-Groome,
our precious "Ted"

CONTENTS

Contents

"WHAT'S THE MENU?"—AFTER FISH ON FRIDAY

What Makes Us Catholic might interest a whole potpourri of people; ranging among the locals from devout faithful to fall-en-away, and then friendly, critical, or curious neighbors. It's for anyone who might wonder, What does it mean to be a Catholic Christian now? At the fore of such motley crew, I'm talking to three friends—Kevin, Jackie, and Bob. Each, in their own way,[1] prompted me to write this book.

Kevin paused pensively after a quaff of beer. I knew there was something on his mind, so I waited. Finally he said, "Yeh know something? When the hospital asked for religious preference, I automatically put down Catholic. Then I wondered what that means for me, if anything anymore."

"Why did you put it down?" I probed. "You could've ticked off 'no preference' or just skipped that part of the form."

"Aw gawd," he drawled in his Boston brogue, "I could never do that. And what if something went wrong during d'operation?"

"But you were only having your appendix out," I reminded him.

"Yeah, but yeh never know," he said with a sage expression, "yeh never know!"

Kevin was reared in a traditional Boston Irish-Catholic family—a bit of a redundancy. His parents likely had never missed Sunday Mass, barring serious illness. Though they didn't agree with everything the pope said, to them he was "The Holy Father," spoken of with reverence. To Kevin, insofar as he bothered to comment, the current pope was—to quote verbatim—"for the birds." Kevin didn't just disagree with the pope on church matters, however; he ignored him. A Boston College MBA gradu-

ate, he was a rising young star at a major company and had long ceased attending church, "never darkenin' the door," as he happily admitted, "not since Granny's funeral."

"Well," I interjected after another pause, "you often say you've left the church. And every faith community should have a well-marked exit sign, leaving members free to leave—and free to stay, whichever they choose. So what's the big deal?"

"Ah, but it's not that simple," Kevin said with an air of explaining things to me. "Yeh see, I didn't feel I'd lied on that form. It felt right to put down Catholic. That's what I am. But then, it should mean something for me. But what . . . ?" and he trailed off again. Before changing the subject, Kevin offered, "Maybe yeh should write a book about that—what it means to be Catholic, even after yeh've left the church."

What Makes Us Catholic is an attempt to engage the Kevins—people steeped in Catholicism but no longer "practicing"—to reflect again on something so significant to their identity. For leaving a local church is easy compared to erasing the traces of Catholic socialization. It has likely shaped their personhood and ways in the world, their defining images and stories, their values, virtues, and vices, their hopes and fears, even their sense of humor. Many Kevins still cherish their "Catholic" identity, albeit in quotes, although they are hard-pressed to say why. I've an atheist friend who insists nonetheless that he's a "Catholic" atheist. Such persistence is particularly true of people soaked in old Catholic marinades, where faith and culture have melded into one; they seep to the marrowbone.

My purpose is not to bring the Kevins back within the fold, though I'd want them to know the breadth of welcome they could find and that they have much to contribute. Rather, I invite them to critically reconsider and deliberately choose what could be life-giving from their faith tradition. In the words of the poet T. S. Eliot, they might come to know it "again . . . for the first time." Kevin's instinct is right; his Catholicism can still *mean* a lot to him and especially to his spirituality for life.

A tall, handsome woman of middle years, Jackie had a dignified bearing and a gentle way about her. I was not surprised when she introduced herself as a lay Franciscan on the first day of my course on Pastoral Theology. Pursuing a doctorate in ministry, she made clear from the start her commitment to the social responsibilities of Christian faith.

Later, in a one-on-one advisement session, Jackie shared some of her faith story. She was brought up a Catholic but "left" as a young woman after some very painful experiences. Her growing feminist consciousness encouraged her departure, and she never intended to return. As she explained, "I felt like the church didn't respect me as a woman, and why be part of an institution that claims to be Christian but doesn't practice Jesus' respect for everyone?"

I was saddened and yet understood why she felt the need to leave. "But, then, whatever brought you back?" I asked.

"Well, over the years, I searched for a church home, found some fine communities of faith, but always felt there was something missing, something valuable I'd left behind. Eventually, and bringing my feminist convictions with me, I decided to return. Of course, it was a little easier to come back through the Franciscans. Francis surely had one of the better renderings of Catholicism." I agreed.

Jackie now helps run a program for "recovering Catholics" in a Franciscan parish. I offered that she was surely ideal for the job but pushed a little. "Can you say more precisely what it was that brought you back to the Catholic church, especially since things don't look any better for women in ordained ministry?"

"Well," she mused, searching for words, "simple enough! I recognized that the greater good here outweighs the sinfulness. I also wanted to work from within for its reform, to keep alive the hope of an inclusive church."

We chatted on about how she now finds her feminism confirmed by her Catholic faith, how the two enrich each other. We agreed that there is a canon within the canon of Scripture and Tradition—a few overarching principles that guide the interpretation of everything else—and that *justice for all* is certainly one of them. We reminded ourselves that "truth will triumph," however long it may take; that the church is a pilgrim people—never stationary. The Spirit surely has surprises in store.

For days thereafter I kept returning to my conversation with Jackie, wondering how to express what she and many like her—educated postmodern women—still find worthwhile in Catholic Christianity. What "greater good" makes it possible for committed feminists—and divorced people and gay people and so on—to hang in with Catholicism? For that matter, why do some quarter of a million adults in the United States choose to become Catholic Christians each year? What attracts them to join or the Jackies to return? That is what I seek to answer in this book.

My workshop in Chicago had only just begun when Bob, a gray-haired older man, slowly rose to his feet. Steadying himself on the back of the folding chair in front of him, his voice quivered as he began, but soon Bob was on a roll. "You asked how we feel about our Catholic identity," he said rhetorically. "Well, let me tell you. I feel betrayed and hurt, and I'm damn mad about it." I was taken aback but urged him to go on. All eyes were now riveted on Bob.

"I grew up in the old church—Catholic school, altar boy, do whatever Father or Sister tells you. Would never dream of missing Sunday Mass or eating meat on Fridays. For my family, the parish was the center of our lives. We said the Rosary together every night and had pictures and statues of Jesus or Mary or the saints in every room. We blessed ourselves coming and going with holy water. For God's sake, kids could tell I was Catholic at the town pool from the medal my mother pinned to my trunks." Many laughed in recognition.

"Then, along came Vatican II in the sixties and all the changes. No one hated them more than me at first, but we had a good staff in our parish, did a lot of adult education. Slowly, I began to like the renewal that was happening in the church; I became a Vatican II Catholic. I felt more at home than ever in my faith, proud of it.

"But then we got a new pope, and a different kind of bishop, and an old style of pastor—though he's still quite young. Now I'm feeling dragged back to a church more like when I was a kid—but less compassionate, and without the fun we had then. Many church leaders don't have a fire in the belly for Vatican II and its efforts at renewal. I know for sure I can't go back, but I don't know where to go instead. I feel lost about what it means to be Catholic anymore."

The people applauded; Bob had struck a chord. I thanked him for his honesty and for riveting our attention on the theme of the workshop.

Many conversations later, this book attempts to respond to the confused and hurting Bobs—the Catholics who will never leave their church but feel torn between the open spirit of Vatican II and signs of a more repressive era being restored. I want to bolster their confidence that the renewal of Vatican II was indeed the work of the

Holy Spirit and will continue to bear its life-giving fruits. The principle proposed two thousand years ago by Gamaliel remains true: whatever is from God, cannot be stopped (see Acts 5:38–39).

What Makes Us Catholic, then, is intended for Catholics who span the spectrum: from the devout to the alienated; from radical reformers to defenders of the status quo; from tired cradle-members to curious catechumens and enthusiastic neophytes; from baby boomers who feel that Vatican II has been betrayed to GenXers who wonder what the boomers are whining about; from returnees who are happier the second time around to those who will never return but could bring with them a rich spiritual legacy.

And because I cast my presentation of Catholicism as a spirituality for life, neighbors in the Body of Christ, and perhaps people of other or no religious persuasion, may find rich resources here for their own journey. It's the spirituality of Catholic Christianity that can transcend the bounds of church institution—even for its own members. At the depth level of spiritual wisdom, the great religious traditions can enhance each other, reminding us that God is greater than all our religions.

As chapter 8 elaborates, Catholic Christianity ought to share its spiritual wisdom at the great table of humankind, as well as welcome all who choose it as their particular home within God's family. Though *catholic* is usually taken to mean "universal," this was more Aristotle's use of the term than how early Christians understood it. Ignatius of Antioch, the first on record to call the Church catholic (circa 107), had *inclusion* in mind more than *universal*. Inclusion, in fact, is closer to the roots of *catholic; katha holos* literally means "gathering in the whole," or, more colloquially, "all are welcome."

To its credit—and often embarrassment—Catholic Christianity has approximated inclusivity, at least by way of saints and sinners. It boasts the Francis of Assisi and Mother Teresa types but also numbers some of the cruelest tyrants of history. The old rumor that Stalin, Hitler, and Mussolini all once served as altar boys is likely true. Today the catholicity of Catholicism endures. Not that I classify any of the following as saint or sinner—and the tradition forbids a rush to judgment—but we can count as Catholic both Frank McCourt and Bill Bennett, Dorothy Day and Mother Angelica, Babe Ruth and Yogi Berra, Ted Kennedy and Pat Buchanan, Madonna and Lawrence Welk, William F. Buckley, Jr., and Anna Quindlen, all studies in contrast.

But what, pray tell, do they share as Catholic identity? Is it as tenuous as what's common to Winnie *the* Pooh and John *the* Baptist—same middle name? Or is it only that statistically they are more likely to feel guilty about sexual sins and to have a keener sense of humor than most? Or are there some deep currents of faith and imagination that these folks share as a river of truth and meaning, some foundations that they might recognize as common spiritual ground? I believe there are and will try to name them here.

My focus throughout this book is Catholic Christian identity—when it seeps into people's perspectives and practices, when it permeates their everyday lives. So, it is not a systematic theology of Catholic beliefs and practices. I try to describe the defining attitudes of Catholic Christianity as these might shape how people engage in the world, how they respond to the great questions of life. In other words, our focus is how Catholics might put faith to work—their spirituality. In fact, I propose that Catholic identity is a spiritual matter.

Social scientists say that we need a sense of identity to live humanly; without it, we can literally feel lost. From the Latin *identitas,* meaning "the same, repeatedly," identity is that which holds together a continuous sense of our human "being" as a person or a community. Read "being" here as both noun and verb; identity is *who* we are and *how* we live. And though our personhood should be ever maturing into new horizons, we need continuity with what went before. In the imagery of the poet William B. Yeats, identity is "the center that holds"; otherwise, "things fall apart."[2]

Social scientists also explain that identity emerges as we absorb the worldview, value system, and sense-of-person reflected in our family of origin and then in the culture and society around us. We interiorize these foundational perspectives in a thousand different ways, but most potent are the symbols that we encounter and make our own. Their national *flag* can touch the very core of people far more effectively than a *definition* of patriotism.

A conspicuous feature of Catholic Christianity is how symbol-laden it is, even raising some to the status of *sacrament*—symbols endowed by God's grace to cause what they symbolize (chapter 4). Until recently, Catholics had myriad symbols that nurtured their identity, tangible things that they could observe, practice, even hang on a wall. "Fish on Friday" was among the most effective.

Christians learned the spiritual practice of fasting from their Jewish forebears in faith, and from the early centuries onward chose to abstain from meat on Fridays. After the sixteenth-century Reformation, Catholics retained Friday abstinence as obligatory, whereas Protestants, preferring to emphasize the gratuity of God's grace, gave up the practice. Thereafter, "fish on Friday" became an identifying symbol for Catholic Christians. As a college student on a summer work site in London, I remember the feeling of distinctiveness when we Catholics had nothing but cheese in our Friday sandwiches, whereas other workers seemed to relish their ham or beef all the more that day. Friday abstinence helped "us" and "them" to know who was who.

Beginning in the 1930s, a great movement of renewal swept through Catholic Christianity, reaching a crescendo with the Second Vatican Council (1962–65). As the Council's agenda, the good Pope John XXIII[3] announced a program of *aggiornamento* for the church, literally, "bringing up to date." Among other things, Vatican II would encourage a personally owned faith with less emphasis on church-made rules. No removal of regulation caused more trauma to Catholic identity than Friday abstinence. In 1966 the church simply changed the law, requiring abstinence only on Ash Wednesday and Good Friday, leaving anything further to the decision of local bishops' conferences.

With hindsight, the change was poorly made—as were many during that tumultuous era of reform. People needed adult education explaining that although the *obligation* was dropped, Friday abstinence could still be a fine spiritual practice and an enduring symbol of Catholic identity. As a Jewish friend explained his observance of kosher to me, "It reminds me to bring my faith into every aspect of my life, even decisions about what to eat." A better catechesis could have invited Catholics beyond the letter of the law—like well-heeled Bostonians feeling obliged to eat lobster on

Fridays—to embrace its spirit of self-denial and solidarity with the hungry of our planet.

Alas, the church simply announced that Friday abstinence was set aside. And though it became only one of a growing swell of discarded symbols—scuttling the statue population of churches, downplaying old pieties like Bob's family Rosary, replacing Latin at Mass with the vernacular, nuns "kicking the habit" for modern clothing—the before and after of *fish on Friday* marked a watershed for Catholic identity.

Almost forty years have passed since those heady days of upheaval and renewal launched by Vatican II. For a few, the Council went too far, making Catholicism indistinguishable from liberal Protestantism. For many more, the spirit of Vatican II has been compromised; they long to get back on track with its movement of *aggiornamento.* And for a whole generation of young people, Vatican II is ancient history. As one GenXer put it to me, "It's like Woodstock, something from the sixties"—long before he was born.

Our agenda, then, is to describe constitutive aspects of Catholic Christian identity for this time. Our statement must be faithful to the tradition at its best and yet offer a fresh horizon that nurtures a spirituality *for life for all* now. So, as two millennia recede and a third begins, it seems timely to restate *what makes us Catholic*— after fish on Friday.

By way of gratitude, I could thank a thousand people whom I've met along the way, but that must wait until "we gather at the river." So, naming a few for now, I remember with deep appreciation my parents Maggie and Terence Groome who, more than any other influence, nurtured my own Catholic identity. I thank John

Loudon, my editor at Harper, and Jim Bitney and Marie Groome for invaluable editorial help. I thank my beloved spouse, Colleen Griffith, who continues to sustain and journey with me into holiness of life together. And I thank our precious little son, Ted, to whom I dedicate this volume. Every day he brings us another joy; he is well named Theodore—"gift of God." Whatever path he chooses to go home to God, I hope the rich spiritual treasury of Catholic Christian faith can help sustain his journey.

November 1, 2001
Feast of All Saints

ONE

"WHAT STORIES TO TELL?"— INTERPRETING CHRISTIAN FAITH

WHAT STORIES TO TELL LUKE?

Marybeth gently cradled Luke out sideways. The priest intoned solemnly, "Luke, I baptize you in the name of the Father, and of the Son, and of the Holy Spirit." Water rolled down the little head into the baptismal font below. The words echoed through the cavernous old New York church with a definitive ring, as if marking a watershed, literally, with things never to be the same again. Ten-week-old Luke rendered some top-lung protest, and then surveyed the ogling assembly as if knowing he was at center stage.

The priest lit a small candle from the big Easter one and handed it to me. "Receive the light of Christ," he said, and then, with a commissioning tone, "Parents and Godparents, this light is entrusted to you to be kept burning brightly." I prayed in my heart to be a good godfather to this new member of the Body of Christ. I resolved to help his parents share with Luke the Christian faith into which, as the priest announced, "he has now been baptized."

The ceremony completed, and it being a lovely April afternoon, we walked up Broadway from Fifty-ninth to Seventy-first for a reception. The newly minted Christian, Luke, led the entourage in a regal-looking pram, a family heirloom. I fell into step with Peter, the proud father and himself brought up as a Lutheran. Peter said the ceremony meant a lot to him, that he thought the priest had done a good job. He was glad so many family and friends could come; likely some had never been at a Catholic baptism before. Then he added reflectively, "Yeh know, a lot of people have negative stereotypes about Catholicism. They think it's only about sin and guilt, but it's a lot cooler than that."

Ah, I thought to myself, now that's the version we should share with Luke—the "cool" one—the Catholic Christianity that encourages fullness of life. It has a thousand stories we could tell to this good end and some that would not serve well at all. I wondered about which is which and how to choose.

By now, however, we had reached the restaurant and I put my musings aside for another time. Then we enacted an old faith story that I would surely tell Luke someday—we had a grand party to celebrate his baptism. With lots of good food and choice wine, laughter and conversation, his Catholic socialization had made a good beginning!

MANY MANSIONS

Party over, the first years being so vital, and Luke already hearing about three blind mice, now's the time to figure out what faith stories to tell him. Every one, of course, will be a particular instance within the great spiritual story of humankind. Luke will live most humanly by honoring his "natural" desire for something more to life than meets the eye, but he also needs good stories to nurture a life-giving spirituality.

Within the spiritual story of humankind, Luke will find dozens of diverse ways for living religiously. Further, among the great religions of God's family, Luke can claim his own particular home. He is now entitled to the life-giving legacy of Christian faith into which we baptized him. And while holding this great Story in common with all Christians, he can inherit a particular version and community of it—a Catholic one.

Now, at its best, Catholic Christianity is a tremendous way to live humanly, religiously, and Christianly. It's a rich resource for growing into fullness of life as a person of God after the way of Jesus—and a lot of fun besides. Peter was right; it can be a "cool" religion. But it's not inevitable that Luke will encounter a life-giving version of Catholicism; the negative stereotypes have their warrant. This brings us back to the question of what stories to tell Luke and how to decide.

So, how to proceed when interpreting Catholicism? I first want to say, "With caution." To proceed with caution is well advised, of course, when approaching identity in any religion. Indeed, when people truly embrace the spirituality of a great religious tradition, they live it in life-giving ways and promote harmony among humankind. On the other hand, there is a surface kind of religious identity that is more sectarian than spiritual; over history, such biased religion has divided with terrifying animosity. Even today, manipulated by opportunist politicians, religion fuels the enmity behind most wars and violent conflicts. This is surely the entire opposite to God's intent in creating us spiritual beings.

For sure, *Christian* faith demands that its adherents live in loving solidarity with all humankind. Our central doctrine *that God loves all people* requires Christians to respect and care for every person, even for those very "other" to us. To claim that Christians are the only ones whom God loves and saves is a narrow sectarianism that nullifies the spirit of the gospel preached by Jesus.

Why would commitment to our own faith ever encourage Christians to be antagonistic toward people of another religion? Shouldn't the opposite be the case? Jesus himself taught, "In my Father's house, there are many mansions" (John 14:2). So, let his disciples cherish their own home within God's family, and yet appreciate—not just tolerate—the great religious pluralism of humankind. *Many* dwellings, indeed! Why would any group need to claim that theirs is the only home?

Every religion must avoid the pitfall of a destructive sectarianism. This being said, however, it's also true that every faith community needs to cherish and claim its own identity; its survival depends on it. In fact, the very future of the world may well turn on how adept we become at respecting differences while claiming particular identity. It will help Christians to juggle the two—cherish identity *and* appreciate diversity—if we remember humanity's spiritual bond as one family of God. We must celebrate what we share in common with other religious traditions, and among ourselves as Protestant and Catholic members of the one Body of Christ.

All the great religions reflect the common human experience of Transcending Mystery; they nourish the heart's desire for the largess of life. They share the conviction that the basis of everything, ourselves included, is the Transcendent—a Presence from beyond us and yet in our midst. Although life in the world may look very material, in fact it's deeply spiritual. What's more, the human spirit shares intimately in this Spirit Realm; it's our true home.

For all the great religions, the Transcendent represents ultimate truth and goodness, justice and peace; thus, people should so live. All the great religions propose religious practices and disciplines to sustain people in living out their human vocation as spiritual beings. All agree that we find more meaning and purpose, more hope and happiness by being anchored (re-ligare) in beliefs, ethics, and rituals that recognize Transcendence. And though we live our spirituality in multiple ways, all of them recommend the way of love. At its best, every great religion helps to turn people toward the neighbor with compassion.

With religions that believe in a personal divinity, Islam, for example, Christianity shares explicit faith in God, and that God embraces all humanity with unconditional love. Theistic traditions also believe that God is actively present within human history, revealing Godself, inviting people into covenant (partnership), and caring for human well-being. These religions emphasize God's great compassion, expecting the same from every people of God, with special favor for those most in need. Likewise, they believe in an afterlife and that God, though merciful, respects our responsibility—even eternally—for our conduct in this one.

With Judaism, Christians share the same roots in Hebrew faith. The Second Vatican Council did much to reaffirm "the great spiritual patrimony common to Christians and Jews."[1] The Council taught that God's covenant with the Jewish people has never been revoked, and that Christians must eradicate every trace of anti-Semitism from their hearts and Church.[2]

Judaism and Christianity share faith in God as Creator and loving Sustainer of all things, as making people in God's very own image and likeness. Both traditions emphasize that God's desire is *shalom,* a lovely and holistic word that includes justice and peace, love and compassion, freedom and fullness of life for all, and the integrity of creation. Further, they believe that God takes humankind into covenant to live as people of God according to the *shalom* that God intends.

Jews and Christians revere the Decalogue—the Ten Commandments—as governing their partnership with God and their responsibilities in the world. Both believe that with God's help people can be faithful to the divine covenant, living their faith in daily life. Both emphasize membership in a faith community, convinced that God comes to us and we go to God most readily as a people—together.

And the bond of all Christians? First and foremost, Catholics must think of themselves as Christian, and cherish their union with Protestant brothers and sisters as one Body of Christ in the world. On the night before he died, Jesus prayed for the disciples, "That they all may be one . . . so the world may believe that you sent me" (John 17:21–22). In other words, Jesus wanted the unity of the Church to be a sign of its credibility. Alas, no wonder that so many doubt it!

Saint Paul explained that Christians are "all baptized into one body" (1 Corinthians 12:13), and "though many, are one body in Christ" (Romans 12:5). What closer bond could there be than the parts of a body functioning together? Vatican II emphasized "the sacramental bond of baptism" among all Christians, making them brothers and sisters in faith.[3] The defining identity of every Christian, first and foremost, is to be a disciple of Jesus within the one Body of Christ—the Church—and it existing "for the life of the world" (John 6:51). (Note: I will capitalize *Church* only when it clearly refers to both Catholic and Protestant.)

All Christians must live what Jesus called "the greatest commandment" by loving God and neighbors—even enemies—as oneself. In fact, our faith calls us to love as Jesus loved. "Love one another as I have loved you" (John 15:12). Christians should function as one body to help realize God's reign of peace, justice, holiness, and fullness of life for all. Beyond these bonds of love and service, we share the Bible as the inspired Word of God, and the same basic profession of faith. All mainline Protestant and Catholic Christians accept the Trinitarian synthesis expressed in the Nicene and Apostles' creeds—the great professions of the Church's common faith.

In one way or another, we "give our hearts" (root meaning of *creed*) in shared profession:

- We profess faith in God as loving Creator who takes humankind into partnership to bring about God's reign for all creation.

- We profess faith in Jesus as fully human and divine, and the promised Messiah—the Christ; whose life models *the way* to live as a Christian people of God; whose death and resurrection empower us to so live and effects God's "liberating salvation"[4] in human history.

- We profess faith in the Holy Spirit as "the giver of life," who "with the Father and the Son is worshipped and glorified"— the third person of the blessed Trinity; that the Spirit guides and graces persons and the whole Church to be faithful to their divine covenant, encouraging them to live in *right relationship* with God, self, others, and creation.

- We claim the same baptism and vocation to become a Church that is *one* in charity and faith, *holy* by God's Spirit working through the lives of its people, *catholic* by its inclusivity and openness of mind and heart, and *apostolic* through its faithfulness to the foundations laid by Jesus.

- Together we aspire to enter the communion of saints; we rejoice in God's mercy that is always on offer; we hope for resurrection as whole persons—body and all; and we trust the promise of eternal life in God's presence.

Whatever stories we tell Luke, we must draw then from this common Christian Story. Its great themes—God, Jesus, Spirit, Church, and so on—intertwine throughout this book, as they must, to reflect the common core of Christian faith. Although I will accent some aspects as central to Catholic identity, at bedrock all disciples of Jesus share the same Christian Story.

And even as Luke is reared Catholic Christian, we should encourage him to appreciate Protestant Christianity as well. We can tell how Pope John Paul II, honoring the five hundredth anniversary of Martin Luther's birth (1983), publicly thanked the great Reformer for helping the whole Church to reclaim the *primacy of faith*, the *centrality of the Bible*, and the *priesthood of all believers*. Rather than reducing the Reformation to one period in history, we will tell how Saint Augustine urged Christians to be "always reforming" the Church. In time, we can teach Luke that the original Protestant principle—to protest everything that is not of God's reign—is the baptismal responsibility of every Christian. In fact, the Catholic church needs good healthy protest to avoid becoming an idol to itself.

Every Christian must promote the unity among disciples for which Jesus prayed. But such work (formally called ecumenism) should never mean blending all beyond distinction, like a bunch of mix-ins swirled to an ice-cream smoothie. *Unity* among Christians should not mean uniformity but *reconciled diversity*. The Christian symbol of the Trinity reflects both unity and diversity within God; the Church should reflect likewise. Each branch and tradition has its particular gifts to contribute to the universal Christian community. Thus, not in spite of but because of an ecumenical spirit we may ask, What makes us Catholic?

Before responding (chapters 2–9), I will review *the theological method* that underlies my attempt; in other words, explain *how* we might decide what stories to tell Luke. I do this, first, to help the reader consider not only *what* I'm proposing but *how* I arrive at such proposals. More important, I invite you to consider adopting such an approach yourself, if you have not already done so. Now, people less interested in the method may want to pass on to chapter 2—skipping the preparations in favor of the meal. But the hard work here may render lasting rewards. After fish on Friday, Catholics need to learn to fish themselves.

An aspect of maturing in faith is learning to think theologically—how to "do" theology. At its best, theology means figuring out how to bring faith and life together. So, the theological method I recommend is that people reflect on their lives from the perspective of faith, and on faith from the perspective of their lives. Quite simply, I will encourage *bringing life to faith, and faith to life*. In fact, whether we advert to it or not, all Christians have their own way of figuring out what their faith means for their daily lives. Before reading my proposal, take a moment to reflect and respond to the following questions.

FOR REFLECTION AND CONVERSATION

- How do you make choices regarding your own faith and spirituality? What are some of the patterns and guidelines you follow?

- Think about sharing Christian faith with a small child, as parent or godparent, family, friend, or catechist. What foundations would you try to lay? How and why do you choose them?

INTERPRETING THE SCRIPTURES AND TRADITIONS OF CHRISTIAN FAITH

The fountain of Christian Faith is God's revelation that finds echo in the human heart. The formal means that God employs to communicate with us—the official media of Christian revelation—are Scripture and Tradition, the latter what has emerged over time as central beliefs and practices of the faith. As chapter 5 will review, Catholics emphasize interpreting God's revelation within the Church—in conversation as a faith community—and lay more store by Tradition than do most Christian denominations. For now it's enough to say that Scripture and Tradition carry forward the deep currents of beliefs, rituals, and ethics that commingle as the great river of Christian Faith.

Our first scriptures are the books of the Old Testament, the vital legacy of Hebrew tradition to Christian faith. Many now favor the term *Hebrew Bible* out of respect for Judaism, avoiding the connotation of "old" as out-of-date or replaced by something "new." Christians are ever indebted to and bonded with Jewish brothers and sisters by sharing their sacred scriptures and Hebrew heritage. The uniquely Christian scriptures are the books of the New Testament: the Gospels, Epistles, Acts of the Apostles, and Book of Revelation—all writings that emerged from the first Christian communities. These two "testaments" of God's revelation make up the Christian Bible.

The Bible's divine revelation had its beginnings within communities of faith that reflected on their experiences of God's presence and saving deeds in their lives. From these reflections on experience, divinely inspired authors wove together written texts, expressing God's revelation through the language and thought patterns of their time and place. These texts ever remain a medium through which people can encounter a "word of God" for their lives now.

Catholics have generally avoided biblical fundamentalism, that is, taking everything in the Bible literally. As Vatican II summarized, the Bible is the word of God "expressed in human language." So, God's revelation is not a direct divine communiqué—a fax from God—but comes "like human discourse."[5] As a result, Scripture and likewise Tradition always require *interpretation*—figuring out what they mean for here and now.

Since the fourth century, Christians have agreed upon the *canon* of the New Testament. These are the books—twenty-seven in all—that the Church formally recognizes as divinely inspired to reflect the "good news" of Jesus Christ, and as establishing the "authoritative guide" *(canonicus)* to Christian faith.

At one time, a controversy raged between Protestants and Catholics concerning the number of books in the Hebrew scriptures. Protestants favored a shorter list, whereas Catholics added some Greek texts not found in the original Hebrew Bible. Today, however, Protestant-sponsored Bible translations (e.g., the prestigious New Revised Standard Version) include both the agreed upon and the additional books, sometimes called apocrypha. With scripture scholars collaborating to translate the ancient texts according to rigorous scholarship, the distinction between the Protestant Bible and the Catholic Bible is largely passé.

Beyond the canon of Scripture, Christian Tradition develops as a medium of revelation down through history. As Christian communities have lived their faith in various times and cultures, facing new questions in each era, the Holy Spirit has guided the whole Church to discern and grow in its understanding of God's original revelation in the Bible. Gradually, with community consensus and the testing of time, great doctrines and commitments have blossomed as central to Christian faith. For example, that the one historical person, Jesus, had two natures—human and divine—is a central doctrine of Christian faith that is not explicitly stated in the New Testament. It is certainly true that the roots are there, but this doctrine was not expressed precisely until the Council of Nicea in 325, and the Council of Chalcedon (451) clarified it further. Since then, belief in the divinity and humanity of Jesus has been a pillar of Christian Tradition.

It's important to remember that not all Christian tradition is of equal weight; not all deserves a capital *T.* Vatican II explained that tradition has "a hierarchy of truths, since they vary in their relationship to the foundation of Christian faith."[6] We might say that Christian faith has teachings that are "major league" (central dogmas and doctrines), "minor league" (common church instruction), and "local league" (favorite emphases in different times or cultures). And though there has never been an official list of what are "major league" articles of faith, clearly something like the divinity-humanity of Jesus belongs at the top of the hierarchy. On the other hand, the common teaching about Limbo, once taken very seriously by Catholics, was, in fact, so close to the bottom that it fell away entirely. The *Catechism of the Catholic Church* (1994) never mentions it.[7]

Catholicism emphasizes interpreting Scripture and Tradition within the faith life of the Church. In other words, it proposes that Christians can best discern their faith, not by themselves individually, but in conversation as a faith community and guided by its magisterium—the Church's official teaching voice. It is enough to say here that this ongoing communal discernment requires dialogue between the faith of *ordinary Christians,* the research of *scholars* in scripture and theology, and—for Catholics—the stewardship of the college of *bishops* in union with the pope. Typically the pope, continuing the leadership of Peter in the first Christian community, expresses the official faith of Catholic Christians as it needs to be clarified or developed. Ideally the pope fulfills this function—the Petrine office—by drawing into consensus the sentiments of *ordinary Christians, scholars,* and *bishops.*

So, again, what stories to tell Luke? At first blush, the response would seem quite straight forward: the Bible and Christian tradition as taught by the Church. Ah, but this is not as simple as it sounds. For the Bible and tradition are in "human language" and reflect the cultures of their origin; we receive them in very different times and cultures. As I will elaborate (chapters 3 and 5), God's presence and self-disclosure continue through all times and cultures; God's ongoing revelation in people's daily lives must also be considered. So, we always need *to interpret* the meaning of Scripture and Tradition for our lives now, to figure things out rather than expect pat answers. Here, the Bible itself is our model, for it reinterprets itself from one book to another. For example, the Hebrew people interpreted the story of Exodus quite differently when they had a powerful monarchy in place than when they were a dispossessed people in exile.

And what of the Bible's contradictions and problematic bits? How could God have made light on the first day of creation and the sun and moon on the fourth (see Genesis 1)? Is it really God's revelation that disobedient teenagers be stoned to death (see Deuteronomy 21:18–21)? More unsettling are instances like the psalmist asking God to bash the heads of enemy children against the rocks (Psalm 137:7–9); or the Israelite leader Jephthah sacrificing his own daughter rather than lose face after a public boast (see Judges 11). Surely such less-than-edifying texts—and there are many—reflect human sinfulness rather than God's revelation. And what of Saint Paul telling wives to be "submissive" to their husbands and slaves to obey their masters (Colossians 3:18, 22)? Surely this was not divine revelation but Paul reflecting the cultural mores of his day. Note that the Risen Christ spent time "opening the minds of disciples, helping them to understand the scriptures" (Luke 24:45); the Christian community has continued this effort ever since.

As the scriptures need interpretation, the same is equally true of Christian tradition. The fact that a tradition emerged after the Bible was written attests that God's revelation continues to unfold—to be ever old and ever new. As Vatican II taught boldly, "The tradition which comes from the apostles *develops* in the Church with the help of the Holy Spirit. For there is a growth in the understanding of the realities and the words which have been handed down."[8] In other words, tradition is enduring but not unchanging. To repeat tradition as just "the same old stuff" is not likely to encourage vital and living faith.

As for telling Luke to "just accept all the teachings of the Church," the simplicity is certainly tempting. But how about the fact that those teachings have been terribly wrong at times—like approving of slavery or encouraging anti-Semitism. Anyhow, the Church's function as teacher requires the whole community to participate, not a small group doing all the teaching and the rest doing all the learning. So, for Luke to mature in Christian faith he should be a player not just a spectator, reaching personal conviction in conversation rather than simply following what "they" say.

While Christians have great formal sources of revelation available to them in Scripture and Tradition, and are guided by the corporate wisdom of their faith community, they have no pat formulas for integrating their lives and faith into "living faith." To figure out the most life-giving version of Christian faith—what stories to tell Luke—the whole Church and each member must take an approach of *interpretation*. In fact, *all* we ever have as human beings is interpretation. This does not mean that our figurings are unreliable. With good guidelines and the help of God's Holy Spirit, we can always know enough from Christian Story to live faithfully as a people of God.

Daily we interpret the meaning of every action, event, and experience that comes our way. To be human is to reflect on our lives, to try to make sense out of them—we are interpreters by nature. When we interpret ancient texts of Scripture and Tradition, however, we are also trying to *bridge the gap* between symbols of meaning from a previous time and our present-life situations. We are trying to uncover what their *original* meaning might mean for *now*.[9]

Theorists say that we can break down interpretation into three moments: *understanding, evaluating,* and *applying.* Even as we try to *understand* something, we are making *judgments* about it and imagining its *application* to life. In practice, the three intertwine, often in the blink of an eye.

You are approaching a green traffic light that turns yellow. In an instant, you (1) recognize what a yellow light means *(understanding)*, (2) wonder whether to speed up or hit the brakes *(judgment)*, and (3) make a choice, deciding to stop *(application)*. Ah, but you forgot the social context of your interpretation (more below). For you are in Boston where the common response to a yellow light is to hit the pedal rather than the brakes. Now the driver behind, who almost rear-ended your car, is honking angrily and flashing hand signs at you. And you are off into a fresh round of interpretation. What *do* those hand signs mean?

Daily life reminds that we can misinterpret even simple things. When it comes to interpreting Christian Story, it would surely help to have guidelines for making reliable interpretations and drawing out what is most life-giving. I will suggest five. In summary, Christian communities and persons should approach their scriptures and traditions: (1) as a great unfolding Story of the vital partnership between God and humankind, and with the Vision of God's Reign; (2) bringing life to interpret Christian Story and Christian Story to interpret life; (3) expecting to encounter old and new spiritual wisdom; (4) being alert for distortions and forgotten legacies; and (5) always choosing *for life for all.*

These five rules of thumb overlap and intermingle as a theological method. When they are followed in conversation with and as the Church, Christians can appropriate as their own the spiritual wisdom of their scriptures and traditions for each time and place.

1. Approach Christian Faith as a Great Unfolding Story of
the Vital Partnership Between God and Humankind, and
with the Vision of God's Reign

If we read a book entitled *The Complete Works of William B. Yeats,* we expect—even before we begin—to encounter some fine poetry. If we're reading Dostoevsky, we expect a good novel and we read it as such. Likewise, the prior sense we have of Christian faith greatly shapes how we interpret a particular text or symbol within it. So, this first suggestion lends one great overarching guideline—a "prior sense"—to shape all our interpretations.

An Unfolding Story. The formal media of Christian revelation are Scripture and Tradition—sometimes I capitalize to remind of their normative status. Rather than fall back into the old Reformation-era debate of "scripture *or* tradition," as if the two could be separated, it is far better to see them as interdependent sources of the one Christian revelation. Likewise, people can mishear both terms as describing something static and final, as declaring divine revelation closed. Indeed, all Christians agree that the canon of Scripture permits no additions, and "tradition" usually implies repeating something over and over—that's how it gets to be a tradition.

Without abandoning these time-honored terms, we may avoid some old arguments and misunderstandings by approaching scripture and tradition as one great *Christian Story* that continues to unfold and is far from over. *Story* can reflect the continuity and vitality of Christian faith, and might make it more engaging for people's lives. All of us love a good story and find in it some reflection of ourselves. Christian Story, like any other, has a great overarching narrative, with characters and plots, the serious and comic, the meaningful and tragic, sins and graces, heroes and villains, a few saints, and sinners galore. And like every great story, it can be retold and embellished from one generation to the next, remaining ever old and ever new.

Christian Story is "told" in many forms. Besides the canon of Scripture, Christian Story has dogmas, doctrines, and creeds; liturgies, sacraments, and symbols; theologies and philosophies; ethics and laws, virtues and values; spiritualities, lifestyles, and models of holiness; songs, music, dance, and drama; art, artifacts, and architecture; community structures and forms of governance; ways to sanctify time and celebrate feasts; and always more. It includes "the whole story" of Christian faith down through history. The enduring story line throughout is God's loving partnership with humankind for our salvation.

A Vital Partnership. Chapter 3 will elaborate a particular way to look at life. For now, we can view our lives in the world and the whole affair of human history as a divine-human *partnership* or *covenant.* God is ever present, reaching out in love to humankind and empowering us to respond as partners in realizing God's best intentions for ourselves and creation. By God's design and grace, the divine-human covenant amounts to a *vital partnership.*

It is *vital* in many senses: as engaging the whole person and the whole community, as lively and to be lived, as invigorating and ever renewing, as revealing who we are and our finest possibilities. The partnership is *vital,* too, in that human participation is of real importance. Although God could bring about God's reign in history without us, God has chosen to wait upon human cooperation. So, God takes us into partnership and graces us with the freedom and capacity to respond by living as people of God.

Christian Story reflects how this partnership has unfolded and continues to unfold, beginning with God's covenant with the Hebrew people, reaching its apex in Jesus the Christ, and continuing as Christian people live their faith throughout history. Through this Story, Christians in all eras and cultures can find identity in faith, discerning what to believe, how to worship, and the ethics to live by.

Vision of God's Reign. I use the term *vision* to describe how the Story challenges Christians to live their faith. Christian Vision includes the invitations and expectations, promises and demands, consolations and corrections that the Story always means for lives now. Every instance of Christian Story has its Vision that should be realized by Christians in the world. The Story that "God loves us" brings the mandate to love others; that "God forgives us," to "forgive those who trespass against us." Jesus' feeding the hungry requires reaching out to the poor of our time and place. Such is the case for every instance of Christian Story; each aspect has its corresponding Vision.

The defining Christian Vision is the *reign of God*. Christians should live all their lives toward this horizon. The later books of the Hebrew scriptures propose *reign of God* as the divine vision for humankind and creation—God's dream for us. Scholars agree that *God's kingdom come* was the guiding passion and defining purpose of Jesus' life as well.

Overall, the Bible represents God's reign as both personal and social, spiritual and political, already and not yet, this-worldly and pointing to eternal life, to be "done on earth as it is in heaven." God's reign summarizes God's unbounded and unconditional regard for all humankind, intending peace and justice, love and freedom, holiness and fullness of life for all people and the integrity of creation. God's reign is the realization of *shalom*.

Because God's reign is the divine desire for humankind, its sentiments are reflected in the human heart. Listening to our own authentic desires, we get an intuitive sense of what the reign of God is about. Our own best hopes alert us to what to look for when interpreting Christian Story. The best sentiments of our hearts can help us to recognize and choose what is *for life for all*.

The reign of God as overarching guideline can help us negotiate the ambiguous aspects of Christian Story. For example, when we hear a "hard saying" of Jesus such as "I came not to bring peace but the sword" (Matthew 10:34), we can intuit that Jesus was not calling people to war; doing so would be contrary to God's reign. Likewise, we can recognize Paul's admonition to women and slaves noted earlier as reflecting the social mores of his time, not God's loving will. On the other hand, Paul's statement that men and women are equal in Jesus (see Galatians 3:28) is integral to God's intentions for us. To discern what is and what isn't divine revelation, then, it helps to ask, Does this promote or diminish the reign of God?

2. Bring Life to Interpret Christian Story and Christian Story to Interpret Life

Bringing life to interpret Christian Story means that we draw upon our whole life in the world to help us figure out what the Story means for now. This guideline advises that we ask reflectively, What does life help us to find in Christian Faith? and what does Christian Faith help us to find in life? This amounts to a kind of conversation between the faith Story and our lives in the world. As always in efforts to make good judgements, whether looking at life, or to Christian faith, or mediating a conversation between them, we have the "built-in" human guidelines of: (a) "what makes sense" in that it is coherent?; (b) "what rings true" to life and lived experience?; (c) "what will be best" for human well-being?

By "life" here I mean everything about us—all our experiences and actions, thoughts and feelings, wisdom of mind and body, as well as what's going on in the community, society, and culture around us. In point of fact, we always bring our lives—with their wisdom and blind spots, healthy passions and distorting prejudices—to interpret everything. But we are often unconscious of our personal perspective. This guideline recommends that we become *conscious* of what we bring to interpret Christian Story. I can think of three reasons why this consciousness is important.

First, because God is ever present in our daily lives, revealing Godself in our ordinary experiences and gracing us to respond. Discerning our faith requires paying attention to what God is revealing through the everyday, and bringing this wisdom to reread scripture and tradition. God's present invitation is precisely what we must discern in the light of Christian Story. So, bringing our own stories—our experiences and activities, the reflections of our minds, the feelings of our hearts, the world of our culture and society—to interpret Christian Story seems imperative if we are to recognize God's word *for now.*

Second and closely related, if we Christians are to live our faith—more than just analyze it—we must look through our own lives toward Christian Story, and through Christian Story toward our own lives. How else can Christians be Christian except by looking at their lives and their faith and putting the two together? Standing back from Christian Story to view it "objectively"—trying to exclude our personal experiences—might appear more scholarly, but at best the interpretation will go to our heads. Christian Story is more likely to go to our hearts and hands if we consciously bring our lives to interpret it.

Third, reliable interpretation requires us to remember our sociocultural location and how this should or should not color our figurings. Recall why you almost got rear-ended in Boston traffic; a yellow light is interpreted differently *there* than elsewhere. But far beyond fitting in, becoming aware of what we bring to Christian Story helps us *to draw upon our positive perspectives* and *to minimize the negative ones.*

The fact is that all of us "have an attitude"—with assets and limitations. Our outlook on life is shaped by our emotional and physical dispositions, by our personal experiences and biography, and most of all by our culture and society. Becoming aware of our tinted lenses requires both personal and social reflection. This means reviewing our perspectives to recognize the influences that shape them, positive and negative.

Our life-giving perspectives can lend insight and worthy passions for interpreting Christian Story. Someone who has personally experienced social oppression will likely be all the more alert to the justice mandate of Christian Faith; likewise with peace, compassion, equality, and so on. For example, contemporary feminist consciousness is helping to uncover the inclusivity demanded by Christian Story and challenging the Church to rid itself of sexism. Interfacing present social consciousness with the ancient wisdom of Christian Story helps the Faith to come alive again in fresh and more life-giving ways.

At the same time, we recognize that every person and community has blind spots and bigotry fostered by their social and cultural world. The Church once cited the biblical curse of Ham upon Canaan (see Genesis 9:18–27) to legitimate slavery; it was blinded by the prejudices of the time. We can do something similar in our own time if not keenly aware of current prejudices.

3. Expect Old and New Spiritual Wisdom from the Treasury

Christian Faith is best approached as a treasury of *spiritual wisdom* rather than as a system of religious knowledge. To uncover the wisdom in Christian Story, however, we must look for as much and expect to find it. Christians should approach their Story with *expectant* hearts and minds. As countless generations have recognized God's will and wisdom through Christian faith, we can be confident to encounter as much.

Instead of expecting the Story to yield "just the same old stuff," however, Christians can anticipate both old and new wisdom. In Matthew's Gospel, Jesus proposed that every scribe who is wise in the reign of God is "like the head of a household who brings forth from the storeroom both the new and the old" (Matthew 13:52). The storeroom (some translations have "treasury") is an analogy for Jesus' own tradition of Hebrew faith. Note that Jesus even mentions the new first.

A great theorist of interpretation, Paul Ricoeur, explains that there is always a "surplus of meaning" in Christian revelation; in other words, we will never exhaust its potency for life. Our most careful and creative interpretations notwithstanding, human words about God's word will never be the last word. Echoing this sentiment, theologian David Tracy proposes that Christian Story functions like a great classic: "Classics are those texts that bear an excess and permanence of meaning . . . they always resist definitive interpretation."[10] Similarly, people can go on forever plumbing the depths of Christian Faith; its wisdom for life is inexhaustible.

Reclaiming old wisdom might well be called *interpretation for retrieval,* and though we may retrieve a rich legacy, there is also an element of rediscovery. Ancestors before us might have known this wisdom well, yet we need to have our own "Aha!" moment when we see for ourselves what it means for today. Instead of passively inheriting "the old," we can come to fresh appreciation for the wisdom of Christian Story.

What, then, of "new" wisdom from the treasury? This may surprise many Catholics, but their faith should be always birthing new possibilities, developments in beliefs, practices, and worship in response to contemporary circumstances. Remember, it is enduring but not unchanging. To repeat the sentiments of Vatican II, "The tradition which comes from the Apostles *develops* in the Church with the help of the Holy Spirit."[11] All such developments must be consistent with biblical revelation, but tested by time and the faith community, the legacy of Christian faith can constantly break new ground.

Here we reach beyond *retrieval* to *creative* interpretation; creative in that it opens new horizons for Christian faith, deepening and enriching the truths already there. This is precisely what can happen when we bring "life" to interpret Christian Story. God's revelation through present experience helps us to find the new in the old. Creative interpretation leads to developments that, given time and testing, may become Tradition. And the cycle continues.

This guideline suggests that we never approach Christian Story as a laundry list of static truths. Instead, we should rediscover the old with freshness *and* create new possibilities out of it. This great river of Christian Faith remains ever fresh because the human quest for truth—even divine truth—is never ending. Vatican II stated this point forcefully: "The Church constantly moves forward toward the fullness of divine truth until the words of God reach their complete fulfillment in her."[12] At the far side of every great truth lies an even greater one. So, we go to the treasury of Christian revelation expecting spiritual wisdom ever old and ever new.

4. Be Alert for Distortions and Forgotten Treasure

From experience we know well the human capacity for error. Our limitations and negative biases can lead us astray. Even when we know clearly what is true and good, we don't always choose them. Should it surprise us, then, that we find the same—error and sin— throughout the history of the Christian people? Besides approaching Christian Story with *retrieval* and *creativity* in mind, therefore, we also need to approach it with a bit of *healthy suspicion*. We should be alert both for distortions to authentic Christian Faith in the reigning version and for life-giving legacies that are being forgotten.

Though very embarrassing, evidence abounds of slavery and racism, of hatred of women and sexism, of intolerance and bigotry in the Church's beliefs, practices, and worship throughout its history. The Church once had its own slave ships and accepted slavery as an inevitable effect of the sin of Adam and Eve. It participated in the destruction of millions of innocent women who were put to death as witches. It fostered anti-Semitism—and thus the Holocaust—by blaming Jewish people for the death of Jesus. And it tortured and killed people for heresy instead of respecting their religious freedom.

Recognizing such sinfulness, Pope John Paul II called on Christians at the beginning of the third millennium to repent "for all those times in history when they . . . indulged in ways of think-ing and acting which were truly *forms of counter-witness and scandal.*[13] To lament and repent for our failures as Christians is the first appropriate response. Then, true repentance requires a firm purpose of amendment—the determination not to repeat such errors. And this requires being alert for similar distortions, though likely more sophisticated, in our own time.

In addition to helping us recognize distortions, healthy ques-tioning can uncover forgotten legacies, truths neglected or fallen out of favor. The treasury of any great people has such items—old valuables overlooked by the dominant perspective. A few exam-ples may stimulate your own search for *subversive memories* in Christian Story, *subversive* in that they shake the status quo and offer more life-giving possibilities.

Only recently did scholars notice umpteen instances of how Jesus included women in his life and ministry, calling them to be disciples and making women the first witnesses to the Resurrection. Indeed, women fulfilled functions in the first Christian communities that later were limited to priests. Such memories could help subvert cur-rent Catholic church polity around women in ministry.

Another example: *ekklesia* (church) originally meant an "assem-bly of equal citizens." This is still a horizon for the Church but clearly was part of its original vision of itself. Likewise, hierarchy, from the Greek *hierarche,* does not refer to levels of command on a power pyramid but rather to the ministry of helping a Christian community to work well together—"holy order"—as opposed to *anarche.* Such forgotten legacies could help to reconfigure ecclesial life and ministry. And there are a thousand more overlooked lega-cies in the treasury of Christian Story. A healthy suspicion—

toward the taken-for-granted version—can ferret them out *for life for all.*

5. Choose For Life for All

As we come away from interpreting Christian Story, we need to choose *a lived response.* It helps to have a pithy rule of thumb that builds upon the previous four and can guide decision making. I propose that Christians complete all interpretations of their Story by choosing *for life for all.*

For life captures well the biblical conviction that God totally favors *life* and calls humankind into life-giving partnership. "I have set before you life and death . . . choose life, then, that you and your descendants may live" (Deuteronomy 30:19). It echoes Jesus' great summary statement, reflected throughout his ministry, "I came that you might have life, and have it to the full" (John 10:10). At its best, Christian tradition stands radically *for life*—a theme developed in the coming chapters.

I use *for life* here in all its multilayered meanings. *For life* suggests something to be lived, done in the everyday. *For life* means favoring human well-being and the integrity of creation. *For life* connotes a lifelong affair, an ever-deepening conversion until we rest in God. And *for all* emphasizes that the choices of Christians should serve the well-being of all others as well as oneself and one's own, with the common good and personal well-being working hand in hand.

In any circumstance, if Christians interpret their Story to choose *for life for all,* they will most likely be faithful to God's loving will and the spiritual wisdom of their revelation. To clarify your own thinking now, take a moment to reflect and respond to the following questions.

FOR REFLECTION AND CONVERSATION

• What are your thoughts or feelings about interpreting Christian Faith? What are the assets of such an approach? What are its liabilities?

• Are any changes emerging in your own approach to your faith?

A CATHOLIC COLLAGE: GIFTS FOR LIFE

It's not easy to capture what lends Catholic Christians their particular identity. Like all Christians, Catholics embrace faith in God, discipleship to Jesus, dependence on the Holy Spirit, and all the great symbols that we hold in common. These make us *Christian* like other Christians and are interwoven constantly throughout this book. So, the foundation of *what makes us Catholic* is the shared faith of the whole Body of Christ; it is certainly not unique to Catholicism.

Nor could we distinguish Catholicism by what is *unique* about it, or at least it wouldn't take a book to do so. The only candidate for something truly unique to Roman Catholicism is the Petrine office, the papacy. Although it is without doubt a significant symbol, most Catholics would hasten to insist that their faith is distinguished by far more than allegiance to the pope.

In pre–Vatican II days, there seemed to be a thousand practices and "real things" that distinguished Catholic Christians. I remember the nightly Rosary in my own home and the vivid picture of the Sacred Heart of Jesus with a small light ever flickering before it. I became aware that my Protestant buddies had no such interference in their evening playtime, nor any picture of a kindly Jesus presiding over their kitchen. For a mixture of reasons—some good, some bad—after the Council such *realia* of Catholic identity seemed to just float away.

The ecumenical dialogue encouraged by Vatican II also helped Catholics to realize how much they hold in common with other Christians, and that our differences are more of emphasis than of kind. For example, all Christian denominations take seriously their call to be a faith community, but Catholicism emphasizes more than most the function of the Church in God's work of salvation. Likewise, all branches of the Christian tree encourage people to *live* their faith, but Catholics emphasize *good works* in ways that others don't.

If Catholic identity became less distinct after *fish on Friday* and less different from that of other Christians with the rising spirit of ecumenism, postmodern thinkers offer an added challenge. These social commentators claim that nothing is "essential" to any human identity, that our cultural context shapes the sense we have of ourselves. Although I don't consider myself a postmodernist, these thinkers challenge me to recognize that my own views here are more provisional than final, more local than universal.

The collage I offer could be configured with other pieces and other emphases and yet be thoroughly "Catholic." Let the reader beware, then, that mine is a very *partial* perspective in both senses of the term—limited and perspectival. So, it is certainly not exhaustive, and my partialities reflect my Irish culture of origin and life in America since young adulthood.

But then, every instance of Christian faith is filtered through some cultural lens. There has never been a cultureless Christianity—a pristine version of "the Gospel" unaffected by its historical surroundings. Jesus himself took on the identity of a first-century Palestinian Jew and remained a devout one all his life. Thereafter, Christian faith was deeply imbued with its cultural setting and soon reflected a diversity of perspectives. Why else do we have four Gospels rather than one, each "partial" in its understanding of Jesus and of Christian faith?

Over history, Catholicism has had a strong tendency to integrate faith and culture. This has produced as many Catholicisms as there are peoples who embrace it—Italian and French, Kenyan and Nigerian, Korean and Vietnamese, and a thousand more. Compare the stoic aura of German Catholicism to the festive style of Hispanic traditions, or traditional Irish acceptance of church authority to the democratic spirit of American Catholics. And multiple spiritual charisms intermingle with Catholicism's cultural diversity. Worship at a Benedictine monastery and then in a Franciscan parish and experience the contrast.

Remember, too, that there are three major expressions of Catholic Christianity, each with its own distinctiveness—Anglicanism, Eastern Orthodoxy, and the Roman communion. Moreover, within these expressions there exists an array of "rites," each with its particular style for being religious, Christian, and Catholic. Within Roman Catholicism (our focus here) one finds a great breadth of theological position and pastoral practice, ranging from conservative to liberal to radical, and many blendings between. Likely there is as much breadth within Catholicism as across the many denominations of Protestantism. Naming what distinguishes Catholic Christianity, then, might be chasing a will-o'-the-wisp.

Yet, part of the genius of Catholicism is precisely its *catholicity*, its ability to maintain unity in faith *and* welcome great diversity of expression. Somehow it manages to etch out consistent marks in very varied cultures, to maintain a common bond throughout many adaptations.

Noted sociologist Fr. Andrew Greeley proposes that Catholics experience their common bond as a characteristic imagination: "There is a distinctively Catholic imagination ... which enables Catholics to see the world through a different set of lenses."[14] Greeley's thesis seems to ring true to the lived experience of Catholics; in fact, he cites copious empirical studies to substantiate his claim.

What fuels this distinctive imagination? My proposal is that it's a combination of some deep-down emphases of Catholic Christianity, which Catholics experience in the everyday as shaping their *perspective on life* in the world. One effective way to uncover these patterns of imagination is around a *typical Catholic response to the great questions of life.* Over the next eight chapters we will review some of the abiding human questions and draw out a response from the depths of Catholic Christianity.

Further, it is my own faith that Catholic responses to the great questions come together as a *life-giving* imagination; they foster an outlook that helps to make and keep life human for ourselves and others. They respond to the deep longings of the human heart for meaning and purpose, for happiness and well-being. These emphases of Catholicism, at their best, are *gifts for life for all* with the breadth of meaning already proposed.

Here again I echo my claim that Catholicism is distinguished by its spirituality. For what else is spirituality but a faith-based outlook that permeates the everyday, a way of *bringing life to faith, and faith to life.* So, when these currents of emphasis flow together, they distinguish the great river of Catholic Christian faith—they describe *what makes us Catholic.* And when embraced as a fundamental outlook—an imagination—then Catholicism becomes a spirituality for life. The great questions:

- **Who do we think we are?** How do we understand our personhood, the possibilities and limitations of the human condition? (chapter 2)

- **What's it all about?** What is our attitude toward life in the world, both the created order and human culture? (chapter 3)

- **Are we made for each other?** How do we view relationships with others, the nature of community, the purposes of society? (chapter 4)

- **What time do we have?** What's our outlook on time, on history and its legacy of tradition? (chapter 5)

- **In what will we invest?** Is the risk of faith worthwhile; what of Christian faith as a life investment? (chapter 6)

- **What are our politics?** What values should guide our lives as citizens and the public worlds we create? (chapter 7)

- **Who is our neighbor?** What are the horizons of Christian concern and care? (chapter 8)

- **What is our heart's desire?** What do we most want out of life? Summarizes a Catholic spirituality—a theme throughout. (chapter 9)

The young musician from Ohio was mesmerized by New York City and excited about her upcoming audition, but as she stood on the corner of Fifty-sixth Street and Seventh Avenue, she felt totally lost. She knew it was around here somewhere, but . . . Then, to her relief, she saw an old man coming toward her, a violin case tucked under his arm. *Ah, he must surely know.* So she inquired, "Excuse me, sir, can you tell me how to get to Carnegie Hall?" The old musician halted, took a pensive moment, and then offered, "Practice, practice, practice."

Practice is integral to a Catholic understanding of faith. Becoming a Catholic Christian requires certain perspectives on life and then lots of practice. In fact, sociologists say that it's our regular "practices" that shape and maintain identity. So each chapter ends by suggesting practices that might help to realize the proposed outlook or imagination.

In addition to perspectives and practices, each chapter begins with a story to engage the reader in thinking about its great life theme. Then, it has three sets of questions throughout to encourage your personal reflections and, when possible, perhaps some conversation with a friend. These elements of each chapter—the focusing story, the questions, the perspectives, and the supporting practices—are crafted to encourage you go bring *your life to your faith* and *your faith to your life*. And that's always the core of what makes people Catholic—*faith at work.*

TWO

"WHO DO WE THINK WE ARE?"— LIVING AS GRACEFUL PEOPLE

OH, DO I EVER REMEMBER JOEY!

My office telephone rang. "Professor?" It was Mary Magennis, the receptionist. "There's a Joey Brown here. He doesn't have an appointment but would love to see you for a few minutes." In the blink of an eye, it all came back—my first year of teaching, and the most miserable of my career. Though a quarter-century ago, the memory remains vivid. Every teacher gets an occasional "student from hell." Joey Brown (name changed to protect the guilty) was mine in spades.

About to say I was busy, I remembered my determination back then not to let Joey force me to reject him—try mightily as he did and close as I came. Why should I lose to him now? "I'll be there in a few minutes," I said to Mary and put down the phone. I needed time to steady myself.

I sat, and the awful memories swirled around me. Had time passed at all? That Joey made himself the class atheist, communist, and anarchist was not the problem, even in theology. Nor that he was disruptive and ill mannered. It was his overt disdain for me and for everyone else in the class. All of us were relieved when Joey skipped, but pity, he usually came.

I imagined what psychologists might say about Joey's behavior—misplaced anger, needing attention, self-hatred—but no explanation relieved the sleepless nights he caused me back then. Joey would have given bad dreams to a seasoned veteran, but for me, a first-year, junior faculty member, he was a nightmare.

I figured out by midsemester that Joey was determined to break my spirit, which would amount to getting me to treat him the way he treated me. Not out of any great virtue on my part—more Irish pigheadedness—I determined not to lose the battle. By the skin of my teeth, I managed to treat him with respect, continuing to appeal to what might be his better self. I thought I'd made it. Then came the final exam.

I caught him cheating, and I lost it. I'd finally had it with Joey; I even relished the thought of turning him in. But then I became suspicious. His cheating was so obvious. Maybe he wanted me to catch him. University statute required me to report cheating. Reporting Joey, however, would mean that he, by then a last-semester senior, would not graduate. What to do? Who was Joey trying to hurt? His parents? Himself? Me? I knew he was capable of reporting me for not reporting him, and I was far from tenure. Yet, I couldn't lose now.

I insisted he take an oral exam in lieu of the written final, and Joey surprisingly agreed. He must not have known his rights to be suspended. He did okay in the oral, pulling a B for the course—brains were never his problem—and so the credits to graduate. I had not seen Joey since. Now, I ever so slowly made my way downstairs.

"Hello, Professor, remember me?" a slightly pudgy man with thinning gray hair greeted me, elation in his voice.

"Joey! Yes, yes, very well," I understated. I reached to shake his hand, but he brushed it aside and took me into a bear hug, like a long-lost buddy. And he held on, and on. Then with obvious pride he introduced his wife and two children, a boy about ten and a girl a little younger. He was clearly delighted to see me, talking a mile a minute with headlines from his life since college.

"Professor, I quote you all the time," said Joey, and his spouse added, *"Oh, yes, yes,"* as if too often. *"I'm back for my twenty-fifth; hard to believe it's that long! But I really came to thank you for all you did for me. You should know that you saved my life. I mean, do you remember the final?"* Happily, Joey seemed embarrassed. I said I did. *"Well, that turned my life around. You see, you finally brought the best out of me."*

I responded, *"Joey, you brought the best out of me, too."* I'm not sure he recognized my sincerity. And now we were both misty-eyed.

We sat and chatted for an hour, and he said good-bye with another bear hug. I marveled at how Joey had changed—and the miracles that God's grace can work.

Going out the door, he turned and said, *"Oh, Joey Junior here thinks he'd like to come to BC for college. I've told him that he must take your course."* I looked at the boy; he had his father's glint in the eye.

"Great. Joey, I'd love to have you," I lied, and made a mental note to inquire about early retirement.

THE QUESTION WE ARE TO OURSELVES

Besides stubbornness, my way of treating Joey Brown reflected the conviction that there is a "best" in every person, if yet to be uncovered. I also believed I had a *choice* about how to treat him. And by God's grace, I managed to choose—in that instance—according to *my* best.

So, allowing for the idealism of my youth, the incident reflects who I thought Joey could be as a person and who I could be—at least on a good day. And though it was God's grace that effected the change in Joey, the Spirit "worked" in part through my way of treating him. So much rides on our attitude toward this human condition of ours, on our opinion of humanity.

There is no more significant question to ask ourselves than "Who do we think we are?" Have no doubt but everyone has a strong opinion, and it affects every aspect of their daily life. The formal name for how we view the human condition is *anthropology*. Our own anthropology amounts to what we expect of others and of ourselves as persons. And it's amazing how those expectations become self-fulfilling prophecies.

Great debates about our human condition continue to rage, and always will. For example, are we shaped more by nature or nurture? Is each personality genetically programmed—through our DNA—or the product of family environment, of social and cultural influences? I don't know the answer, but it seems wise to straddle the fence. So, who we are and become as persons is shaped by *both* nature and nurture. Our natural disposition to do good things is enhanced by positive family formation; our tendency to do bad things will flourish in a negative environment.

In fact, I'd say that nature and nurture shape not only *who we are* but also *the opinion* we have of who we are. Friends of mine who have identical twins swear that one has been an optimist and the other more cautious about people from the day they were born. On the other hand, they also recognize that both kids have taken on—variously—their parents' perspective on people.

Every person is one of a kind; note how our law courts believe fingerprints. Still, even with each person being truly unique, and nature and nurture creating endless diversity, our human condition is a shared one. There is a profound commonality among us—a "human nature" that is native to every person, even the Jerry Browns. Let's take a moment just to list the obvious.

First, the most notable aspect of our condition is that we are alive *bodies,* and we share similar bodily functions. People's everyday needs for food and elimination, activity and rest, clothing, shelter, and safety, as well as our extraordinary capacities for emotion, communication, creativity, and relationship with one another and the world, all engage our bodies—including our ultimate capacity to love and be loved.

Second, we have minds with which we can think, weaving together reason, memory, and imagination. This reflective capacity enables us to understand the world and ourselves. We can even think about our own thinking, becoming conscious of our consciousness. Now that's a high level of reflection!

Following on, we have the capacity of will that enables us to make decisions, and some freedom to choose between good and evil, true and false. Add into this mix our emotional life, a whole kaleidoscope of feelings that works together with thought and will to make us real players in the world, active agents instead of passive blobs. A thousand times a day, our bodies and minds, wills and emotions combine to act upon the world around us, even influencing who we ourselves become. What an amazing power!

Then, people are relational to the core; we are literally made for each other. This is why we naturally create networks of relationship—family and friends, community and society at large. And within these relationships, we have a gut sense of our rights and responsibilities, that we are participants who deserve respect as human beings.

Isn't it fascinating that every person tries somehow to "make meaning" out of life, to have an outlook and a sense of purpose that holds things together. We search for meaning in spite of experiencing our mortality—that we get sick and will die. Though we may exaggerate our own importance at times, in saner moments we recognize that some day soon the world will go on merrily without us, that the cemeteries are full of indispensable people. And yet, though death is certain, we have a gut-level confidence that there is more to being human than eat, drink, and be merry. In fact, there is much more to us than meets the eye—which would start another round of the obvious that people have in common.

Every aspect of the person can be studied as a serious science. All the social sciences—sociology, psychology, anthropology, and so on—investigate the human condition. So do the natural sciences such as biology and chemistry, at least indirectly. And every school of philosophy addresses this question we are to ourselves.

We can learn from all the sciences and philosophies, and yet—think about it—we can respond adequately to "Who are we?" only from the perspective of faith. Beyond the DNA and social analysis, human beings need a faith perspective around questions of meaning and purpose, especially when we face realities like sickness and mortality. Even to address the first obvious characteristic I listed— that we are *alive bodies*—pushes toward a faith perspective. What is this vitality by which we are alive?

Christian faith, with its great doctrines such as that everyone reflects the divine image and that God became a person in Jesus, can lend a very life-giving imagination on our human condition. Catholicism is particularly rich in its theological anthropology. Remember, however, that we will never fully comprehend ourselves. Scientists now claim to have mapped the 3.1 billion biochemical "letters" of human DNA—the operating instructions for human beings. Yet be assured, given whose image we reflect, mystery will ever remain.

FOR REFLECTION AND CONVERSATION

- What is your own estimation of the human condition? Note your imaginings about who we are and what we can expect of each other.

- How does your faith perspective affect your understanding of people? Reflect on some of the other influences on your anthropology—significant experiences and relationships, cultural and social influences.

CATHOLIC IMAGINATION OF THE PERSON:
A GIFT FOR LIFE

Two Catholic images of the person can serve as summary guides while the details unfold. The first reflects who we *essentially* are; the second, more our *attitude* toward ourselves and the life we have. Both are a gift for life.

If human nature were placed on the scale of "good or bad," to which side would it tip? Pick up any morning paper and you'll find weighty evidence for both: tremendous goodness, generosity, and creativity on one side, but malevolent meanness, evil, and destruction on the other. How do *you* weigh the scales? Even a fraction favoring either side will be significant. The great theologian Bernard Lonergan (1904–1984) summarized the classic Catholic weighing as "a realistic optimism."

Note that *optimism* is the noun and so the defining sentiment about human nature. Catholic Christianity tips the scales to the positive side, however slightly. Essentially, humankind is more prone to choose the good, the true, and the beautiful than the evil, false, and ugly. As the psalmist wrote, God has made us "just a little less than the angels" (Psalm 8:6).

Yet, let's not be naive about ourselves. We can and too often do choose sin and evil, hatred and destruction. Plus, all of us get sick and will die—the ultimate counter to naive optimism about our existence. As the same psalmist also wrote, people "resemble the beasts that perish" (Psalm 49:12). But over against the realities of sin and death, Christian faith claims that Jesus has conquered sin and made death to go backward, not into the abyss but opening into new life. A cautious optimism seems in order.

My second summary is that Catholicism at its best prompts a joie de vivre outlook, encouraging people to embrace each day as a gift to enjoy. Some of this spirit is captured in the old Latin term *humanitas*. Difficult to translate, *humanitas* carries the meaning of benevolence and compassion—being humane—toward ourselves and others, and likewise appreciation for the good things of life. A *humanitas* outlook recognizes human shortcomings but leans toward hope and goodness, mercy and forgiveness, appealing to what is best in us.

Within these two "spins" of *realistic optimism* and *humanitas*, I offer five elaborations of a Catholic Christian anthropology. They are: (1) to affirm and celebrate the whole person and all people; (2) to recognize that we are terribly capable of sin but remain basically good; (3) to believe that by divine grace we can live as partners with God and each other; (4) to embrace our human vocation as becoming fully alive to the glory of God; and (5) to become lovers forever.

These images do not exhaust who we are, and in one way or another, every subsequent chapter adds something about the human condition. Taken cumulatively, however, these are the contours of Catholicism's response to the question we are to ourselves.

1. Affirming and Celebrating the Whole Person and All People

Affirmation. Two great strains of Christian Story give unqualified affirmation to the human condition: the accounts of *creation* and *incarnation*. The first reflects that *human life shares in the very life of God;* the second, that *God shares our very human life* in Jesus. How could our condition be any more affirmed?

The Bible has two great mythic accounts of creation in the Book of Genesis, and they reverberate throughout subsequent books. Genesis 1 portrays humankind as the climax of divine creation, completed on the afternoon of the sixth day. It represents God as making a considered choice, as if ruminating with consultants; "Let us make humankind in our image, after our own likeness" (Genesis 1:26). Apparently reaching consensus: "God created humankind in God's image, in the divine image God created them; male and female God created them" (Genesis 1:27).

The sacred author notes that God paused after each of the five previous days of creation and "saw that it was good." After creating women and men, however, God saw that day's work as *very* good" (Genesis 1:31); note the superlative. Catholic Christianity maintains that human goodness thereafter is never lost, that we ever remain in the divine image—even after "the Fall" (Genesis 3).

The second creation account in Genesis 2, gives symbolic detail of how God created humankind, crafting from clay "a person of the earth" (gender-inclusive)[1] and then blowing into its nostrils *the divine breath of life* (Genesis 2:7). Notice how the story affirms our materiality but then adds the amazing claim that we become alive by the very life of God. God's own life is our animating principle. What an affirmation of the person!

Beyond creation, God's ultimate endorsement of the human condition is that the divine "became flesh and dwelt among us" (John 1:14) in Jesus, the Christ. What a fantastic claim: that God came among us as one of ourselves. We could have no greater affirmation of our worth than for God to "dwell" in this human condition, becoming like us in all things "but sin" (Hebrews 4:15).

Celebration. Echoing this affirmation, Catholicism encourages people to embrace life as a gift, to let the joy of living far outweigh its burdens. Some religions and spiritualities see life more as a test to endure or a cross to carry. Indeed, there are strong strains of these sentiments throughout Catholic Christianity as well. But at its best, the more authentic Catholic perspective is that life is a blessing to be enjoyed and celebrated. We are to live life to the full, relishing every day and favoring fullness of life for all.

The Bible is very realistic about the options before us, but its resounding wisdom is that we *choose life*. God sets out the classic choice in the Book of Deuteronomy: "I have set before you life and death. . . . *Choose life* so that you and your descendants may live" (30:19). The Bible urges this choice precisely because God totally favors life. Remember that God's ultimate desire for humankind is *shalom*—wholeness and fullness of life. Because God wills *shalom*, God's people should live accordingly: *for life for all*.

Fullness of life is also Jesus' best hope for humanity; commitment *for life* marks his whole public ministry but is most explicit in John's Gospel. Jesus described himself as "the bread of life" given "for the life of the world" (John 6:35, 51). Presenting himself as the Good Shepherd, he declared, "I came that you might have life, and have it to the full" (10:10). He said, "I am the resurrection and the life" (11:25) and "I am the way, the truth, and the life" (14:6). He taught that "eternal life" is found in "knowing" God and the one God sent, Jesus Christ (17:3).

The first Christians encouraged being for life, embracing and celebrating it as gift. Saint Irenaeus (130–200), an early Christian author, summarized well this imagining of the human, that "the glory of God is the person fully alive."[2] In other words, the more completely we become human—develop our talents, fulfill our responsibilities, live to the full—the more God is praised. Our very being alive is a priestly estate, a celebration to God's glory.

Of the Whole Person. In Western culture, we readily refer to the person as "body *and* soul." The problem is that we tend to hear those terms as naming separate parts. This dualism is a legacy from ancient Greek philosophers who thought of body and soul as antagonists, with the material body dragging down the spiritual soul from its lofty heights, causing sin, sickness, and death. Plato even saw death as a blessed liberation of the captive soul from the prison of the body.

The Hebrew tradition, by contrast, had no such dualism or negativity toward the body. It understood the person as a body-soul unity. If we return to the creation stories, Genesis 1 makes clear that the whole person reflects the divine image and all is "very good." Note, too, that God made "humankind . . . as male and female" (Genesis 1:27), two sexually identified persons. Clearly, sexuality is integral to personhood and enjoys divine blessing.

Remember that in the Genesis 2 story God creates physical beings from the earth and then enlivens them with God's own life. But rather than dualism or antagonism, the story implies that both aspects are needed to constitute a person, a unity of body and soul—a bodied soul. And the whole person is divine handiwork.

When I use the word *soul* throughout this book, I mean it in the Hebrew rather than the Greek sense. It is not an aspect of the person apart from the corporeal, not "the ghost in the machine of the body"—the philosopher Descartes's summary of "soul" in

Western culture. Rather, think of soul as what the poet Yeats called "the deep heart's core" of the person—one's very person-hood.

The Hebrew word *nephesh*, usually translated as soul, literally means "alive as a person." So, in that second Genesis account, when God breathes the divine life into the body, it becomes *nephesh* (2:7). We can say, then, that the human soul is *the animating principle by which the person is alive with God's own life.* Soul symbolizes the aliveness of the whole person, which is the divine life within us.

The New Testament continues the Hebrew sense of the unity and goodness of the whole person—epitomized in the person of Jesus. Note how John's Gospel states that "the Word *became flesh,*" not entered into, not took on, but "became" (some translations have "was made"). When some overly pious Christians claimed that Jesus was only pretending to be human and could not have really become flesh, the Church condemned them as heretics. Eventually it proclaimed a dogma of Christian faith that the divine and human natures were united as one person in Jesus.

The early Christians were also convinced that the whole person and all people are saved precisely because Jesus took on our full humanity; thus, all was raised up in the Risen Christ. They went so far as to profess faith "in the resurrection of the body" (Apostles' Creed), making the point that even in eternity we will be *whole* persons, not disembodied spirits.

Since those early years, however, Christians have struggled with the unity and goodness of the whole person. Many heresies have strongly favored dualism of body and soul, portraying the body as evil. Undoubtedly, these negative movements rubbed off on the Christian community and—let's face it—especially on Catholicism. For example, few religious traditions seem more uptight about sexuality. Yet, officially at least, such movements were condemned. At its best, Catholic Christianity held out for the unity and goodness of the whole person.

Of All People. Christian affirmation and celebration pertains to all people, in every time and place and without exception. This is reflected in Christianity's insistence on the *dignity and equality, rights and responsibilities* of every person.

Dignity and Equality of All. From the beginning, Christian theologians recognized the *imago Dei* (image of God) tenet as establishing the *equality and dignity* of every person, no matter what their sex, race, class, or creed. Endorsed by the divine life within, all people have an essential dignity and deserve to be treated with reverence and respect. This pertains equally; no one is any more made in God's image than anyone else. Before God we are all equal, by birthright. As the *Catechism of the Catholic Church* summarizes well, "Created in the image of the one God and equally endowed with rational souls, all [people] have the same nature and the same origin . . . all enjoy an equal dignity."[3]

Rights and Responsibilities of All. Their faith demands that Christians commit themselves to basic human rights for every person. No one should ever be denied what is needed to live humanly. Pope John XXIII offered a now-classic listing of inalienable human rights: to life and to a worthy manner of living; to respect as persons without discrimination on any basis; to pursue and express the truth; to be informed and educated; to worship God freely; to choose a state in life; to have gainful employment, decent labor conditions, and just wages for work; to organize and associate with others; to participate in public affairs and contribute to the common good.[4]

Pope John also insisted that each right has a companion responsibility—to promote the same for everyone else. Rights and responsibilities are two sides of the same coin of personhood. Just as we claim and exercise our own rights, so we always remain responsible for promoting the rights of all. In fact, it's by fulfilling our responsibilities to the "other" that we recognize the Other and realize our own personhood. Oh, we always need God's help to fulfill our responsibilities, but we cannot delegate them. Responsibility and accountability are integral to being human.

2. Capable of Sin but Basically Good

The mythic stories of Genesis 1 and 2 offer inspiring accounts of our creation, but how about Genesis 3, the story of first parents eating "the forbidden fruit" and being banished to "east of Eden" (Genesis 3:24)? In describing the human condition, we must recognize our terrible capacity for sin and that we "originate" with sinful tendencies. To do otherwise is to play the ostrich.

From the story of the Fall, reflecting the evil of which human beings are capable, Christian theologians of the West constructed the doctrine of original sin. It proposes that procreation passes on to humankind the lasting consequences of the disobedience of Adam and Eve, which are temptation and sin, suffering, sickness, and death. From birth, then, our human condition is a broken one, with "a strong inclination to evil," as the Baltimore Catechism put it.

Very few Christians believe the story of the Fall literally or take it as a historical explanation. Yet this great mythic story reflects something very true to our human condition. Except for Jesus—and his mother, Mary, in Catholic faith—every person who has ever lived has been disposed to make wrong choices, to sin by commission and omission. Not only our personal lives but also our social structures and cultural mores reflect this proclivity for sin.

Catholics would never think of their tradition as minimizing human sinfulness. On the contrary, many experience it as creating excessive feelings of guilt and sinfulness. We make jokes about "good old Catholic guilt" and laugh because they ring so true. But just how *sinful* are we? Most Catholics are surprised to hear the "official" Catholic response: that we are not nearly as sinful as we are graced.

Are people inherently evil? Do we inevitably choose to sin? Or are we essentially good and, with God's help, capable of free choice? The Catholic position tilts well in favor of humanity's essential goodness. Though its pastoral practice may often reflect otherwise, Catholic Christianity does not take sinfulness as defining people. In fact, we are good to the core and, with God's help augmented in Jesus, we have the free-will capacity to choose accordingly. This position came into clarity through controversy with the first great Protestant Reformers.

Martin Luther (1483–1546), and John Calvin (1509–1564) even more so, took the position that the human condition is essentially sinful and corrupt. Calvin described humanity as *massa peccati*—a mass of sin. In fairness, the Reformers were trying to make an important pastoral point in emphasizing human depravity. By saying that we are totally sinful and yet can be saved, they wanted to highlight the gratuity of God's grace. This was much needed over against Catholic freneticism about performing pious practices as if we need to *earn* salvation by our own efforts. Unfortunately, in the midst of Reformation-era polemics, Catholicism did not recognize the pastoral concern but instead saw a theological error.

At the Council of Trent (1545–63), Catholic Christianity officially rejected the notion of human depravity. It reiterated that though we have a "fallen" nature and are ever in need of God's grace, we are essentially good, not inherently corrupt. Although "original sin" is pervasive in our lives and world, even more so is "original grace." The divine spark in us is never extinguished, the *imago Dei* never lost.[5] As the *Catechism* states, though "human nature bears the wound of original sin," we still "desire the good" and "remain an image of our Creator."[6]

Christians also believe that by his life, death, and resurrection, Jesus broke the hold of sin on people and renewed our capacity for doing good. Catholicism highlights that God in Jesus transformed the human condition and restored us as God's "sons and daughters by adoption" (see Galatians 4:5–6). Thomas Aquinas explained that Jesus "renovated" humanity from within, building upon the "original grace" that was never lost to human nature. What this all means for Catholic imagination: because we are made and remain in God's image, and because of God's grace through Jesus Christ, the defining human orientation is for good and for God.

3. Partners by Grace with God and Each Other

So, people are basically good. Still, we can't save ourselves by our own efforts alone. We need God's help. The traditional Christian term for divine help is *grace*. Summarizing a long Catholic tradition, Karl Rahner described grace as God's personal-presence-in-love to human beings. Further, Christians traditionally name their experience of divine presence and help as the work of God's Spirit in the world. So, we can say that *grace is the Spirit lovingly at work in our lives, empowering our own best efforts.*

God's grace is gratuitous love—free; *gratis* means "not earned." And because our nature is not depraved, we can respond to grace as partners with God and one another. We can make our own best efforts—with the Spirit's help—and those efforts are significant to the outcome. In the classic phrase of Thomas Aquinas, "God's grace works through nature." This means that the Spirit works with and through us to advance the reign of God in our lives and world.

We noted that Calvin claimed total human depravity and thus our complete dependence on God's grace; *sola gratia* was a great slogan of the Reformers. In this, Calvin was at the opposite end of the spectrum from Pelagianism, an ancient movement that the Church condemned as heresy but that still enjoys much favor among Catholics.

Pelagius, a Celtic monk of the fifth century, was overly confident in our ability to save ourselves. Apparently he claimed that by personal effort alone people can lead good and moral lives, and that the sin of Adam and Eve was no more than bad example, reflecting no loss to the human condition. For Pelagius and "the work of salvation" (see Philippians 2:12), all the eggs are in the human basket.

The classic Catholic position imagines a middle ground between Pelagius's self-sufficiency and Calvin's total dependence on God.

Against Pelagianism, Catholic Christianity took the position that "people cannot rise from the depths of sin by their own free will unless the grace of the merciful God lifts them up."[7] In other words, human agency for good always depends on God's grace. Against Calvinism and its sentiments, Catholic Christianity insisted that because we are inherently good we are capable of partnership with God. Human efforts and cooperation are needed for doing good, though ever sustained by God's grace. If the official Catholic teaching were on a bumper sticker, it might read: "Without God, we can't. Without us, God won't."

In pastoral practice Catholicism has often failed to walk the tightrope between God's grace, what God does for us, and human efforts, what we must do ourselves. Its classic theology, however, balances a partnership between God and humankind, avoiding the extremes of God doing everything for us, on the one hand, and human self-sufficiency, on the other.

People in recovery from addiction will be the first to say that although they depend entirely on the help of Higher Power, such help "works" through other people and requires their own best efforts. After twenty-four years of sobriety, my friend Sean often remarks, "Every day is a struggle, but I make it with the help of God and my AA buddies." And Sean would never take a job in a pub. The Spirit works through our own spirits, other people, and the everyday world.

The biblical notion of covenant reflects this same delicate balance between God's grace and human efforts. In all the biblical covenants, including the new one made in Jesus, God bonds humankind with one another and Godself and empowers people to live according to the divine dream for creation. Both divine and human partners must play their parts; and we are capable of such partnership with the help of God.

In chapter 4—on sociology—I will elaborate on how our partnership with one another actualizes our partnership with God. I emphasize that the human condition is realized as a *community-of-persons*. But here we can highlight the flip side of this coin—that we are ever *persons-in-community*. Our human identity is first and foremost relational; we become who we are through relationship with other people.

It is not that we become a person first and then relate; rather we become persons only by relating. This is why I favor the word *person* to describe us, rather than *individual*. The latter is from *individuare*—literally, "to stand apart"—whereas *person* is from the Greek *prosopon,* meaning "turned toward the other." The very term *person* bespeaks that we become human through partnership with others.

4. Becoming Fully Alive to the Glory of God

Because we image our God, being a person is never a static state or a finished product. The human vocation is a lifelong journey into fullness of life. With the Spirit working through our own good efforts and gifts, we have endless potential as human beings—finally fulfilled only in eternity.

To repeat the lovely phrase of the early Church theologian Irenaeus, "The glory of God is the person fully alive." That God glories in our becoming fully human may come as a surprise to many Catholic Christians. So often they experience their tradition as a stricture, as curtailing their human development. The truth should be the opposite. Christian faith ought to be a great spiritual resource for fullness of life for ourselves and empowering our responsibility for others.

What does it mean to become "fully alive to the glory of God"? What are our innate capacities and horizons as human beings? There couldn't be an exhaustive list, but a general schema of categories may be suggestive. Here we echo some of the common characteristics listed at the outset.

Reflecting, Knowing, and Making Meaning. Our gift of mind enables us to reflect on experience, to know the world, to recognize the truth, to make meaning out of life. Within the mind we can distinguish *reason, memory,* and *imagination,* though these capacities always function together. Acting in concert, they enable us first to become *aware* of the data that comes through our senses, second to reflect on sense data to *understand* what we experience, third to make *judgments* regarding what we understand, and finally to reach *decisions* about it. This is how we come to know the world and life in a meaningful way.

We can even turn our reflective capacities upon ourselves, becoming self-reflective. This allows us to understand, judge, and decide about ourselves as persons, to take on great questions like "Who are we?" and "What's it all about?" And the more we develop our capacities of the mind, the more we give glory to God.

Choosing and Becoming Free. Between the morning decision to get out of bed and the nightly one to turn out the lights, we make thousands of choices every day. Human beings are not programmed robots but fairly free agents who choose and make decisions. In traditional philosophical terms, we have the gift of free will. It functions in concert with mind and emotion to make us agents in life—real players. Our choices can even influence our own becoming.

Catholic anthropology insists that we have free will because, as noted earlier, it refuses to see human nature as depraved. We do not inevitably choose evil and we can choose good. It grants that cultural influences and social forces can impair our will, and drugs or alcohol can temporarily suspend it. Normally, however, we retain enough freedom to be held responsible for our actions. And while God's grace prompts and sustains good choices, God never does so at the expense of *our* choosing. For grace is God's love at work in our lives, and true love empowers—never diminishes—the human condition and our responsibilities.

The Hebrew scriptures portray God as championing human freedom. The great freedom story is Exodus, when God intervened in human history to free the Israelites from slavery in Egypt. In the New Testament, Jesus is represented as setting people free: from personal sin and social oppression, from hunger and fear, from closed-mindedness and hard-heartedness, from hatred and despair, from sickness—spiritual, physical, and emotional—and even from death. This is one way that Saint Paul summarized what Jesus achieved for humankind: "Freedom is what we have, Christ has set us free. Remain, then, as free people and do not become slaves again" (Galatians 5:1).

God has made free will indigenous to the human condition. And the more we live into responsible freedom, the more we give glory to God.

Relating, Creating, and Making History. We simply cannot "keep to ourselves." We are persons precisely by relating with other people and the world, and this again because we are made like unto God. In Christian faith, God is a Trinity of Loving Relationships, both within Godself and toward humankind. No wonder our innate nature is relational; nothing less would reflect the divine image.

Because "God is love" (1 John 4:8), the pinnacle of our human potential is to love and be loved; I elaborate this as my crowning point—number 5 below. Here I highlight that our relationality grounds our ability to reach beyond ourselves—to be self-transcendent. And self-transcendence is the ground of our spirituality. It prompts us to reach for the Transcendent—for relationship with God—who is first reaching out to us. And only relationship with God can fully satisfy our capacity to love and be loved.

Because we are made in the Creator's likeness, our relating with others and the world can be wonderfully creative. As we relate, we employ our imaginations and creativity; we develop skills, crafts, and arts to produce the culture that surrounds us and the aesthetics that nurture our spirits. Human beings even have the amazing capacity to procreate and then to parent new persons into life.

When we create what is good for humankind, what sustains and improves the world, what is beautiful to enjoy, when we procreate responsibly and parent well, we give glory to God. Catholic Christianity insists that by God's grace our human agency and creativity can make a lasting contribution to the well-being of self, others, and world. We can "make history" *for life for all* and this to the glory of God.

Living the "Natural" Law. Natural law is a foundation stone of Catholic ethics. It reflects the conviction that God has built into human nature the ability to know what is right and what is wrong, and the disposition to choose rightly. Although this law feels "natural," it reflects the divine law implanted in human hearts. Every culture and the most primitive of peoples have known intuitively that things like murder, cheating, and lying are wrong, and that love, honesty, and truth-telling are right.

Building on natural law, Catholicism claims that there are universal and timeless moral values, and that people can recognize them by human reason alone. In the Catholic tradition of ethics, the Bible confirms and amplifies what we can already know by natural law. For the classic Protestant ethic, murder is wrong *because* the Bible condemns it; for the classic Catholic ethic, murder is wrong, which is *why* the Bible condemns it.

Growing in God-likeness. Contemporary Christology makes the point that Jesus revealed both who God is *and* who we can be—the possibilities for humankind. In Jesus we recognize what it means to become fully alive to the glory of God; he is our human potential "writ large."

Looking to the actual life of Jesus, we recognize that becoming fully alive includes becoming free and responsible, just and peaceable, merciful and compassionate, kind and respectful, hospitable and inclusive, prayerful and centered, balanced and integrated, hopeful and faith-filled, and—above all—loving. Fullness of life after the example of *the historical Jesus* means growing into the best virtues and values that the human heart desires.

What, then, about *the Risen Christ of faith?* What does faith in

Jesus as the Christ mean for whom people can become? We will return to this question many times and approach it from different angles. Here, let's focus on the Christian conviction that *the fullness of divinity and humanity were united in Jesus Christ.*

The great ecumenical Council of Chalcedon (451) stated that "Our Lord Jesus Christ is complete in deity and complete in humanity, truly God and truly a human being" and yet remained "one person."[8] Christian Story carries many interpretations of the meaning of this doctrine for the human condition. In general, however, the unity of divinity and humanity in Jesus Christ is an analogy for all humankind, that our becoming fully human means becoming more divine.

This is a rich emphasis of Eastern Catholicism that all Christians would do well to reclaim: by growing into full humanity we become more like unto our God. Orthodox Catholics stress that we are created in the divine image and must grow in divine likeness. They call this *theosis,* literally "becoming divine." Such is what Jesus Christ empowers for all people. In the lovely phrase of Saint Athanasius, "God became human so that humans could become more like God."[9]

5. Becoming Lovers Forever

Near the end of the New Testament we find Saint John's three-word description of God that had been unfolding throughout biblical history: "God is love" (1 John 4:16). If we arch a rainbow from the Genesis stories of creation to John's closing "definition," we recognize that God's life in us is God's love for us and through us to the world. Every person is alive by the love of God. The breath we breathe is God's love for us; our lifeblood is divine life and love coursing through our veins. God literally made us out of love to become lovers.

Our highest calling, then, the fullest realization of our humanity, is to love and be loved. And given the divine-human partnership, God's love is the model for humanity's. So, human love is not some easy romanticism or license but requires *right* and *loving* relationship with God, self, others, and creation—love that demands justice and responsibility to the neighbor. Echoing his Hebrew faith, Jesus preached such radical love as "the greatest commandment" (Mark 12:31): love for God with all one's mind, heart, soul, and strength, and for neighbors as for oneself—including even enemies.

This call to love reaches beyond death into eternity to reunite us with the Love whence we came. At birth we move from our mother's womb into a new life here; at death we experience rebirth into new life in God's eternal presence, a passage far more amazing than from the womb to here. The Preface prayer for the Mass of the Resurrection states that "the sadness of death gives way to the bright promise of immortality," for in death "life is changed, not ended." Lifelong growth into eternity as true lovers; such is the human vocation. We could have no higher calling.

Although human beings are destined to return to the Love whence we came, Christian faith teaches that this reward is not inevitable. Why? Precisely because God respects human freedom. Even though God continually invites us into right and loving relationship, we have the amazing ability to say no to the divine covenant. If that be our lasting choice, then God respects it, not condemning us as much as allowing us to decide our own fate.

Thus, God holds us responsible for how we live our lives. Anything less would not honor us as human beings. Chapter 25 of Matthew's Gospel offers a riveting account of the Last Judgment. It seems that the decisive criterion by which our lives will be measured is how we cared for neighbors most in need, how well we lived the greatest commandment. Saint Paul wrote wisely that, in the end, "faith, hope, and love endure . . . and the greatest of these is love" (1 Corinthians 13:13). Indeed!

FOR REFLECTION AND CONVERSATION

- With what do you agree or disagree regarding the imagining of the human condition proposed so far? What would you add to this Catholic perspective?

- What spiritual practices might nurture people in becoming more fully human?

PRACTICING A HUMANIZING SPIRITUALITY

The image I've proposed of the person has far-reaching implications for putting spirituality to work in the everyday. I've already hinted at some. Now, to stimulate your own imaginings, I propose three spiritual practices that can support a *humanitas* outlook on ourselves. Two are general; the third is a bit more specific.

1. Love and Respect Yourself

I place this practice first because Christians tend to overlook the third leg of the love commandment, "as yourself." Yet, there it stands—a law of God. The Catholic anthropology proposed here would encourage authentic self-love as a spiritual practice. Love of self as person is grounded in God's unconditional love. It is certainly different from the self-pandering of a consumerist society. What, then, does responsible self-love amount to for Christian spirituality? I imagine three features.

First, authentic self-love *cherishes one's own personhood as of infinite worth* regardless of achievements, simply because of God's unconditional love. Just by being alive, we give glory to God. This conviction can be an antidote to toxicities like self-doubt, shame and blame, and the social compulsion to prove one's worth. Authentic self-love is convinced with the psalmist that "You knit me together in my mother's womb . . . I am fearfully, wonderfully made" (Psalm 139:13); that God says of each of us, "I called you by name, you are mine" (Isaiah 43:1).

Second, self-love *encourages a balanced life*—since we don't have to prove ourselves or earn our worth. It helps us to keep our priorities straight, to remember what matters most, to maintain a healthy balance between work and recreation, between the personal and the professional, between discipline and indulgence, between our own efforts and God's grace.

A friend asked recently why I seemed to be too busy. I responded, "Poor spirituality" and was confident of my self-diagnosis. Whenever we find ourselves taking on too much, not making time for rest and relaxation, not keeping up with family, friends, and support community, not taking sabbath or time for prayer and reflection, we are failing to practice self-love.

Third, Christian self-love entails *caring for our bodies* with regular exercise, a balanced diet, avoidance of alcohol or drug abuse, and general health care. One of the most positive features of New Age spirituality is its holistic emphasis, encouraging people to care for their health as a spiritual practice. Christian faith should do as much or more.

Christianity has always prompted care for the sick, listing it among the "works of mercy" required of every Christian. Healing was an integral aspect of Jesus' public ministry, and the early disciples were noted for their care of the ill and dying. Thereafter, from the medical attention provided by the ancient monasteries down to the vast network of church-sponsored hospitals and clinics around the world today, the Catholic community has evidenced a strong commitment to health care. It undertakes such efforts, however, as fulfilling the second leg of the greatest commandment—"love your neighbor." It is less noted for good care and appreciation for one's own body.

The seeds of a more holistic spirituality are strewn throughout Christian tradition, though needing to be nurtured. Remember that we are a body-soul unity, that the whole person is basically good, that "the Word became *flesh*" in Jesus. If taken seriously, such affirmations should encourage good care for our physical well-being.

2. *Render Unconditional Respect to Other Persons*

We return to love of neighbor many times throughout this book; it could not be otherwise when we are proposing the practices of a Christian spirituality. Here I highlight that a Catholic anthropology requires the spiritual practice of *unconditional respect* for others. Such respect amounts to *reverencing* other people as reflections of God, recognizing the divine presence in them regardless of their successes or failures, their sameness or otherness to ourselves. This loving regard should encourage a common bond with all humankind, prompting us to treat every person as "one of the family"—God's.

My thesaurus offers *prejudice* as an antonym to respect. How accurate! Surely every instance of prejudice—racism and sexism, classism and sectarianism, ageism and homophobia—is, at base, a refusal to respect certain people as persons, or a claim that some are more "person" than others. Sexism, for example, is the prejudice that men are more "person" than women; like all prejudice, absurd! Over against this, Christian spirituality requires us to treat all people as equally made in God's image, equally affirmed by God's incarnation in Jesus.

Most of us have prejudices of one kind or another, despite protestations otherwise. The point here is that eradicating prejudice from one's personal life (as well as from society; see chapter 7) is a spiritual practice required by Christian faith.

It helps to honestly name our prejudices and to reflect critically on them. This means to recognize their negative origins and destructive consequences. It helps to make friends among those against whom we are prejudiced. Statistics indicate that straight people are far less likely to be homophobic if they have friends or family members in the gay community. Finally, we should remember that human efforts alone cannot root out the evil of discrimination from our hearts or from society. That requires God's grace; which brings us to a third spiritual practice.

3. Pray for the Graces You Need

Given the partnership between divine grace and human effort, we should ask often for the particular graces we need to make our own best efforts. Saint Ignatius of Loyola (1491–1556), founder of the Jesuits, strongly encouraged people to figure out the graces of which they are most in need, and then to "pray their desire" to God.

So, the recovering alcoholic prays to sustain the struggle for sobriety, the worried parent to respond appropriately to a child in distress, a spouse to be loving around a particular tension. We can be confident that the Spirit always provides when we pray for the grace to sustain our own best efforts.

FOR REFLECTION AND CONVERSATION

- Add your own suggestions for spiritual practices that can enhance your personhood.

- Is there an adjustment or a new decision emerging regarding your anthropology? If so, how will you respond?

THREE

"WHAT'S IT ALL ABOUT?"— TAKING A SACRAMENTAL VIEW

A BIT O' GOOD

When I rented the car at Dublin Airport, they said it was brand-new, and sure enough it was. On my way back to the airport five days later, after two seminars that had gone well and a delightful visit with family, the last thing I expected was car trouble. The sun rose slowly on a lovely autumn morning, phasing the Wicklow Mountains into focus on the horizon. Birds were singing among the last of the leaves, and I was humming along.

About a half-hour from the airport, I thought I saw steam rising from under the hood but assumed it was the dew vaporizing with the morning sun. Then the temperature gauge jumped to boiling point, and, as I pulled over, the car cut out, enveloped in a cloud of steam.

No phone or gas station was in sight. I had to make that flight or I would miss my class next morning, and my restricted air ticket would be useless as well. I stood beside the steaming car looking plaintive but doubted anyone would stop. Then, to my surprise, an old red Ford Escort pulled over. The driver, a weatherworn middle-aged man by himself, asked in a thick Dublin accent, "Are y'in trubble?"

I explained my plight and he said "Hop in," nodding to the seat beside him. I grabbed my luggage and we were off. My good Samaritan was Joe Carroll, "an ould Dub" he claimed proudly, and on his way to work—on a building site. I asked him to drop me at the next village where I could call a cab, but he rejoined, "Naw, none out here at this hour. I'll drop yeh at d'airport." I protested feebly that it was out of his way. He said, "Yeah, 'tis. But not that much," adding, "and besides, I've got a daughter in New York"—as if that explained something. Relieved, I accepted with, "Well, I'll pay you."

Joe inquired what county I was from, what brought me back to Ireland, what kind of seminars was I giving. When he heard I was some kind of theologian, he fell silent for a while, and then asked, "So, what's it all about?"

I faltered, "What's what all about?"

"Life, yeh know—the whole thing—does it amount t'anthin'?" Joe asked, giving a half-circle wave to the horizon. I thought to myself, Where else but in Ireland would this question be raised so early in the morning?

Since my mentioning theology seemed to prompt Joe's question, I stumbled around about how faith can help us to respond to the great questions, to find happiness, meaning, and purpose in life; otherwise, it can all seem a bit absurd. Then Joe, relishing and rising to the occasion, wanted to know what I meant by "faith" and by "happiness" and by "meaning" and whether these "had anthin' to do with goin' t'church at all." I was happy to reach the airport!

I thanked Joe profusely, told him he was living proof that the old hospitality hadn't been lost, and insisted on paying him, at least what I would have paid for a taxi. He refused, "But I can't take yer money." I was adamant, whereupon Joe pleaded, "Ah, don't ruin the first bit o' good I did today." With that, I had to relent.

We said good-bye like old friends. As I hurried away to drop the keys at the rental company, tell them where to find the broken-down car, and catch my plane, I stopped and turned. Joe was still there, as if seeing me off. I called back to him, "Hey Joe, I think you know well what it's all about." He gave a soft chuckle and waved—again a half-circle to the horizon.

WE ALL HAVE AN ATTITUDE

I once had a wise soul friend—now gone to God—who, regardless of what concern I raised, would inquire, "Are you gettin' a good night's sleep?" I was young and sometimes felt he wasn't taking my problems seriously. Was this the best he could do by way of spiritual wisdom? But I've come to appreciate the point he was making. With a good night's sleep, everything looks different and usually a bit brighter.

Our perspective makes a huge difference to how we live in the world and experience life. It was Joe's outlook—imagination—that prompted him to stop and do what he did that early morning. Thank God he had the one he had! With another attitude, he would have passed me by and not given it another thought.

Our worldview, of course, depends on more than a good night's sleep—important as that may be. Genetic factors and a myriad of familial, social, and cultural influences commingle to produce our personal perspective on the world and on our lives within it. Joe's summary of all those influences was to describe himself as "an ould Dub," and for those in the know, that speaks volumes. However we come by it, we all "have an attitude" that tints every-thing with our own inimitable hue.

Like Joe Carroll, ancient philosophers also asked, "What's it all about?" They called their study *cosmology*. I mention the technical term only because it hints at an original outlook. The Greek word *cosmos* means "ordered universe" and is the opposite to *chaos*. Clearly, those early sages began their study assuming that "the world" *has* an order to it, a design that the human mind can comprehend. It all already makes sense; we just need to uncover the sense it makes.

Contemporary philosophers still ask this age-old question, but they focus as much on "the looker" as on the world being looked at, thus broadening the reflection to *human life in the world*. They also take "world" to mean both the created order of nature and the culture that human beings create. So, Joe's wave to the horizon was fitting. The question "What's it all about?" encompasses "the whole world" and our outlook on it as well.

To really take the question seriously invites us to become conscious of our own view of life, to recognize what and who has formed it, to discern what is *for life for all* and what is not, being willing to adjust our attitude as needed. If we passively accept our perspective as a given or canonize it as the only way to see things, then it can effectively blind us. On the other hand, being critically conscious of our worldview can enhance our freedom and agency, can open up new horizons.

This chapter focuses on what Christian faith might lend to people's outlook on life. Indeed, this theme echoes through every chapter—they all intertwine—but here we focus on people's bedrock worldview. What would it mean for Christian faith, and Catholicism in particular, to permeate people's imagination about daily life in the world, shaping how they experience, interpret, and respond to it?

FOR REFLECTION AND CONVERSATION

- When do you find yourself asking "What's it all about?" How do you typically respond?

- Who or what has most influenced your outlook on life in the world? How? Why? With what consequences?

THE CATHOLIC WORLDVIEW: A GIFT FOR LIFE

The backdrop of a Catholic worldview is the covenant between God and humankind described in chapters 1 and 2. We can summarize the divine-human partnership as *God's grace enabling human cooperation to achieve God's desires for creation, the reign of justice and peace, holiness and fullness of life, here and hereafter; with the Spirit's help, people can become agents for life for all, and God holds us so responsible.* Given this divine milieu of human existence, we can recognize that life in the world is *good* and *gracious, meaningful* and *worthwhile.*

A Good and Gracious World. Echoing the positive sentiments about the person (chapter 2), we can say that everything God creates, whether directly in nature or in partnership with humankind, is essentially *good.* Like the person, the world is more graced than sinful. Love more than hate, goodness more than evil are the generative forces of life in the world.

As with the person, of course, we cannot romanticize or be naive about the world. The dynamics of nature—operating with their own freedom—can wreak havoc and bring great suffering to humankind. Likewise, human beings can bring as much on themselves through unwise or sinful choices. Yet, a Catholic Christian worldview comes down on the side that nothing that God has made, makes, or causes to be made is essentially evil. Our lifeworld is basically good. To quote an old youth-ministry poster, "God does not make junk."

In tandem with goodness, life in the world is fundamentally *gracious,* coming to meet us as gift. Oh, indeed, we must make our own best efforts to live the covenant—there is no cheap grace. Yet before and far beyond what we earn, life in the world comes to meet us as gracious, ever offering us "more in the midst of the ordinary." This morning I awoke to the birds singing. I lay and listened awhile to a grand symphony of nature and knew again that all is gift.

The world is *gracious* because God's *grace* (same root) takes the initiative. This means that the Spirit is ever abroad in the world with loving intent, working prior to and more generously than all human efforts. We experience the Spirit working through our own spirits and through the whole created order. So, it's God's Spirit that makes life in the world a gift.

A frequent descriptor of God in the Hebrew scriptures is *hesed;* the corresponding Greek word is *charis,* the root of "grace." A favored translation is "loving-kindness." With such a Spirit at work in the world, we can experience the core of life as loving-kindness.

Have you ever worked hard and achieved something, only to realize that it came as a gift. Pull back the veil a little, and we discover that life in the world is like that. Imagine recognizing that every day is a gift to be lived with gratitude instead of a problem to be solved or a burden to bear. What a life-giving attitude! My grandmother would often say, "Every morning you wake up, stretch out your arms and don't feel the side of a coffin, that's a great day." Granny had a Catholic imagination about life in the world.

Life as Meaningful and Worthwhile. If life comes to meet us as a gracious gift, what about our own agency in the world—our side of the covenant? Do our efforts amount to anything? So much of society is beset by boredom; so many people feel that their lives lack meaning or purpose. By contrast, Christian faith encourages the fundamental attitude that life is meaningful and worthwhile. Here again, God's grace empowers our efforts to make it so.

All of us try to find or create meaning in our lives; that's our human disposition. At the same time, we find ourselves born into a world already chock-full of meaning. We discover here—in place long before we arrived—a *meaning-full world* of language, culture, and society. Within these meaning-laden realities, we discover a vast array of beliefs and traditions, customs and attitudes, relationships and roles, rules and laws, values and virtues, structures and expectations, artifacts and arts, tools and technologies, and everything else that human beings create to effect *cosmos* and resist *chaos*.

From our first days of life, we are socialized into the world of meaning around us. Although we can and should resist some of what we find, it all does shape our outlook. Nor do we take on our world of meaning just by instinct—the way bees in a beehive appear to act in meaningful ways. Instead, we consciously appropriate the world of meaning that was here already and then add some of our own.

Being convinced that the world is meaningful should not make us naive about countersigns. We don't have to look far to recognize that besides truth there is falsehood, besides good there is evil, besides honesty there is deceit, besides peaceful rhythm things can go terribly awry. The absurd constantly threatens our hold on meaning. It helps to remember, then, that the meaningfulness of life does not depend primarily on our own efforts nor on how we *make* meaning. Indeed, as agents in the divine-human covenant we have a responsible part to play, but meaning is not really "made" by human efforts. Life is meaningful first and foremost by divine design, and then because God's Spirit continues to work in and through the world.

Christian faith proposes that life in the world is meaningful because all is grounded in Ultimate Meaning. As Loving Creator and Sustainer, God provides the amazing design, pattern, and possibility of nature and of human culture. According to the first creation myth, God created *cosmos* out of *chaos*. Note that "in the beginning" the world was "a formless wasteland" and "darkness covered the abyss," but "God said . . ." and a meaningful world began to emerge (Genesis 1:1–3). The philosopher Heidegger proposed that the backdrop of human being-in-the-world is the abyss. By contrast, Christian faith insists that life's backdrop and its foreground are Ultimate Meaning—God's Spirit lovingly at work.

In addition, human agency in the world is *worthwhile.* Surely there is no greater pain than feeling worthless, that even our best efforts are a waste, with no purpose or lasting legacy. Conversely, a Christian perspective adamantly asserts that life in the world *is* worthwhile, that every life has a purpose, that all work—unless it diminishes human well-being—is valuable. By the power of the Spirit, every person can be a responsible partner in realizing God's dream for creation.

The dominant attitude of society is that our worth depends on what we do, possess, or achieve. Christian faith, by contrast, holds that the worthwhileness of life—like its meaningfulness—does not depend on our efforts alone. Rather, life in the world is worthwhile because of God's providence, presence, and partnership with us. Within God's sustaining love, life is worthy for its own sake, regardless of our accomplishments or accolades. We give glory to God just by being alive as reflections of the divine in the world. What more worthwhile purpose could we have?

THE SACRAMENTAL PRINCIPLE

Catholic Christianity emphasizes that the divine-human covenant is enacted within the everyday of life; *here* is where "it's at" between ourselves and God. *Here* God outreaches and engages with us. *Here* we respond as responsive partners. Catholic tradition gathers up this conviction that our covenant is realized through the ordinary of life in the principle of sacramentality. Nothing is more significant to *what make us Catholic* than the sacramental principle. It epitomizes a Catholic outlook on life in the world; if allowed only one word to describe Catholic imagination, we'd have to say *sacramental*.

Theologian Richard McBrien writes, "No theological principle or focus is more characteristic of Catholicism or more central to its identity than the principle of sacramentality."[1] Although this is surely true, Catholic Christians tend to associate sacramentality too exclusively with what happens in church, with the celebration of the seven sacraments. The principle of sacramentality, however, reaches far beyond liturgical rites. In fact, the great sacraments are simply climactic celebrations of the sacramentality of life.

The sacramental principle means that *God is present to humankind and we respond to God's grace through the ordinary and everyday of life in the world.* In other words, God's Spirit and humankind work together through nature and creation, through culture and society, through our minds and bodies, hearts and souls, through our labors and efforts, creativity and generativity, in the depth of our own being and in community with others, through the events and experiences that come our way, through what we are doing and what is "going on" around us, through everything and anything of life. *Life in the world is sacramental*—the medium of God's outreach and of human response.

Saint Augustine defined a sacrament as "a visible sign of invisible grace." The sacramental principle proposes that everything in our life-world can be such a sign. In the classic phrase of Ignatius of Loyola, Christians are invited "to see God in all things."

Christian faith also claims that God's saving work in Jesus has heightened the sacramentality of life. Christians believe that Jesus was the primary sacrament of God to the world; empowered by the Spirit, Jesus was God's saving presence as one of ourselves. What could be more "ordinary" that that? And the Spirit continues the sacramental effect of Jesus throughout human history.

Understood within the sacramentality of life in the world, the seven sacraments are sacred symbols that mediate God's grace in Jesus with heightened effect. This they do by the power of the Holy Spirit working through the Christian community. Each sacrament is a way of encountering the Risen Christ and of receiving the particular grace that the sacrament symbolizes, be that of initiating, empowering, sustaining, forgiving, healing, serving, or bonding. But Catholic Christians should never think of the seven sacraments as apart from life. All must be appreciated as apex moments that heighten and celebrate the sacramentality of life in the world.

Note that all the sacraments are symbolized by the "ordinary" of life, by bread, wine, water, oil, touch, words, gestures, and love-making in marriage. Each symbolizes something profoundly everyday that by the power of God's Spirit continues the saving mission of Jesus, enacting a climactic moment in the divine-human partnership. As theologian Rosemary Haughton writes, "Sacraments are extraordinary experiences of the ordinary."[2]

Baptism symbolizes all human experiences of partnership and community, of belonging and vocation, as it initiates people into the Body of Christ—the Church—to live as disciples of Jesus toward the reign of God.

Confirmation symbolizes the human *spirit* of faith, hope, and love, and continues to initiate into Christian community by "sealing" Christians with the gifts of the Holy Spirit, strengthening them to live their faith in the world.

Eucharist symbolizes all that reflects vitality and responsibility, peace and justice, care and compassion—everything that fulfills the covenant—as it celebrates the *real* presence of the Risen Christ, makes "an offering of praise" to God, bonds Christians into community, sustains them with the "bread of life," and empowers them "for the life of the world" (John 6:51). Eucharist is "the sacrament of sacraments" (Aquinas's phrase)—for Christian faith the most eminent instance of divine-human encounter.

Reconciliation symbolizes all human efforts at forgiveness, peacemaking, and clemency as it celebrates God's never-ending mercy for repentant sinners, mediated through a Christian community.

Anointing of the Sick symbolizes all human efforts at healing the ill, sustaining the elderly, and consoling the dying as it celebrates and mediates God's power to restore people to health—spiritual, physical, and psychological—or to give hope for eternal life.

Holy Orders symbolizes the vocation that everyone has to worthwhile work as it officially ordains a person to function as a leader in the Christian community's ministries of preaching, celebrating sacraments, and enabling the gifts of all to work well together—with "holy order."

Matrimony symbolizes all experiences of friendship and support, all of human intimacy and sexuality, as it celebrates the covenant of life and love between a married couple.

In traditional Catholic theology, the effectiveness of a sacrament depends both on the action of the Spirit and on the response of the person and community celebrating it—as always, a covenant. There is nothing magical about sacraments. True, they mediate God's grace but also bring the response-ability to live as graced people. For example, Eucharist enables people to encounter the real presence of the Risen Christ *and* it sends them to "love and serve" after *the way* of Jesus.

We must say likewise for the sacramentality of life in general. God's grace works through the ordinary and everyday but also expects our partnership and responsibility. Though enabled by God's Spirit, we must make our own good choices and best efforts. In sum, Catholicism invites people to adopt a sacramental outlook on all of life in the world. In the words of the poet Gerard Manley Hopkins (1844–1889), "The world is charged with the grandeur of God. / It will flame out, like shining from shook foil."[3] That's a Catholic imagination.

GOD'S SPIRIT AT WORK IN THE WORLD

Christian faith sees Jesus as the primary sacrament of God in human history. Jesus perfectly fulfilled in his person and life the divine-human partnership. Likewise, he models and empowers disciples to live this new covenant of Christian faith. The broader principle of sacramentality, however, reflects an understanding of God and of God's Spirit at work in the world.

Sacramentality reflects a God who intervenes lovingly in human history—the Spirit at work—and engages humankind in partnership toward God's reign. Too often, even believers imagine God as removed from the ordinary and everyday, as of no consequence to the Mondays of their lives. Even to say "I believe in *a* God" can sound as if God is just one more thing within a larger frame of reality, and usually located "off out there." Better to say, "I believe God *is*." For a sacramental consciousness imagines God as the ground of all that is and the loving dynamic of life, and yet ever Transcendent and more than all creation.

In ancient times, we find a marked contrast between the God of Greek philosophy and of Hebrew faith. For Aristotle, God is a Cosmic Reason who designed creation, set it in motion, and now has nothing further to do with it. For Plato, likewise, God is an Ideal Form who totally transcends creation and never engages in human history. For both, God created the world but then absconded to some heavenly realm, leaving us to our own devices.

The God of Hebrew faith is also Transcendent Other—"God of the Heavens" (Psalm 136:26). In contrast to the Greek image, however, God is also the Immanent One who pours out upon the earth divine goodness (Psalm 33:5) and mercy (Psalm 119:64); God visits and cares for the earth and all its people (Psalm 65); God is as near as our own heartbeat (Psalm 73:26), by whose very breath we breathe (Genesis 2:7). God intervenes and acts within history to favor humankind—especially those most in need. God promises to be "ever present in your midst" and to "go with you wherever you go" (see Leviticus 26:11–13).

The God of biblical faith has the best of intentions for creation and humankind. For all, God's desire is faith, hope, and love, peace, justice, and freedom, compassion, wholeness, and holiness—the best of everything. And God takes humankind into partnership on behalf of these desires.

The classic instance of this two-sided covenant is how God intervened to set free the oppressed from slavery and then immediately gave Israel the laws for how to live on in freedom. "I am the Lord your God who brought you out of Egypt, that place of slavery" (Exodus 20:2)—and then the Decalogue follows. So, people are to do God's loving will, not as a whimsical test but in order to remain free; all idols enslave. God's law is truly for our own good.

For Christian faith, God's decisive sacrament in human history was Jesus Christ, in whom the first disciples experienced God present as savior and liberator. Matthew's Gospel gives Jesus the name Emmanuel, "which means, God is with us" (1:23). Throughout his ministry, Jesus promised a new outpouring of God's Spirit to continue the work of saving the world. That promise was fulfilled at the First Pentecost (see Acts 2:1–13). And at the end of Matthew, the Risen Christ assured disciples, "I will be with you always until the end of time" (Matthew 28:20). Such faith in "God with us," saving, engaging, and enabling humankind as covenant partners, is all reflected in the principle of sacramentality.

The principle of sacramentality also reflects the Christian doctrine of God as Triune. For this doctrine symbolizes that God is a Trinity of loving relationships. It is God's very nature to be in relationship both within Godself and with humankind; as emerald is green, so God is loving relationship. Given this relational nature, God cannot leave us and our world to our own devices, to muddle along by ourselves. And so God's Spirit constantly outreaches into human history, renewing creation and continuing the saving work of Jesus.

And the divine outreach to humankind, as Saint Thomas Aquinas argued convincingly, is always according to the mode of the receiver. In other words, God's initiative comes through the ordinary and everyday media of life. The Trinity means that God is always at work in the world—creating, liberating, and sanctifying—and inviting our responsible participation in God's dream for us all. That's what life is all about!

ENOUGH TO TEST ANYONE'S FAITH

But doesn't the sacramental principle sound a bit too cozy, as if everything about life in the world is hunky-dory. Surely there is a massive stumbling block to a sacramental outlook? *If God is lovingly present, and life in the world is basically good, then how come there is so much suffering and evil?* Here is a problem for all people of faith, but the principle of sacramentality requires Christians to address it head-on. Surely it lands us knee-deep in paradox, in mystery, facing how little we know and testing faith to the limits.

Let's admit immediately that believers—theists—have no convincing *explanation* for evil and suffering, much as atheists are stumped by goodness and love. Even the Bible explicitly recognizes that suffering is beyond human ken. Although Job is ever our hero for questioning God about it, his eventual sentiments are: "I have dealt with great things that I do not understand; things too wonderful for me, which I cannot know" (Job 42:3). Beyond acquiescence, however, we can make a few summary statements from Christian Story. Though not explaining sin and suffering, they can make the principle of sacramentality seem not unreasonable.

First, God never causes human evil or natural suffering. God laments both but allows them out of respect for human freedom and the dynamics of nature. It is as if God chooses to limit the divine omnipotence, waiting upon human cooperation so that we might be free partners in the covenant. Likewise, natural disasters such as hurricanes and earthquakes happen because of the "freedom" granted to the dynamics of creation by its Creator.

Second, the overarching biblical revelation is that God does not use suffering as a quid pro quo punishment for sin. Indeed, sinful choices often bring suffering, but from the natural sequence of cause and effect, not from a punitive God.

Third, even when human beings make sinful choices, God may draw some good out of them. The *Catechism* summarizes, "God is in no way, directly or indirectly, the cause of moral evil. [God] permits it, however, because [God] respects the freedom of creatures and, *mysteriously, knows how to derive good from it.*"[4]

Fourth, though Jesus offered no final explanation for sin and suffering, he taught disciples to avoid the first and alleviate the latter. He urged people to resist sin's power, personally and socially; to repent as needed and be assured of God's mercy. Likewise regarding suffering, Jesus healed the sick, fed the hungry, condemned injustice, defended victims, included the marginalized, showed deep compassion for the poor and afflicted, and told disciples to do likewise.

Fifth, in his agony and death, Jesus symbolized God's solidarity with people who suffer, upholding all who carry the crosses of life. In his Resurrection, Jesus defeated the powers of evil—they cannot finally triumph—and reversed suffering and death to go backward into new life.

Sixth, Christians must recognize whatever in the world is not of God's reign. In other words, a sacramental outlook requires a critical consciousness as much as an alert one. This includes a healthy suspicion for human sinfulness—personal and social. A sacramental perspective looks critically at life in the world, probing and questioning everything for the absence as well as the presence of what God intends.

Beyond this, we can only say that to recognize the reality of sin and suffering, and still to affirm the sacramentality of life in the world, poses a paradox for Christians; yet, faith is so often paradox-laden. And think about it; it really doesn't take much faith to say that suffering and evil have the last word. Real faith is required, however, to see beyond them, in spite of them, to the goodness of life in the world.

A SACRAMENTAL CONSCIOUSNESS—IMAGINE!

As a rule of thumb, we can say that sacramental consciousness amounts to being *alert to the more in the midst of the ordinary.* True, it looks *at* the world, but also looks *through* it, convinced that there is always more than meets the eye. A sacramental consciousness recognizes and responds to the Transcendent in the everyday, the Creator in the created order, the Divine in the human, the Supernatural in the natural, the Cosmos in the grain of sand, and the connectedness of all in God's Spirit. A sacramental consciousness helps us to responsibly participate in everyday life as a divine-human partnership.

People with a sacramental consciousness are able to "pull back the curtain" *(revelare)* on God's presence and grace in the everyday. Such a consciousness heightens the vitality and élan of life, enabling people to make the most of it. It encourages us to "choose life" for ourselves, others, and the world (Deuteronomy 30:19) and to live it to the full (John 10:10). It puts a spin on everything *for life for all*.

As a sacramental outlook is fundamental to Catholic imagination, so activating our own imagination is key to developing a sacramental consciousness. For sure, God's Spirit "works" through every aspect of ourselves and creation, but I suspect especially through human imagination.

Jesus' frequent benediction "Blessed are those who have the eyes to see" and "the ears to hear" was surely a call to imagination. But perhaps Jesus' strongest encouragement of disciples to imagine was "Unless you become as little children, you cannot enter the reign of God" (Luke 18:17). The child's fresh, playful, and creative approach to life is required for belonging to God's reign.

On occasion, "the more in the midst" may be patently obvious. A couple stand holding their newborn child and have a felt sense of Loving Mystery. We participate in a memorable celebration of Eucharist when the Real Presence in assembly, word, and sacrament is palpable. Such immediate experiences are what Celtic spirituality calls "thin moments," when the veil between human and divine becomes gossamer-thin—almost lifted. But for more ordinary moments, we need imagination to recognize "the more."

Otherwise, the grandmother's hug and the baby's smile can be missed as God's love in our lives.

We use imagination to see what is truly "here," how things really are, beyond the obvious and routine. This is precisely how its greatest exponents—poets and artists—use it; they imagine and unveil for the rest of us a little more of the real. Oftentimes, they explicitly name its sacramentality. Echo here the lovely line of Gerard Manley Hopkins: "The world is charged with the grandeur of God." Patrick Kavanagh (1904–1967) wrote of encountering God "in the bits and pieces of Everyday."[5] And in her epic poem *Aurora Leigh*, Elizabeth Barrett Browning said:

> *Earth is crammed with heaven,*
> *And every common bush afire with God;*
> *But only he who sees takes off his shoes—*
> *The rest sit round it and pluck blackberries.*[6]

With a sacramental imagination, we might well go shoeless all the time. For we are ever before the burning bush—encountering the sacredness of the ordinary, the divine presence in the everyday.

The Trappist monk Thomas Merton recounted standing on a street corner of downtown Louisville and having a mystical experience of God's presence in the bustling city before him. That took imagination. We see the morning sun rising over the horizon. Of course, we can explain the sky's pink to red hue meteorologically. Still, its beauty and the gift of the new day can lend a felt sense of the Presence in which we dwell—if we allow imagination to work!

We also need imagination to discern how best to respond to God's presence in the midst of life. Only by imagining possibilities and likely consequences can we discern how to live the covenant. And although memory and reason lend clarity to the will, imagination fuels the emotions to make the choices we should make. Imagination is crucial to doing the right thing as a people of God.

Imagination is necessary, too, for critical consciousness, that is, for recognizing what is not of God's reign, resisting it, and living otherwise. Personal and social myopia can blind us to people in need, to what we ought to do as God's reign in the world. Recall Jesus' description of the final judgment (Matthew 25:31–46).

God will divide sheep from goats by who gave food and drink to the hungry, clothing and shelter to those in need, care to the stranger, the sick, and imprisoned. Ironically, both sheep and goats will confess to God: "We did not *see you*." The sheep, however, did see the poor and cared for them, whereas the goats did not. The sacramental imagination, it seems, is not so much to see God first and then to act—who would not respond upon clearly seeing God? Rather, we must "see" and respond to the poor and oppressed—often hidden by social blindness. In their faces, then, we may imagine the face of God.

FOR REFLECTION AND CONVERSATION

- How do you respond to a sacramental imagination about life in the world? Note your agreements, disagreements, additions.

- What are some spiritual practices that might sustain a sacramental consciousness?

PRACTICING A SACRAMENTAL OUTLOOK

I propose three practices to encourage a sacramental perspective on life. Again, two suggestions are general and a third is more specific.

1. Develop the Habit of Sacramental Imagination

The more we practice this consciousness, the more it becomes a habit. Here are four suggestions.

First, *pause for a few moments at the beginning of each day* to refresh your sense of life as a gift in the presence of God. In the hubbub of daily cares, it is easy to forget the gift of it all and God's loving presence. Indeed, on some days life can feel more like a burden than a gift. Or we can experience what spiritual writers call "a dark night of the soul," when God's Spirit seems more absent than present. Saint Paul wrote that "we see now through a glass, darkly" (1 Corinthians 13:12). Some days the glass can be darker than others. And yet, every day is surely a gift. Begin each morning with an intentional pause to recognize as much before God, and to ask for the grace to live this day with gratitude.

Second, *be alert throughout the day for particular "God-moments."* Flying out for a speaking engagement at a conference, I got to Logan Airport only to find it closed by an approaching thunderstorm. A 1:30 flight finally left at 9:30 P.M., and I had missed the first of my scheduled presentations. I sat frustrated, exaggerating how my absence would diminish the conference, forgetting that the cemeteries are full of indispensable people. Then, a little boy about two years old left his mother across the way—she had started to doze off—came over, climbed up on my lap, and with the biggest smile said, "Hi." Suddenly the delayed plane didn't seem important, and I knew the conference would do fine without me. We have such epiphanies of God's love every day; too often we miss them. It helps to be on the alert.

Third, *take time for faith reflections.* Reflection is pausing to figure out what's going on; we do it a thousand times a day. But then, it's a great spiritual practice consciously to bring our faith to our reflections, to let faith guide how we interpret life. The old philosophical adage that "the unexamined life is not worth living" is surely true; a sacramental outlook encourages reflecting on life from a faith perspective. And when we take extended pauses for faith reflection, we can call it meditation.

Meditation takes many forms. A favorite in Christian tradition is to read and reflect prayerfully on a text of scripture, talking to God about what it might mean for life now. But the focus of meditation can be any aspect of life in the world—an experience of nature, a contemporary event, an issue of concern. So, we can meditate by pausing to reflect on what's going on, bringing our faith to discern what is or is not of God's reign, what the Spirit may be inviting, and how to respond in a faith-filled way.

Fourth, *stop to smell the roses.* Besides meditative moments, take contemplative ones. The typical distinction in Western spirituality is that meditation is more active on our part—we figure things out by talking to God, we work at it—whereas contemplation is more noticing and receiving the gifts that are there, often staring us in the face. Essentially, contemplation is "stopping to smell the roses." It can be as simple as pausing with a particular gift, focusing on it, letting it speak to the heart, enjoying it for a few moments.

I've heard the mother of a newborn describe her favorite moment of contemplation as the quiet time at the end of breast-feeding when the baby falls asleep at her breast. She finds herself just sitting and gazing with great love on the contented little face. And somehow, she also has a felt sense of God's love as well. God offers all of us countless opportunities for pause to receive a gift, even one as obvious as our own breathing. Take at least a few each day!

Not only do meditation and contemplation nurture a sacramental consciousness, but doctors now say that these practices can be antidotes to all kinds of maladies, can lower high blood pressure, and more. We shouldn't be surprised, given our body-soul unity as whole persons.

2. Be a Good Steward of Creation

New Age spirituality has a keen sense of creation, encouraging people to enjoy and care for nature. Although mainline Christianity has often failed in this regard, a sacramental outlook should foster tremendous appreciation and responsibility for creation. Given the dire threats that modern consumerism, pollution, warfare, and waste now pose to the environment, stewardship of creation is surely an urgent spiritual practice required of Christians.

Before technology became so developed, human beings couldn't do much to harm the environment. With the Industrial Revolution, however, we began to waste and destroy the air, land, water, and the ozone layer over it all, at a dreadful pace. Christian faith did little to challenge the abuse.

In fact, some critics claim that Christian interpretation of the creation stories was part of the problem. We had read them as placing "man" at the center of creation with dominion over everything else. This encouraged the assumption of male *power over* nature—in addition to women and children—as if creation is at the whim of human appetites. Instead of stewardship we claimed ownership; we forgot that "the earth is the Lord's and all that is in it" (Psalm 24:1).

The first Genesis story indeed directs humankind "to fill the earth and subdue it, to have dominion . . . over every living thing" (Genesis 1:28). However, we must read this alongside the second account, in which God mandates people to be good stewards of creation. The key verse is Genesis 2:15; it has many translations. The terms of commission to humankind are *shamar* and *abad*. *Shamar* means "to sustain with loving care" and *abad* is typically translated as "cultivate."

Thereafter, the overarching biblical sentiment is that creation is a divine gift and humankind must be its responsible steward in God's name. Of all the sacred authors, the psalmists had the keenest sense of the sacramentality of creation. They experienced the Creator coming to meet them through the created order and called upon it to join them in worshiping God. "Sun and moon and shining stars . . . fire and hail, snow and mist, storm winds . . . mountains and hills . . . fruit trees and cedars"—all of creation must join in praising God (Psalm 148). Both as gift and as responsibility, creation is a sacrament of the divine-human covenant.

The spiritualities of many ancient peoples have a strong sense of divine presence in creation and of human responsibility to care for it. Over the years, there were always pockets of creation spirituality among Christians, too. Celtic spirituality—my own original—has a beautiful sense of God's presence through nature. Likewise, many medieval women mystics reflect a creation spirituality. Saint Hildegard of Bingen (1098–1179) is an eminent instance. The Franciscan charism also has a strong ecological strain; Francis's appreciation of "brother sun and sister moon" has lived on in his community. Such a spirituality must now become the currency of *all* Christians.

This means to relish and enjoy the beauty of nature, pausing often to recognize God's presence "in the great book of creation."[7] We must also become rigorists in ecological stewardship, and everyone *can do* something in this regard. Even the simple three R's of environmental care—*reduce, reuse, recycle*—if widely practiced, will make a huge difference to the well-being of the environment. A sacramental outlook requires Christians to make stewardship of creation integral to their spirituality.

3. Celebrate Life—and Eucharist

Catholics have a well-deserved reputation for their spirit of celebration. For many years I lived in the Italian section of Boston— the North End—which holds a religious festival every Sunday throughout the summer. Just to walk the streets during festival time, with their riot of color, parades, music, singing, dancing, and the best of food and wine, is exhilarating—a spiritual experience.

The two strands of chapters 2 and 3—a positive understanding of the person and of life in the world—come together to encourage Catholic festivity. They amount to saying that all creation is essentially good and a gift from God. So, within proper limits, we should enjoy it. This is why Catholics can sometimes have a little more fun. For example, many Christian traditions condemn alcohol as evil, but the Catholic attitude is that it, too, comes from divine bounty. Although people can abuse it, if used responsibly and in moderation, alcohol is a gift to be enjoyed.

A sacramental outlook epitomizes this spirit of celebrating life. That the ordinary and everyday is the arena of divine-human partnership should lend a deep joy to our lives. In his final words to the disciples, Jesus repeated his hope "that your joy may be complete" (see John 15:11; 16:24). The constant presence of God's Spirit in the everyday—the more in the midst of the ordinary—always warrants celebration.

Catholic Christianity has long cherished the celebration of Eucharist as the apex of the seven sacraments and, indeed, of the whole sacramentality of life. Here by the power of the Spirit, the faith community can encounter the Risen Christ in its assembly, in the scriptures proclaimed, and climactically in the consecrated bread and wine as Jesus' "body and blood" presence. After Mass has ended, Catholics reverence the Real Presence that continues in the Eucharist reserved in the tabernacle.

For Catholic Christians, Mass is the central symbol of divine-human encounter, the most sacred event at which God and people come together. Vatican II described Eucharist as "the fount and apex of the whole Christian life."[8] Its enactment is well named a celebration.

The Mass is celebrated in two major parts, the Liturgy of Word and the Liturgy of Eucharist. Each reflects the pattern of "our lives to God, and God's life to us, for the life of the world."[9] In other words, participants can experience here the core dynamics of Christian spirituality—*bringing life to faith and faith to life.*

Liturgy of the Word begins with the assembling, the call to worship, and an act of repentance—participants bringing their lives to God, warts and all. Then God's life comes to the assembly through the scripture readings and homily. In the Creed and prayers of the faithful, the assembly recommits itself to living faith in the world.

Liturgy of Eucharist begins with a presentation of gifts; the bread and wine are symbols of people's lives being offered to God. By the power of the Holy Spirit, they are consecrated into the Body and Blood of Christ, which participants can receive in Holy Communion—God's life to us. Mass ends with the assembly being sent *(missa)* to "love and serve" for the life of the world.

Catholics are known to complain loudly, often with good reason, about the quality of their Sunday liturgy, and especially the often poor standard of preaching. A negative pastoral situation can put a strain on anyone's faith. And yet, the Second Vatican Council tried mightily to convince Catholics that "the people" are the Church, that all baptized members must participate in its life, and that this should be eminently true in the celebration of Mass. All are called to "full, conscious, and active participation . . . demanded by the very nature of the liturgy." And "such participation by the Christian people . . . is their right and duty by reason of their baptism."[10]

Notice that "right and duty" go together. Catholic Christians have a "right" to Eucharist. Parenthetically, this raises the issue of the growing priest shortage. It would appear that the Western church is insisting upon celibacy and maleness for priesthood at the expense of people's access to Eucharist—so central to Catholic identity and spirituality. Further, people have a right to a decent quality of liturgy. But even in cases where the liturgy is not what people are entitled to, Catholics remain responsible to make the most of their Mass. For it always assembles a community of Christian people, lends access to the word of God in scripture, and offers Holy Communion, rebonding the community within the Body of Christ. This is ever worth celebrating!

FOR REFLECTION AND CONVERSATION

- Has your own worldview changed any from your conversation with this chapter?

- What practices are inviting you to deepen your sacramental outlook on life?

FOUR

"ARE WE MADE FOR EACH OTHER?"— GETTING TOGETHER FOR GOOD

A THIN PLACE AND A WIDE COMMUNITY

The storm howled through the rafters of the great stone Abbey of Iona as if gathering us from the four winds. We were a rainbow community, with all the hues of humanity, assembled around the high altar to share "the bread of life."

Although our diversity was dramatic, more amazing still was the local inclusivity. For old neighboring enemies—English Anglicans, Scottish Calvinists, Ulster Presbyterians, and Irish Catholics—were assembled here to celebrate as one Body of Christ. I'd never imagined a gathering like it this side of eternity, if then.

A few days before, my companions and I had looked over the western rim of the rugged Isle of Mull and seen for the first time the fabled Iona. I had longed to visit here since childhood.

Growing up, I heard a hundred stories of the legendary Saint Columba (521–597), known to me first by his Gaelic name, Colum Cille. His biographers claimed that Columba left Ireland as a "pilgrim for Christ." But an old tradition ran that he was banished as penance for some terrible public sin, endearing him all the more to childhood imagination.

For whatever reason he sailed, Columba and twelve companions landed on this little knob of an island in the Scottish Hebrides on Pentecost Sunday, 563. Here they established a renowned monastery that became a beacon of sanctity and scholarship, later acclaimed "the savior of civilization" during Europe's darkest age.

In the footsteps of Columba, thousands of pilgrims and penitents have come to Iona, finding here what the Celts called "a thin place"—where the veil between Creator and created is gossamer-thin. To this day it is the hallowed heart of Celtic spirituality.

We were four in our pilgrim band: myself; Colleen, my spouse; and two dear friends, Sr. Jane Silk and Sr. Jeanne Snyder, both celebrating fifty years of vowed religious life. For the next four days we steeped ourselves in the ethos of Iona. We walked the little island from Saint Columba's Bay at the southern tip to the Strand of the Monks at its northernmost end. We participated in the prayer life of the Abbey. Most memorable there was its intensity of community experience.

The spirit of Columba lives on in the present Iona community. It was founded in 1938 by George MacLeod to forge new ways of living the gospel together. Members dedicate themselves to a "rule" that unites work and worship, politics and prayer, life and faith. Steeped in Celtic spirituality, the Iona community is deeply committed to peace and justice, to integrating the feminine and masculine, to stewardship of creation, and to hospitality toward all.

As the sacred drama unfolded on this sabbath morning, the presider invited us "to come to the table of company with Jesus . . . the table of sharing with the poor of the world . . . the table of communion with the earth in which Christ became incarnate." What Christian could refuse such an invitation?

It felt as if the whole world came forward as one grand communion, the living and dead, the saints and sinners. Perhaps my eyes deceived me or imagination ran wild, but for a moment I could swear I saw an old, old monk leading the way with the lilt of a jig in his step. Columba?

CAIN'S OLD QUESTION EVER NEW

Can you imagine what life would be like if you had this whole world to yourself? Or what if there were as many people as there are but with none of us relating in any way, a bunch of self-sufficient monads? The prospect of living without community seems totally inhuman, a nightmare. *To be a person is to be in relationship with other people and the world.* With that said, great questions remain about our communality.

To what extent are we relational beings? Are relationships a precondition or an add-on to personhood? Do human beings become an "I" only through a "we," or are we first and foremost individuals who then enter tit-for-tat contracts for personal benefit? If we are essentially communal, must we sacrifice our personhood to some group? If we don't, is a community anything more than a collection of individuals? Within society, what are the limits to our rights and responsibilities, and who sets them? Is the Iona community, with its inclusivity and commitments, a symbol of hope for humanity or a foolhardy attempt at a pipe dream?

All these questions were implied in Cain's ancient and eternal query of God, "Am I my brother's keeper?" (Genesis 4:9). Wasn't he really asking, Should I care for myself alone or for brothers and sisters as well? Might it be wisest to respond with *both/and* instead of *either/or;* to care for ourselves as "persons-in-community" and to care for each other as a "community-of-persons"?

The theme of this chapter is sociology and what might be a Christian perspective on human sociality. Patently, our everyday attitude about community greatly affects how we live with others in the world. Wherever we come down between the extremes of rugged individualism and communal dictatorship greatly influences how we realize our human vocation, and thus our Christian one.

As we shall see, Christian faith proposes a distinctive social perspective. In particular, Catholic Christianity has its own way of affirming *both* person *and* community. And Christians should integrate their faith perspective on sociology into their spirituality for life.

FOR REFLECTION AND CONVERSATION

• Recall a significant experience you've had of community. Why does it stand out for you? What bonded the community together?

• Thinking more broadly, how do you understand human relationality? For example, does it constitute who we are as persons, or are we first and foremost "individuals"?

CATHOLIC IMAGINATION ABOUT SOCIETY: A GIFT FOR LIFE

Chapter 2 proposed a Catholicism that celebrates the person, affirming our basic goodness and dignity as human beings. Following on, it has a consistent attitude toward society, precisely because this is how God intends us to be together—*we are social beings by divine design.* At its best, then, Catholic Christianity affirms both person and society, not favoring one over the other but holding the two in mutuality. It teaches that society must ensure the rights, dignity, and well-being of each member and, likewise, that every person must contribute according to circumstances to the *common good* of society.

Beginning with Augustine, there is a strong strain of Christian thought that looks upon society with suspicion, as a "city of sin." Augustine placed this public realm over against the "city of God," which reigns in the hearts of saints here and in heaven hereafter. Protestant Reformers embraced a two-kingdoms view, separating what is "of God" from what is "of man." Five hundred years later, the morning paper gives ample grounds to argue such a divide.

Catholic Christianity, on the other hand, generally maintained a positive view of society. God made us relational beings, so society could not be inherently evil. Instead, society is how we sustain our human nature; we create a common world to sustain our dignity and destiny as persons. Of course, like the human condition itself, society is never perfect. But we can always improve it, reform it, and, if necessary, revolt against its oppressions. Avoiding the extremes of totalitarianism and individualism, society is responsible for promoting the *common good* of all, which includes the *personal good* of every member.

We noted in chapter 2 that the best word for oneself is *person* precisely because it is a communal word—from the Greek *prosopon*, "turned toward the other." Every one of us is a person-in-community if we are a person at all. Now, turning the coin, by nature we flourish best as a community-of-persons. Thus, being human gives rise to community, and community is essential to being human. Our word *idiot* is also from the Greek; *idiotes* literally means "one who stands alone."

Although affirming society and the *common good* may sound a bit self-evident, it is actually countercultural. Beginning with the modern era—from the Industrial Revolution onward—there has quite been a strong sentiment in Western culture to favor the individual as autonomous and standing alone. The English philosopher John Locke (1632–1704) was its champion in politics.

Now, only extreme anarchists reject the need for society. But after Locke, Western democracies—and especially the United States—tilted heavily to favor individual rights and private property over against social responsibility and the common good. Locke insisted upon the "absolute liberty" of the individual. He claimed that society, instead of being a natural bonding, emerges from a "social contract"—a tit-for-tat kind of agreement. Within society, individual rights reign supreme, limited only by the precept "Do not infringe upon the rights of others." Such thinking encouraged a utilitarian attitude toward society—take from it what you can get—with little emphasis on shared responsibility for the common good.

By contrast, Catholic social thought continued to place equal emphasis on person *and* society, stressing that the welfare of each works in cooperation rather than being in competition. In this sense, Catholicism clung more tenaciously than did modernity to the old-world consensus, reaching back to Plato and Aristotle, that society is the *natural* arrangement for persons, and its function is to promote the *common good* and the good of *each person*. Ultimately, only what benefits all, benefits me.

ALL FOR ONE AND ONE FOR ALL

There can be problems in making an argument from *nature* to favor society or social arrangements. For example, there has been much gender and racial bias in how the dominant culture has interpreted "nature." As late as 1880, the Massachusetts Medical Society argued that women were unsuited "by nature" to be physicians. This is not unlike the argument that the Catholic church still makes against women becoming priests.

Besides bias in what is natural to whom, we must also recognize that nature is not static. It evolves across history and cultures. That is, what emerges as people's nature is influenced by their nurture as well. So we need to be cautious and socially conscious when arguing that any social arrangement is "natural." Even so, we can surely say that some aspects endure as natural to our human condition, and the urge to form society is one of them. At least, such is the philosophical claim of Catholic Christianity.

In addition to the argument from nature, Catholicism claims good theological reasons for holding a community-of-persons sociology. Again, we can cite the symbol of the Trinity. That the interior life of God is a community-of-persons surely means that people created in God's image are made for community as well. For our theological rationale in this chapter, however, I will highlight Catholicism's emphasis on the Church being a community for God's work of salvation. Its sentiments about society in general reflect the function it sees for the Church. In Catholic thought, sociology and ecclesiology intertwine, with community essential to being good disciples and good citizens.

A "private Christian" is a contradiction in terms. To live as disciples of Jesus, people need to bond with a living community of Christians and with ancestors in faith; this faith community is a prime medium of God's grace. As Jesus was God's sacrament of salvation to the world, so the Church is now the sacrament of Jesus. By the power of the Holy Spirit it continues as a community to do Christ's work of "liberating salvation."

Community is a central theme of the Hebrew scriptures. God called Abraham and Sarah to become "a great nation" in whom "all the peoples of the earth shall find blessing" (Genesis 12:2–3). Ever after, the Hebrews embraced their identity as "the *people* of God." They entered the covenant to live as God's people, and God made them responsible for and to each other. Every good done benefited the doer and the community; every sin hurt the sinner and the community. Repentance had to be both personal and communal. Theirs was no communalism, however; the Hebrews were keenly aware that each person deserved respect and care, with special favor for those most in need—the poor, the widow, the orphan, and the alien. Yet they always recognized themselves as "a people," not an assortment of individuals.

Reared in this Hebrew sociology, Jesus invited people into a community of disciples. Although the New Testament does not offer a blueprint for Church organization, Jesus made clear that he intended his followers to forge a deep bond of community to continue his ministry to the world. Scholars point to Jesus' table fellowship as symbolic of his communal intent; he welcomed all and sundry to eat with him, with special outreach to those who were socially unacceptable. In a culture for which eating together had great symbolism, this action epitomized Jesus' deep respect for every person and the inclusive community he intended among disciples.

When preaching the greatest commandment (Matthew 22:34–40, Mark 12:28–34, and Luke 10:25–28), Jesus united as one the three loves—of God, of oneself, and of neighbor. Thus, Jesus' response to Cain's question was that indeed we must love our brothers and sisters with the same measure as ourselves, and that this is how we love God. As chapter 7 will elaborate, this love command applies both personally and socially; Christian love cannot be limited to one-on-one charity but requires justice in society.

The first Christians understood themselves as a community-of-persons. We know this from the metaphors they chose to describe their group. None captures this better than "Body of Christ," the great communal image that Saint Paul gave to Christian imagination. As the historical Jesus was present in his physical body, Paul imagined that the Risen Christ continues in the world through the community of disciples. He wrote to the church at Corinth, and to all Christians thereafter, "You are Christ's body, and individually members of it" (1 Corinthians 12:27).

Note that Paul's understanding of the Church as Christ's Body places equal stress on the personal and the communal. In the Body of Christ, each member is cherished, cared for, and has a unique role that no one else can play. Still, each part needs the whole for its proper functioning. A hand or foot by itself would be dead, or "If the whole body were an eye, where would the hearing be?" (1 Corinthians 12:17). So the well-being of the community is crucial to that of each member and vice versa (see 1 Corinthians 12:12).

With mutuality among the parts and between the whole and the parts, Paul proposed an amazing sense of equality within this Body of Christ. "For in one Spirit we were all baptized into one body, whether Jew or Greek, slave or free person, and we were all given to drink of one Spirit" (1 Corinthians 12:13). Baptism, then, calls Christians to become what the scripture scholar Elisabeth Schussler Fiorenza has aptly named "a community of equal disciples." In the Body of Christ, no one is any more baptized than anyone else.

Although Catholic theology emphasizes both person and community, in practice Catholicism has often failed to maintain the balance. It can be so intent on touting the Church that it forgets the rights and responsibilities of individual members. It is unrivaled for making its clergy a favored elite—clericalism—with complete power in all matters of sanctifying, teaching, and ruling. Few dictators have claimed as much hegemony as popes have done over history. At times, the institutional church can idolize itself, becoming its own end—an empire—instead of a sacrament of God's reign.

The sixteenth-century Protestant Reformers, led by Martin Luther and John Calvin, had eminent good cause to revolt. They rightly challenged the church's corruption, but equally its authoritarianism and exaggerated sense of its own importance. Their intent—biblically well grounded—was to reaffirm the "priesthood of all believers." This is the notion that baptism requires every Christian to participate in the mission of Jesus. Likewise, they insisted that the scriptures should be at the heart of Christian faith, with every person entitled to read and interpret them.

The efforts of the Reformers bore some rich social as well as spiritual fruits. For example, the movement toward democracy received great impetus from the Reformation's advance of personal responsibility and the rights of the person. These are values that Catholicism, when faithful to its best theology, should champion as well. In the polemics of the time, however, Catholicism saw

Protestantism as underrepresenting the communal aspect of Christian faith.

Given the widespread corruption and need for reform, it was understandable that the Reformers might downplay the function of the institutional church. But did their criticisms collapse the healthy tension between person and community, favoring the rights of the individual? From a Catholic perspective, it appeared so.

When Catholic Christianity regrouped at the Council of Trent (1545–63), it agreed that everyone should have a personal relationship with God. But rejecting the individualism it perceived in the Reformers, Trent strongly reaffirmed the necessity of the Church for living the Christian faith. Since then, though often failing egregiously to practice the balance, Catholicism has claimed a theology that emphasizes both personal discipleship and Christian community.

Over the past forty years and inspired by Vatican II, Catholicism has moved closer to "walking the walk," although the Council's full vision is still a horizon for us. Regarding the person, the Council reclaimed for Catholics the "priesthood of all believers"—Luther would be happy—and reaffirmed that all the baptized are called to holiness of life. According to personal gifts and circumstances, all Christians must participate in the mission of the Church in the world. The Christian community is every member's business rather than being a service station with a few in charge of dispensing to the rest.

On the other hand, Vatican II championed a communal understanding of the Church, insisting that its primary nature is to be "a people of God" rather than a hierarchical institution. It placed priority on the community of members rather than on its leadership with "the led" as an afterthought. Further, Vatican II consciously expanded Christian community to include *all* the baptized—Protestant and

Catholic—as full members of the Body of Christ. "All those justified by faith through baptism are incorporated into Christ."[1]

At least the theology is in place now for personal rights and responsibilities within a bonded faith community—a Church that is all for one and one for all. Such communal faith should overflow into the social realm, championing the personal good of every member and the *common good* of the whole.

SOCIETY FOR THE COMMON GOOD AND CHURCH FOR THE REIGN OF GOD

Catholic Christianity has consistently understood society's function as serving the *common good. Common* does not mean totalitarian, as if the group counts for everything. Rather, the good served is *common* precisely because society serves the personal good of every member. On the other hand, the Catholic understanding avoids rugged individualism, instead making each person responsible for the good of neighbor and community. It is the two together—society's responsibilities to the person and the person's responsibilities to society—that realizes the *common good.*

That society exists for the *common good* has a parallel in the Church's function for the reign of God. Catholicism has a long tradition of locating the Church in the midst of society, not above, over against, or apart from it. In this spirit, a compelling way to understand the purpose of the Church is to think of it as *a sacrament of God's reign in the world.*[2] What does this mean?

We noted already that the reign of God is both a personal and a social symbol; God is to rule in people's hearts and lives, and in the public world of society and culture. Now add to this mix the classic definition of *a sacrament* by Thomas Aquinas: "an effective symbol that causes to happen what it symbolizes."[3]

Being a sacrament of God's reign, then, requires that the Church work effectively in society to help bring about the values of that reign. Every Christian community must be a catalyst for realizing God's intent of peace and justice, love and compassion, inclusion and fullness of life for all, and the integrity of creation. The Church's purpose is always spiritual, first and foremost, with its mission rooted in Christian faith. Yet, it is precisely its spiritual mission and communal faith that give it, and likewise every Christian, great social responsibilities. When we pray "your kingdom come," we must choose to do God's will of *shalom* "on earth as it is in heaven."

The early Christians imagined the Church to possess specific tasks or ministries in service to God's reign. Although they are variously listed to include from three to six, I suggest the following five, using their ancient Greek names:

- *Koinonia:* to be an inclusive community of faith, hope, and love; a truly "catholic" community that welcomes all people into partnership; that engages each member's gifts "for the life of the world" (a *welcoming* community).

- *Kerygma:* to evangelize, preach, and teach God's word of liberating salvation that we know through Jesus and the New Testament, through the Hebrew scriptures, and through Christian Tradition (a *word* of God community).

- *Leitourgia:* to worship God publicly as an assembly of Christian people, celebrating God's covenant in Jesus Christ and the hope of salvation for all humankind (a *worshiping* community).

- *Diakonia:* to care for human needs—spiritual, psychological, and physical—helping to build up God's reign of peace and justice in the world, with special favor for the poor and disadvantaged (a community of *welfare*).

- *Marturia:* to bear credible public witness to Christian faith through lifestyle and example, living as an effective symbol of God's reign even to the point of suffering and death (a *witnessing* community).

The point I wish to highlight is that these ministerial functions should not be confined within the Christian community itself; the very mission of the Church demands that Christians realize them in society as well. Everything the Church does should serve the common good of society, and everything in society that realizes the values of God's reign should have the support of the Christian community. Christians should be citizen-disciples, uniting the realms of church and society by faith that is lived in the world.

FOR REFLECTION AND CONVERSATION

- How do you respond to a community-of-persons sociology— for Church and society? What rings true? False? Needing addition?

- What might this social imagination mean for Christian spirituality?

PRACTICING A SOCIAL SPIRITUALITY

Following our pattern, I make three suggestions for integrating a community-of-persons sociology into Christian spirituality. Again, the first two are generic, and the third is more specific. Let my suggestions stimulate your own.

1. Good Citizenship as Integral to Spirituality

Think about it for a moment: Christian spirituality must entail serious social responsibilities. How can Christians fulfill the great commandment of love and live as a Church for the reign of God in the world unless they bring their faith to bear on their communal life and participation in society.

Now, there was a time in Western history when church and state were totally intertwined—the era of Christendom. (It had a high point about the year 800.) That structural arrangement, however, was not a wise one. For one thing, it gave the church too much power, allowing it to commit some of its worst sins: leading crusading wars in the name of God, executing anyone considered heretical, and persecuting people perceived as "other," especially Jews. It was a blessing when modern democracies decided to divide the turf between church and state.

Once it was divided, however, the pendulum swung to the opposite extreme. Now people were encouraged to keep their faith very private, never letting it impinge on the social realm except for one-on-one charity. The influential French philosopher Jean-Jacques Rousseau (1712–1778) made the persuasive argument for this neat separation. He reasoned that the public and private are two separate spheres of life, that the state should care for the former, leaving the private realm to the church.

Rousseau had good intentions. He wanted to keep the state from interfering in people's personal lives. However, his proposal—which spread like wildfire—made faith a totally private matter, situating it apart from public life. This amounts to a kind of atheism, because it establishes a whole sphere from which God is excluded.

No democracy has outdone the United States in its structural separation of church and state. The touchstone of the divide is the First Amendment to the Constitution, which states that "Congress shall make no law respecting an establishment of religion, or prohibiting the free exercise thereof." Passed in 1791, the amendment's original intent was to protect the church from undue interference by the state. This wise constitutional arrangement, however, became a "wall of separation" between the two institutions and—even more debilitating—between people's faith and their participation in society.

Chapter 7 will elaborate on how Christian faith demands social justice. For now, in response to a community-of-persons sociology, let us renew the simple notion of good citizenship as a spiritual practice. For no matter how we view the relationship between church and state or what we think is the best way to promote social justice, faith mandates that every Christian be *a responsible citizen.* Good citizenship is a required spiritual practice.

We just reviewed the fivefold functions of Christian ministry for the reign of God. These functions can also be suggestive for Christian citizenship. Stretching the categories a bit, we can imagine how citizen-disciples might function in society through works of welcome *(koinonia)*, welfare *(diakonia)*, witness *(marturia)*, word *(kerygma)*, and worship *(leitourgia)*.

Welcome. Even in modern democracies, there is much discrimination—on the basis of race, gender, ethnicity, religion, orientation, class, and so on. In fact, anyone who is "other" to the dominant group is considered inferior and unwelcome. We are far from being a truly inclusive society that welcomes diversity and resolutely defends the equal rights and dignity of all. Christians should be at the forefront of forging communities and a society that welcomes "the other," honoring their God-given dignity without insisting that they become "the same."

Welfare. Given the social connotation of *welfare,* the Greek word *diakonia* may be better rendered here as *being a good neighbor.* Chapter 7 elaborates that *diakonia* demands social justice. But here, let's keep it very down-home. Who does not have a hundred opportunities a day—in family or community, at work or recreation—to be kind and helpful to others? Over against the terrible trend of "random acts of violence," their faith should compel Christians to do "random acts of kindness" and as a habit *for life.*

Witness. Every Christian should exemplify in lifestyle the best social values. These include the socially significant values of honesty, integrity, truth-telling, loyalty to commitments, respect for each person, and common courtesy—now all too uncommon. To these we can add civic virtues such as caring for personal and public property, paying fair taxes, and protecting the environment; and democratic values such as respect for just government, equal opportunity in every endeavor, due process under law, voting as an informed citizen, and participating in public discourse. Living such values and virtues is integral to the spirituality of Christians; their faith demands it.

Word. Traditionally, Catholics have understood evangelization quite narrowly as converting people to Christian faith. But an amazing development has emerged over the past twenty-five years, beginning with Pope Paul VI's "On Evangelization in the Modern World" (1976). This document emphasized evangelization not as "bringing them in" but rather as "bringing Christians out"—out into the world with God's word of "liberating salvation." "Evangelization means bringing the good news into all the strata of [society] . . . transforming humanity from within and making it new."[4]

So, evangelization for Christians comes down to living their faith in society, doing in daily life what they profess to believe. In a lovely phrase attributed to Saint Francis of Assisi, "Christians should always preach the gospel, sometimes using words."

Christian spirituality should also include bringing words of faith, hope, and love into the public realm, and mostly without using religious language. Indeed, when appropriate, Christians must share their faith—always with respect and ecumenical sensitivity for other faith traditions. But to every conversation, they can bring the values of God's reign, with or without "God talk." I think of a former student who works with street gangs in an inner city; among other things, she teaches rival gang members how to "talk" to each other instead of becoming violent. What a "ministry" of word!

Worship. There is a strong constitutional consensus in the United States that religious worship should be confined to faith communities. All things considered, this is likely a wise arrangement. So, instead of proposing things like prayer in public schools—a tokenism—it seems wiser for Christian citizens to be discerning about the rituals and symbols that *are* "sacred" to their society at large.

Here the term *liturgy* serves us better than the fifth *W* word, *worship*. In ancient Greek society, *leitourgia* literally meant "a public work," something that symbolized the life of society. Every society has such "public works" that represent its soul; rituals and symbols that are sacred to its identity. Christians should bring their spirituality to review the "public works" of society, seeing to it that they function *for life for all*.

2. Participate in a Faith Community

A gift that Catholicism brings to contemporary spirituality is its emphasis on faith community. Instead of the individualism that often marks the New Age movement, Catholic spirituality is at once personal and communal. It encourages people to form an intimate relationship with God *and* to do so within a community of shared faith.

This being said, many Catholics give up on their local parish. And they often have good reasons for dropping out. The institutional church can appear closed-minded on issues that cry out for debate. It can seem hardhearted with its rules and regulations, often appearing to miss the spirit of the gospel for the letter of the law. Many a local parish makes poor attempts at the ministries of *welcome, word, worship, witness,* and *welfare*.

While one can always find reasons to give up on a parish, the fact remains that living as a Catholic Christian requires participating in a local faith community. Moreover, a social spirituality reminds that the church is not "them" but "us." "We" are the church and must accept responsibility for it; the baptismal vocation requires active participation in some local community. It may be necessary to "shop around" for a good parish; the current *Code of Canon Law* even permits this rather than requiring people to belong to the parish of their geographic location. But every Christian is to contribute their time, talent, and treasure to the ministries of a local parish or base community.

By working for personal holiness and community renewal, we can help to make the Church—local and universal—what it ought to be: a sacrament of God's reign in the world. Beyond general participation in parish life, each Christian can take on a particular service according to personal gifts and community need. Again, the fivefold schema of ministries may be suggestive.

Every Christian should assemble regularly with their faith community for *leitourgia* (worship) and, according to time-honored tradition, with serious responsibility to do so for the sabbath—on Saturday evening or Sunday. Beyond "full, conscious, and active participation" in the liturgy by everyone present,[5] many liturgical functions are now open to laypeople: lector, song leader, acolyte, eucharistic minister, hospitality, choir, and more. If one has the appropriate gifts, it is an enriching spiritual practice to serve the liturgical life of one's Christian community.

The functions of *koinonia* (welcome) and *marturia* (witness) require all Christians to build up their particular faith community, to help it practice what it preaches by living their faith. Again, some people will have particular gifts for building up the community life, for enabling others to grow in faith, hope, and love. Every parish needs priestly people to maintain its common life and prophetic characters to work for its reform.

The ministry of *kerygma* (word) requires each Christian community to evangelize, preach, and teach the "word of God" that comes through Scripture and Tradition. The parish must see to it that all members have ready access to Christian Story—from cradle to grave. Everyone can participate in sharing their faith, and within the parish community some have gifts for the designated ministries of the word—evangelist, preacher, and catechist.

The ministry of *diakonia* (welfare) must be the concern of every Christian. Here again, some people have a particular charism to work for justice, both within the church and in society. This will be our focus in chapter 7. Every Christian, however, has ample opportunity every day to participate in ministries of compassion and the works of mercy.

Catholic tradition offers two lists of mercy works: *corporal* and *spiritual*. The seven *corporal works of mercy* are feed the hungry, give drink to the thirsty, clothe the naked, shelter the homeless, visit the sick, minister to prisoners, and bury the dead. The seven *spiritual works of mercy* are convert the sinner, instruct the ignorant, counsel the doubtful, comfort the sorrowful, bear wrongs patiently, forgive injuries, and pray for the living and the dead. Who cannot find regular opportunities for some such "works"? They are integral to a social spirituality.

3. Pray to the Saints and for the Souls

To the Saints. The "communion of saints and sinners" is a particular instance—some would say an extreme one—of Catholicism's community-of-persons spirituality. It reflects the radical notion that the faith community reaches beyond the grave, that even death does not break the bond of baptism. This is an old conviction; since the first centuries, Christians have practiced praying to the saints and for the souls.

Catholicism takes the attitude that the dead are still with us, though in a whole new way. As the Preface of the Mass of Resurrection states, their lives have been "changed, not ended." The saints remain bonded with the living in the Body of Christ and are now in the eternal presence of God. This is why they can add their prayers to our own. Strictly speaking, we don't pray *to* the saints, at least not as if *they* can respond. Instead, we ask them to pray *with* us and *for* us to God, much as we might ask living persons for their prayers.

Within the communion of saints, Mary holds pride of place—and rightly so; look at the fine son she reared. Christian faith holds that the divine and human natures in Jesus never interfered with each other. So, as human, Jesus had to be reared and taught like any person. Luke's Gospel explicitly states that Jesus *"grew* in wisdom, age, and grace before God and all the people" (Luke 2:52).

Who else but Mary—and Joseph—nurtured Jesus' capacity for love and compassion, his commitment to justice and peace, his care for the poor and oppressed, and all his life-giving values. Mary was present during his public ministry, there at the foot of the cross, and with the disciples on the First Pentecost. No person other than Jesus played a greater role than Mary in "the work of salvation."

Some Marian devotion arose from the very human instinct that, as children have a special affection for their mother, Jesus must have had the same. Now, if Mary prays with us, how can Jesus refuse—his own mother? Remember that he worked his first miracle at Mary's request at the wedding feast of Cana, making a lot of great wine— as Catholics like to point out to teetotaling Protestants. The early Christians came to revere Mary with the sacred title of *Theotokos*— literally, "God-bearer"—since Jesus' human and divine natures were united in the one person she bore.

Over history, the more the Church preached a punitive and patriarchal image of God, the more devotion to Mary increased among the common people. She reminded them of the mother-love of God. And Mary's own image of God now inspires the struggles for liberation. For her, God "puts down the mighty from their thrones and raises up the lowly, fills the hungry with good things and sends the rich away empty-handed" (Luke 1:52–53). No doubt for Mary as to whose side God takes, implying the same mandate for God's people. Devotion to Mary remains both consoling and demanding for a contemporary spirituality.

For the Souls. The very earliest liturgies in the Church included intercessory prayers on behalf of "those who have gone before us, marked with the sign of faith" (an ancient phrase still used in the First Eucharistic Prayer). The custom reflects a fairly common human sentiment; spiritual care for departed ancestors is practiced by more than half of humankind.

When faced with the radical demands of baptism—becoming "other Christs"— the early Christians needed to remember God's great mercy. For those who tried without much success, or who repented on their deathbeds without righting the wrongs they had done, the Church intuited that God provides some intermediate state of purgation between death and eternal judgment.

My own image of Purgatory is of a big room where we come face-to-face with all the people whom we were hoping never, ever, to see again. And we must put things right before proceeding onward. Likely this gets done "in the wink of an eye," or as some authors now propose, coincident with death.

Anyhow, since the earliest days, Catholic Christians have been convinced that the departed souls are still bonded in the Body of Christ. Thus, the living can pray for them, do an act of mercy, love, or justice on their behalf, and somehow such good works can work to their benefit. A favorite Catholic practice is to have mass celebrated "for the eternal rest" of a departed loved one. Of course, eternal life is never earned by human efforts on either side of the grave; this is the gift of God's mercy. Still, to pray that the dead will be admitted to God's eternal presence can be a consolation to the bereaved.

Practices associated with the communion of saints and sinners have led to many abuses within Catholicism. In popular piety it could appear at times that people were *worshiping* the saints—idolatry. The scandal of the Church's taking money for "indulgences"—benefit to the dead—was the last straw that prompted Martin Luther to put the match to the powder keg that became the Protestant Reformation.

Challenged to reform such pastoral abuses, Catholicism yet continued to claim that the bond of baptism transcends the grave. It remains one striking instance of what a community-of-persons sociology might mean for a Catholic spirituality.

Do you have a favorite saint—birth-patron or namesake, grandparent or old teacher—with whom you feel a special bond? Ask them to pray with you to God concerning some need or issue. Or do you have a recently deceased family member or friend whom you still mourn? Consider praying for their eternal rest, or offering to God on their behalf some good deed done in faith. If needed, your prayers or action will redound to their benefit. How? We don't really know, nor do we need to.

FOR REFLECTION AND CONVERSATION

- What other practices might nurture a community-of-persons spirituality in your life?

- Does this chapter prompt any decisions for your own practice of a social spirituality?

FIVE

"WHAT TIME DO WE HAVE?"— MINING THE TREASURY OF SCRIPTURE AND TRADITION

THAT CLOCK'S FAST

When we visit my family in Ireland, that first night home my broth-
er Bar (Bernard) just refuses to go to bed. My other sisters and
brothers who are still with us—Kieran, Peg, Maureen, and Jim—
their spouses, and maybe some nieces and nephews, are likely to
gather the night we arrive to welcome back the "stray one." Good
food and fine libations abound, and the best of chat. Heaven will be
pressed to do better.

Eventually people trickle away to their homes or to bed, but not
Bar. He stokes up the fire with fresh sods of turf; Doreen, our gra-
cious sister-in-law, replenishes the edibles and potables; and we
settle in, with Bar assuring us, "Ah, the night's young yet."

Now the sweep of time and eternity is our only horizon. We
review the births and deaths, marriages and milestones since last
we met. We want to hear and tell the whole story.

Do you ever have moments when it feels as if time stands still,
as if "now" is an eternal present? The poet Patrick Kavanagh
lamented:

My birthday comes as usual,
As birthdays will.
You can't keep the eastern sun,
On Cassidy's hill.[1]

But on a first night around the fire in Kinnegad, it feels as if we might actually keep the sun in tether.

It could be the present or thirty years ago, the way we talk. We summon up family and friends long gone, and we freshen the traces they left on our lives. Time has not really "gone by," for we still have its cherished legacy. We talk about the problems of the world, the state, the church, the family, but with an air that things will come right in time, even if we never "see it." Indeed, all time seems ready at hand to us, as past, present, and future weave into one—our time now.

The turf tries to burn down but is replenished. Bar may doze off briefly, only to return to the stories, revived by the catnap. And the last thing he'll say is, "Time for bed!" We do go eventually. I can't remember how or why, but not because "it's late," more that "it's time."

On one memorable winter's night, the jet lag had won out and I was longing for bed. Bar was more dozing than conversing by now, but still making no signs of a move. Eventually, I thought of appealing to the clock. Ah yes, the clock, that custodian of time and with a big one hanging on the wall.

So gently I announced the chronological time, or more suggested it with a diffident air and no hint of implication. Ever true to eternal time, Bar drowsily rebutted, "Ah Tom, that clock's fast!" And he put another sod on the fire.

WHAT TIME IS IT?

We speak all the time about time in everyday conversation; about spending and saving time, finding and losing time, investing and wasting time, not enough and too much time, about time flying or dragging, being on time or after time, having a good or bad time, a fun or sad time; we check the time, have a busy time, wish people a nice time, and wonder about the right time. Despite all our talk, do we really embrace *this* time that we have now? So little of my time has the quality of a first night back in Kinnegad.

Oh, indeed, we can obsess about schedules—what time to begin, to end, how to spend the in-between time. Modern lives are under the tyranny of the clock. But do we embrace and enjoy our time, relish it, or just let it drift by? Maybe Bar was right; that clock is always fast, robbing us of our time now.

Social commentators say that the modern fixation on time came with the ubiquity of watches. Perhaps it's true that the ancients, with the occasional sundial in a flower garden, "had" more time than we do. At least, our image is that they lived at a slower pace and worried less about time. If true, how ironic, especially with all the "timesaving" devices we have today. Could it be that our attitude toward time is at issue—how we imagine it?

About sixteen hundred years ago, Saint Augustine queried, "What then is time?" He mused, "If no one asks me, I know; if I want to explain it . . . I do not know."[2] How right he was! We dwell in time, like fish in water, and yet find it very difficult to understand.

The favored image is that time is linear, as if it were three different times—past, present, and future—rather than three aspects of the same experience. For Aristotle, time grinds backward along a straight line, coming from the future into the present and disappearing into the past. This separating of time into three could rob people of present time, for the present becomes past immediately that it comes from the future. So, the present is already *gone* as soon as it arrives. Such linear thinking can diminish people's embrace of their own time now. And if we don't have a sense of agency in our present time, then we live superficially and accept whatever comes—fatalism.

It's surely true that people's perspective on time greatly influences how they live—spend their time. It makes a big difference whether we imagine ourselves as agents with purpose and meaning or as cogs in a wheel of fate, whether we embrace and shape our time or let it roll by us as dozing spectators. I also raise the question of *time* because our attitude toward it is so crucial to how we view *tradition*. For *what else is tradition but the legacy of time-over-time—of history?* Tradition is everything we find here when we arrive, the cultural heirloom of those who "did time" before us and now bequeath to us.

People often take liberal or conservative positions regarding tradition—and so of time—sometimes to the extreme. The liberals tend to be biased against tradition, assuming that "the new" is always better than what went before. Whereas, conservatives tend to romanticize tradition as if the old ways were inevitably best and the norm for how things should be now. One relishes the future; the other cherishes the past. But both can miss out on the present and the real value of tradition.

It's imperative that we embrace the time we have and be agents within it, that we reflectively inherit the past and its legacy, and that we be responsible in the present toward the future. This is precisely the image of time and tradition suggested by Christian faith and particularly by Catholicism. When brought to life—integrated into people's spirituality—it can be a gift *for life for all.*

FOR REFLECTION AND CONVERSATION

- How would you describe your own image of time?

- Locate yourself on a continuum between tradition as something antiquated and to be left behind and tradition as the way things should be and to be repeated over and over. Explain why you place yourself where you do.

CATHOLIC IMAGINATION ON TIME AND TRADITION: A GIFT FOR LIFE

Catholic Christians are as likely as any to hold a linear and tripartite image of time, and there are conservatives and liberals among us. Yet, Catholicism carries the roots and sometimes the fruits of a holistic perspective on time, and on a good day can walk the tightrope of a *critical appreciation* of tradition. Let me summarize and then elaborate.

Undoubtedly we experience time as yesterday, today, and tomorrow. For the Other Partner within the divine-human covenant, however, time is eternal. To God, time is present, with the past remaining and the future already. Although incapable of comprehending eternity (the suspension of duration), human beings can intuitively sense the unity of time, and can recognize that time past is still with us and that our present lives can shape the future. Within our consciousness, we can detect that we *have* much more than just this fleeting moment.

Think about it: your past is very much with you now. You could not read these words nor I write them if our pasts were totally gone; we would have no resources of language, concepts, and culture. It seems ridiculous even to imagine being without the past, but a purely linear sense of time encourages such amnesia. Truth is that we are who we are and can have the present we have precisely because the legacy of the past is still present. And instead of the future invading and our accepting whatever comes, we can help shape it by present behavior.

We live more humanly if we recognize ourselves as "dwelling in time" instead of as spectators who watch time flow by. It is more life-giving to think of time holistically, to embrace and engage time present, inheriting within it the legacy of time past and making our own unique contribution to time future. The Latin poet Horace advised people, *Carpe diem,* "seize the day." What great advice. But seizing the day means more than "grasping" the one before us, as if the immediate present is the only time we have. If we want to choose it, "we've all the time in the world." So, a holistic sense of time means that we make the most of this day, *and* inherit within it the legacy of the past, *and* leave a legacy from the present to the future.

Such a holistic sense of time is more life-giving for communities as well as for the person. Societies and cultures become totally impoverished without the wisdom, art, and science that is the legacy of past to present. Likewise, present generations have a profound responsibility to leave a *life-for-all* legacy to the future, a responsibility made all the more urgent by our heightened capacity for destroying creation.

The linear understanding of time dates back to ancient Greek philosophers; they imagined time as *chronos,* which is the measuring and dating of sequential events—clock time. The Bible, too, has a sense of *chronos* time, with the past and present leaning into a future promise. However, the Bible's dominant perspective is *kairos* time. This is the kind I've experienced around the fire in Kinnegad. The New Testament uses *kairos* for the due time or the right time. So, Jesus could say at the beginning of his mission, "This is the *time* of fulfillment" (Mark 1:15), to his mother at Cana, "My *time* has not yet come" (John 7:6; his mother didn't agree), and at the end, "My appointed *time* draws near" (Matthew 26:18). Note, too, that the *kairos* moment is "appointed" by God, not by human timekeeping.

Such *kairos* moments can evolve from previous events but may also come as an apocalypse—something unexpected and not caused by anything before it. To the biblical mentality, too, every *kairos* time gathers the past and future into the present. So Jesus could announce to disciples, "The kingdom of God is already among you" and, without contradiction, urge them to pray and work for its coming. Biblically, then, time is more *spiral* than linear, with the present carrying forward the past and helping to forge the future.

This holistic time pertains especially to God's saving deeds. The Hebrew emphasis on *remembering* reflects the conviction that what God has done to save the people in the past can be remembered with saving effect in the present and will continue to save in the future. When, for example, the Hebrews recalled the story of Exodus, they experienced God's liberating power again. They never thought of the Exodus as a "thing of the past" but as an ever-present event that promised a future of freedom.

Christians inherited this *kairos* sense of time from their Hebrew roots. They were convinced that Jesus' life, death, and resurrection continue as a permanent event throughout history. For Catholic Christians, such *real remembering* is epitomized in the celebration of Eucharist. When the Church obeys Jesus' directive, "Do this in memory of me," it reenacts his deeds of liberating salvation in *this* present time and nurtures the hope of the heavenly banquet. Here people can experience again Jesus' life, death, and resurrection for their present and future. No wonder Catholics refer to Eucharist as "real presence."

A holistic sense of time lived on, though often as a subtradition, throughout Western consciousness. In responding to his own question "What is time?" Augustine found the linear view to be inadequate, arguing that the three times are not separate but aspects of the same reality. He wrote, "If future and past times exist . . . they are there neither as future nor as past, but as present." Augustine conceded that everyday speech may need three different terms, but we should use them to mean "the present of things past, the present of things present, and the present of things future."[3]

Other chapters of this book attend to the "present of things present" and the "present of things future." For example, Catholicism honors the "present of things *present*" in its principle of sacramentality—that God partners with humankind now through the ordinary and everyday of life (chapter 3). The "present of things *future*" is central to Christian partnership in working for God's reign (chapter 6), in the struggle for social justice (see chapter 7), and in the hope of salvation for all humankind (chapter 8).

With lots of attention to the *future* and *present* in other chapters, our focus here will be the *past* that is present through Christian tradition. It is this legacy of time—tradition—that modern people are most likely to misunderstand or miss out on.

The philosopher Hans-Georg Gadamer argues convincingly that the Enlightenment movement—modernity, if you will—had a "bias against tradition." It portrayed tradition as limiting people's lives, as a controlling past imposed upon the present. The Enlightenment had the battle cry "Dare to think for yourself." To think critically for oneself is a fine sentiment, but it came to mean "Refuse the authority of tradition."

To dismiss tradition is to lose out on the wisdom of the past; this, in fact, is "irrational." As Gadamer argues, when we recognize that tradition represents the hard-won wisdom of foreparents, it seems eminently *reasonable* to appreciate its legacy as a resource for living humanly in the present. For what others discovered and bequeathed as tradition "is not irrational and arbitrary but can be discovered to be true." So, instead of dismissing it or falling into "blind obedience" to the past, to appreciate tradition can be "an act of reason and freedom."[4]

In general, Catholicism resisted the Enlightenment bias and continued to appreciate tradition. In fact, the Protestant theologian Langdon Gilkey lists appreciation for tradition as a distinguishing feature of Catholic Christianity. For Gilkey, Catholicism emphasizes "the reality, importance, and 'weight' of tradition and history." He cautions that if made absolute or given too much weight—as Catholics are wont to do—tradition becomes "stifling and corrupt," whereas, if critically appropriated, tradition "can be a source of vast strength."[5] To appreciate Gilkey's positive point, let us review Catholicism's theology of tradition, and then return to his caution.

GOD REVEALS IN HISTORY

Catholic Christianity is well described as a "historical" faith, meaning that it arises from history, intertwines with its historical context, and should be lived in the everyday of life. There are faith communities that place themselves above the fray of history, or over against the society around them. By contrast and in keeping with its sense of the person, of life, and of society (chapters 2, 3, and 4), Catholicism encourages engagement with the world, celebrates its goodness, works for social reform and the realization of God's reign "*on earth* as in heaven." Here I highlight that the mode of divine revelation—not only the workings of God's grace but divine wisdom for our lives as well—also emerges in and through history. Grace and revelation are the work of God's Spirit in the world.

Thomas Aquinas emphasized the self-evident but crucial point that God's revelation comes to humankind "according to the mode of the receiver." In other words, God's Spirit reveals through the normal channels by which human beings come to know anything—through activity and experience, through curiosity and discovery, through reflection, conversation, and community. This is precisely the mode of "knowing" reflected in the Bible.

The Bible arose from people's experiences of historical events, great and small, first in the story of God's people Israel and then through the life of Jesus, the Christ. Gradually, the faith that emerged from reflection on these experiences was written down and the writings compiled. Although the sacred authors were divinely inspired, the revelation originated through historical events and everyday life—according to the mode of the receivers.

Echoing the principle of sacramentality, revelation in history means that the Spirit works through daily life to enlighten and inspire people, enabling them to know God's loving will and wisdom. This is true of our time and throughout time. As Vatican II explained, history is the medium through which "God . . . *uninterruptedly* converses" with humanity.[6] And as the sacramentality of life climaxes in the seven sacraments, so within present experience we can inherit the legacy of God's revelation as encountered through Scripture and Tradition.

God's self-disclosure to the Hebrew people began with the call of Abraham and Sarah, sometime about two thousand years before the common era. Thereafter, their faith Story unfolds, taking as much as a thousand years to come into its present written form. The Hebrew Bible has many literary genres: legal codes and priestly instructions, prophecies and proverbs, poems and plays, historical accounts and records. Yet all arise from the history of this people of God and are set forth within an overall narrative, a long-winded story of creation, fall, promise, call, slavery, exodus, covenant, followed by land, judges, kings, prophets, exile, and return.

With their holistic sense of time, the Hebrews told their Story over and over, highlighting God's saving deeds on their behalf and experiencing again God's liberating power as ever present. When children asked about their identity in faith, often in teachable moments such as at the Passover meal—"Why is this night different from every other night?"—parents recounted their Story as a people of God (see Deuteronomy 6:20–25). This was God's revelation to them through their history, and through them to the present.

For Christianity, Jesus Christ is the divine "Word made flesh" within history (John 1:14) and thus the summit of God's self-disclosure. But note well, Jesus was a historical person, living life at a certain time and place. God's revelation could not have been more "according to the mode of the receiver" than to become human like ourselves. As God incarnate, Jesus Christ reveals God to us and us to ourselves—the human face of God and the divine face of humanity. In Christian faith, Jesus represents the fullness of divine revelation (John 1:16). Yet, this does not mean that he explained all mysteries or suspended the normal ways of knowing. Rather, for this side of eternity, Christians now have their normative revelation of God and humanity in Jesus.

After their experience of Jesus' life, death, and resurrection, the first disciples set about living their faith, expecting the Risen Christ to return soon in glory. As this hope faded and the first eyewitnesses began to die off, the Christian communities became concerned to write down the oral traditions that had emerged from people's direct experiences of Jesus. Eventually, and with the inspiration of the Spirit, these "pericopes" (snippets) came together in the Gospels, and other inspired texts emerged from the lived faith of the first communities.

Gradually, Christians agreed upon a "canon" of official texts for their Bible. They accepted the books of the Hebrew scriptures, and then added twenty-seven texts of the New Testament: Gospels according to Matthew, Mark, Luke, and John; fourteen epistles attributed to Paul (though some were written by disciples in his name); seven letters attributed to James, Peter, John, and Jude; the Acts of the Apostles recounting the life of the first Christian communities; and the Book of Revelation. Christians believe that all the canonical books were divinely inspired—God's Spirit at work—and they revere the whole Bible as the primary medium of "the word of God." Now we may ask, What about thereafter?

A deep Catholic conviction is that God's revelation did not end with the Apostolic era and is not limited to the Bible's pages. Rather, by the presence of God's Spirit, revelation continues to unfold throughout human experience—history. A battle cry of the Reformers was *Scriptura sola* ("Scripture alone") as the sole rule of faith. By contrast, Catholicism held out for Scripture *and* Tradition.

Catholicism's rationale for appreciating Tradition was quite straightforward and reflects a holistic sense of time. Jesus promised to send God's Holy Spirit to guide and enlighten the community of disciples, the Church. This promise was fulfilled at the First Pentecost. Since then, and as new eras, questions, and issues emerged, the Spirit has guided Christians to reflect on their historical experience in the light of faith and thus to develop their understanding of God's revelation in the Bible. Of course, every development must carry forward and be in continuity with biblical revelation. Yet biblical revelation needs ongoing development in order to sustain a vibrant faith over the ages and across cultures.

Guided by the Spirit and after time, testing, and consensus, the Christian community can embrace a development in its faith as a Tradition—with a capital *T.* Such Tradition, developing biblical revelation through contemporary experience, reflects that Christian faith is an ongoing journey into divine truth. This sentiment was championed by Vatican II: "The tradition which comes from the apostles *develops* in the Church with the help of the Holy Spirit. For there is a *growth* in the understanding of the realities and the words which have been handed down. . . . [A]s the centuries succeed one another, the Church constantly *moves forward* toward the fullness of divine truth."[7]

Without the developments represented by Tradition, Christian faith could become a stagnant pool instead of a great river of living waters. Cardinal John Henry Newman (1801–1890) called this "the dynamic identity" of Christianity; he meant that it should be ever developing for changing circumstances and yet always in continuity with its biblical roots. Together, then, Scripture and Tradition function as two media of one divine revelation, handing on the vital legacy of Christian Faith from one generation to the next.

Let us return now to Gilkey's caution. If we approach either Scripture or Tradition in a closed-minded way, as if they are static heirlooms, they could become deadening to Christian faith. While Protestant fundamentalism emerges around the Bible, Catholic fundamentalism is more apt to attach to Tradition, making it appear fixed and finished, as if the past is "a dead letter" rather than a source of new life for the present and future.

We cannot be sanguine about the risks of canonizing Tradition; as Gilkey warned, we can make it seem "stifling." Official Catholicism can use Tradition to discourage developments, to silence questioning and critique, highlighting only what favors the current party line. Interpreting every aspect of Christian Tradition calls for great care—appreciation, questioning, and creativity. Let us now revisit and elaborate a theme first raised in chapter 1.

CAUTIONS FOR INTERPRETING CHRISTIAN STORY

Scripture and Tradition are "the word of God in human language."[8] The second part of this phrase reminds us that they reflect the world and time in which they emerged—"the mode of the receiver." Echoing chapter 1, this means that the Church must *interpret* Christian Story. It is not a direct communiqué from God; we must figure out its meaning for now.

We can imagine such interpretation as a great conversation *among* the Christian community and *by* the whole community with the "texts" of Scripture and Tradition. As in a good conversation, there is give-and-take, talking and listening to each other. We bring our lives to read these sacred texts and we bring these sacred texts to help us read our lives, all with a view to living as people of God. Ultimately, that's the revelation we seek—divine wisdom for life.

And the conversation is not just now but stretches across history. Each generation is invited to the table; there it can inherit the wisdom that emerged from the experiences of foreparents in faith, and then make its own contribution. So, Scripture and Tradition ever prompt a great conversation, down through history, as the Christian community interprets its own Story in dialogue with present experience. This makes for a never-ending exchange between life-in-the-world and the Faith-handed-on.

Chapter 1 offered five guidelines for such interpretation. In summary:

1. Approach Christian faith as a great unfolding Story of the vital partnership between God and humankind, and with the Vision of God's Reign.

2. Bring life to interpret Christian Story and Christian Story to interpret life.

3. Expect to encounter old and new spiritual wisdom.

4. Be alert for distortions and forgotten legacies.

5. Choose *for life for all.*

Here I add some cautions that might help Catholics like myself to avoid our favorite pitfalls regarding Christian *Tradition.* Harkening back to Gilkey's alert, I can think of three:

1. Forgetting the primacy of Scripture and allowing Tradition alone to hold center stage;

2. Passively inheriting Tradition—being neither critical nor creative about it;

3. Leaving interpretation of Tradition entirely in the hands of the Church's papal magisterium.

I have three counter-suggestions to offset these dangers:

1. Honor Scripture and Tradition as symbiotic sources of God's revelation;

2. Approach Christian Story with critical appreciation and creative appropriation;

3. Interpret Scripture and Tradition within the whole Christian community and in dialogue with life in the world.

1. Honor Scripture and Tradition as Symbiotic
Sources of God's Revelation

Let's be honest. Catholicism claims allegiance to *both* Scripture and Tradition, but until lately that has been little more than lip service. For we have generally neglected the Bible, functioning as if Tradition alone represents divine revelation. This is an unfortunate legacy of Reformation polemics, which drove both Protestants and Catholics to exaggerate their positions. For the more the Reformers cried "Scripture alone!" the more Catholics downplayed the Bible and played up Tradition; whereas the more Catholics emphasized Tradition, the more Protestants turned to the Bible alone.

Although we have miles to travel, the post–Vatican II era has strongly encouraged Catholics to recenter the Bible at the core of their faith. Vatican II decreed that "easy access to sacred Scripture should be provided for all the Christian faithful."[9] Probably nothing has prompted more renewal than implementing this mandate. Catholics are studying, praying with, and sharing their faith around the Bible as never before. We are beginning to cite Scripture the way we once recited the catechism, the epitome of Tradition.

In this scriptural renewal, we have been inspired by the faithfulness of Protestant brothers and sisters. As Pope John Paul II formally recognized when celebrating the five hundredth anniversary of Luther's birth (1983), Catholics owe a great debt to Protestants for maintaining the centrality of the Bible to Christian faith.

Vatican II also tried to move beyond Reformation arguments, proposing a partnership between Scripture and Tradition, as if there is *one revelation with two manifestations:* "Sacred tradition and sacred Scripture form one sacred deposit of the word of God." For this reason, "both sacred tradition and sacred Scripture are to be accepted and venerated with the same sense of devotion and reverence." And the two should be interpreted within a Christian community. Scripture, Tradition, and Church "are so linked and joined together that one cannot stand without the others"; they "all work together . . . under the action of the one Holy Spirit" for "the salvation of souls."[10]

So, biblical faith retains its vitality through the developments that become Tradition, whereas Tradition needs Scripture to provide inspiration and ensure continuity across time. This unfolding of the "surplus of meaning" that ever remains in God's revelation needs the guidance of the whole Church—my third point below.

2. Approach Christian Story with Critical Appreciation and
Creative Appropriation

Their faith requires Christians to approach Scripture and Tradition with an attitude of deep *appreciation*. They should be confident that these ancient symbols can mediate a "word of God" for lives now. They have been revelatory for countless generations before us, and faith in the God who reveals here leads us to anticipate that they will be revelatory for this generation, too. So, Christians should go to their Story with real appreciation and *expecting* to encounter God's revelation for their lives.

Now, what may at first sound a little contradictory, this appreciation should be thoroughly *critical*. I don't mean this in any negative sense; on the contrary. At its best, *critical,* from the Greek *krinein,* means to *discern* carefully. In other words, *critical appreciation* means to think carefully and reflectively about Christian Story; why would we ever do less! Such discernment is essential if we are to take these old texts of meaning from "back then" and figure out what they mean for here and now. Let us unpack *critical appreciation* a bit further.

First, it will mean interpreting for *retrieval* as outlined in chapter 1. This means reclaiming for ourselves and with freshness the old truths to be found in Christian Story. It is as if we must learn again and for our time the spiritual wisdom that our parents already knew well. Such retrieval nurtures our Christian identity, gives us an anchor in "the wisdom of the ages," makes the Faith our own. With critical appreciation we recognize for ourselves the great value of our Story, and it confirms us as a Christian people of God.

Even as Christian Story affirms, however, it also confronts us and calls us in question. It may even condemn some aspects of my life or of society. Its intent is to invite more faithful living for God's reign, but this means alerting to the reality of our sins and failures. So, as Christian Story comes to our lives, it judges and challenges us to grow in living our faith.

By the same token, as we bring our lives and contemporary consciousness to Christian Story, we can detect aspects that we don't want to repeat at all, that we should resist. Not all our traditions have been wise and life-giving; in fact, we must recognize lots of sins and errors in the history of the Christian people—our practice and approval of slavery, discrimination against women, encouraging anti-Semitism, and so on. Though these sins are not Tradition with a capital *T,* they are certainly there with a small *t.* They must be rejected.

Also, some beliefs and practices may have been fine for another day but might not be wise now. Or the dominant version currently in place may not reflect "the whole story" at all. Christian Story has lots of life-giving memories that can be easily forgotten or fall out of favor. For all of these reasons, Christians should approach their Story with a *questioning* attitude; instead of blindly accepting, they should question the "in vogue" version of Christian Story. Such *questioning* is integral to a critical appreciation of Christian faith.

We turn now to *creative appropriation*. As I've said before, each generation must make Christian Story its own through present experience, discerning what this Faith means for now, what it asks of people in the present. But the Faith is less likely to become our own if we just passively receive it, as if the present should simply repeat the past. Instead, there needs to be a bit of creativity in how we appropriate the tradition—if for no other reason than to make it resonant to our own situation. Because each historical context is unique, every interpretation of Christian Story is, in a sense, a "new" one. Each era should have its own contribution to the future—a holistic sense of time.

Remember, too, that Christian Story is like a great classic (chapter 1) that ever yields old and new possibilities. This echoes Jesus' saying that the scribe learned in the reign of God is like the head of a household who can take from the storeroom both the old and the new (Matthew 13:52). Every generation needs to do as much if Christian Story is to nurture a vital and living faith for each time and place.

We are more likely to be creative in our fidelity to Christian Story if we bring our lives to interpret it. For it is our own lives that enable us to reclaim the tried and true from the Story and to create new possibilities from it as well. The horizons of Scripture and Tradition broaden our own, and present horizons—what the Spirit is revealing through the experiences, perspectives, and wisdom of this generation—can broaden what others have seen thus far in Christian Story. The outcome is ongoing vitality and creative fidelity in the faith of Christians.

3. Interpret Scripture and Tradition Within the Whole Christian Community and in Dialogue with the World

Many times we have noted that Christians should interpret Scripture and Tradition within the community of faith—the Church. This seems like a reasonable and wise proposal. Prudent people do not rely on their own opinion alone in important matters. Why do so in matters of faith?

Note, too, that all the sciences of knowledge function as communities of conversation, with colleagues bouncing ideas off each other in mutual support and correction, and building on each other's work. Surely as much should prevail in the Church. What a blessing to have a community of shared Christian faith whose members nurture and stretch, affirm and correct, teach and learn together. It was Saint Thomas Aquinas who argued that the "teaching Church" and the "learning Church" should be one and the same community of faith.

So far, so good! Nevertheless, we cannot skip lightly over a weighty aspect of Catholic identity—the teaching authority of the Church. Many would wonder how interpreting Christian Story with *retrieval, questioning,* and *creativity* reconciles with the stereotypical image of the Catholic church as authoritarian. And even apart from stereotypes, that Catholicism expects obedience to its magisterium—literally, "authoritative teacher"—is an accurate portrayal.

In Roman Catholic consciousness, *the* symbol of Church authority is the papacy. As successor to Saint Peter, first among the apostles, the pope has primacy in teaching authority. Richard McBrien notes that this Petrine office is the "one characteristic . . . which sets the Catholic Church apart from all other churches."[11] The richest Catholic tradition is that the pope should teach in collegiality with the bishops of the world and represent the consensus faith of the whole Church.[12] Even with such nuance, the magisterium of the institutional church functions as authoritative teacher for Catholic Christians.

Matthew's Gospel tells of the Risen Christ gathering the small Christian community on a hillside in Galilee. As a final mandate, Christ gave all present the commission to "go teach"—to make disciples among all peoples (see Matthew 28:16–20). Since then, the Church has understood itself as continuing Jesus' *teaching* mission for the reign of God.

It is imperative to remember, however, that the "Church" is the whole community of the Body of Christ—a constant theme of Vatican II—not just its papal leaders. All baptized Christians, therefore, are called to teach and learn together. So, the Church's teaching authority is symbolized by but certainly not limited to the papacy.

That the whole Catholic people should participate in their church's teaching/learning dynamic is not a new idea. Again, we can cite Saint Thomas Aquinas, writing almost eight hundred years ago, and the seeds of it were planted on that hillside in

Galilee. Aquinas clarified that the Church has three cooperative sources of *teaching/learning*: (1) the research of *scholars;* (2) the lived faith of ordinary people, called the *sensus fidelium* ("sense of the faithful"); and (3) the official *magisterium* of the papacy cum episcopacy.[13] All three should work in concert, mutually supporting and correcting one another.

The official *magisterium* draws together and teaches the shared Faith of the whole community. In this, it must be faithful to Scripture and Tradition, be well informed by the research of *scholars,* and be listening to the *sense of the faithful*. Likewise, *faithful Christians* should trust their own discernment, be guided by the consensus of the *magisterium,* and appreciate the research of *scholars*. Similarly, scripture scholars and theologians need to place their scholarship in dialogue with the *sense of the faithful* and be guided by the consensus taught by the *magisterium*. When all three function in partnership, it's a great system of checks and balances, enabling the Church to navigate between relativism and authoritarianism.

As its three-way conversation unfolds, the Christian community should also be in dialogue with the world. In matters of faith, as well as in everything else, we must listen to the sciences of knowledge and the traditions of wisdom that are all around. This is an old Catholic attitude, to be open to every source of knowledge and wisdom, confident that all truth is of God. In fact, Saint Augustine said that one meaning of being "catholic" is "to be open to the truth, wherever it can be found."

In the context of the Church's teaching authority, I add an important note. Let us remember that *freedom of conscience* has been a core tenet of Catholic Christianity since its beginning—

though often more honored in the breach than the observance. Reflecting a long legacy, Vatican II referred to conscience as "the most secret core and sanctuary of a [person]" where we are "alone with God, whose voice echoes in [our] depths." A Catholic not only *may* follow conscience, but "is *bound* to follow . . . conscience faithfully, in order [to] come to God."[14] The teaching authority of the Church notwithstanding, conscience is the last court of appeal!

FOR REFLECTION AND CONVERSATION

• What are some of your responses to these proposals about time and its legacy of tradition? Is any new insight emerging for you?

• What spiritual practices might help you to live a holistic sense of time? To draw new life from Christian tradition?

PRACTICING A SPIRITUALITY OF
TIME AND TRADITION

Let the following suggestions stimulate your own imaginings of how to integrate a holistic sense of time and its legacy of tradition into your spirituality—your faith at work! The first two suggestions are general, the third more specific.

1. Sanctify Your Whole Time

Most religious traditions have the practice of praying at appointed moments throughout the day, week, and year. The sentiment is that by setting aside certain times as holy, those holy times gather in the time before and after, sanctifying all time. This was the conviction of the Hebrew people from whom the first Christians inherited this rich spiritual practice.

The young Christian community met daily for shared prayer and "breaking of the bread" (see Acts 2:42–47). They designated particular times throughout the day for personal prayer, and days of the week for holy fasting. They also embraced the great Hebrew tradition of sabbath, though moved to Sunday—the day of Jesus' resurrection.

Sabbath then and now is the weekly pause to recognize the sacramentality of life, to remember that everything belongs to God and thus to give thanks, to renew partnership in God's ongoing work of salvation. Sabbath celebrates God's creation, remembers the Story of salvation since then, and anticipates the fullness of God's reign to come. By keeping sabbath, and especially through their celebration of Eucharist, Christians reenact Jesus' death and resurrection and look forward to the heavenly banquet.

So, sabbath looks backward and forward, and yet is a holy day of rest, setting aside the works and cares of the everyday. As such, the sabbath epitomizes a holistic sense of time. With each week flowing into and out of this day of rest, sabbath is like an inbreaking of eternity, gathering all time into this time now and urging us to embrace it as our own. Of this day above all days, we must heed the counsel "Carpe diem."

With the flowering of monasticism in the fourth century, the Church organized a pattern of daily prayer into the "divine office." This community prayer of praise and thanksgiving, built around the psalms and selected scripture readings, was prayed by the monks at certain "hours." Traditionally, it began with Matins just after midnight or in the very early morning and Lauds at rising, continued with some minor "hours" throughout the day, and ended with Vespers at evening and Compline at bedtime.

Though the "divine office" is practiced most faithfully in monastic communities, the Church always thought of it as part of its public prayer. In 1971, in fulfillment of a directive of Vatican II, the divine office was revised as "The Liturgy of the Hours" and simplified to encourage lay Christians to participate throughout the day.

Ordinary Christians, by the by, developed their own lay traditions of daily prayers. They favored morning and night prayers and "grace" before and after meals. The tolling of monastery and abbey bells for the divine office reminded people in the villages and fields to pray as well. Many Catholic cultures developed the practice of pausing three times each day (at 6:00 A.M., noon, and 6:00 P.M.) for the Angelus. This is a meditative prayer on the Incarnation of Jesus, interwoven with devotion to Mary.

Many Catholics, too, had a strong tradition of reciting the Rosary daily, dubbed "the poor person's divine office." The complete Rosary has fifteen decades of Hail Marys, each introduced by the Our Father and ending with the Glory Be. People usually say five decades each day. Every decade is designated to remember some "mystery" of faith, and the fifteen are divided into three sets of Joyful, Sorrowful, and Glorious mysteries. They focus on the Incarnation, Passion, and Glorification of Christ, respectively.[15] For many Catholics, the Rosary still serves as a mantralike prayer that they can say while working, driving, falling asleep—anytime at all—counting the decades on their fingers if beads are not available.

Sanctifying time is eminently reflected in the Liturgical Year, which melds the unfolding seasons with the great events in Jesus' life, death, and resurrection. More than a facile recalling, the Liturgical Year reenacts God's saving deeds in Jesus. It has two great "cycles": Christmas, beginning with Advent preparation and closing with the Feast of Epiphany; and Easter, beginning with the repentance of Lent, climaxing at the Triduum and Easter Sunday, and culminating with Pentecost. In between these two cycles we have what is aptly called ordinary time. Here the liturgy revisits other great events and teachings from the life of Jesus and celebrates feasts of Mary and the saints as well.

From this brief review, we can see that to sanctify time is an integral aspect of Catholic spirituality, and all Christians—not just the ones in monasteries—are invited to do so. We can still find rich suggestions in the practices of our foreparents in faith.

By participating regularly in sabbath worship with a faith community, we can experience firsthand the cycle of the Liturgical Year. This reminds us that all time is holy, the times of high feast days and ordinary time as well. Through the Liturgical Year we experience the sense that human history and salvation history blend as one, making all time sanctified.

Observing the sabbath as a day of real rest helps to keep things in perspective, reminding us of who and what should come first in our lives. It can save us from idolatry—for example, of our work—and thus from self-imposed slaveries. It reminds us that we can afford to rest precisely because God is God and not ourselves.

If ever an era was in need of sabbath, it's surely ours. Compared with observant Jews, Christians are generally poor at sabbath keeping. There is great wisdom in keeping a day of rest and re-creation, but Christians should also remember that this is a law of God. God must have known that the only way some of us would take a day off was to make sabbath a law of the covenant.

We can pause throughout every day for moments of raising mind and heart to God. Chapter 9 will recommend a routine of daily prayer with some extended set-aside time. Besides this, we can have a hundred prayer moments throughout every day as well. Upon rising, at bedtime, before and after meals are old favorites for prayer pauses. And then we can find other moments and reminders—to sanctify time.

A friend tells me that she uses the waiting time at traffic lights and supermarket checkout lines as opportunities for a prayer pause. Now, whenever stopped at a light or waiting in line, she "automatically" has a prayer moment. She says she now gets less impatient with the wait, so it's good for her health as well. All of us can find moments and our own reminders throughout the day, pausing to recognize God's presence in our present. In this way we place our own time within eternity and know that all time is ours.

2. Steep in the Wisdom of Christian Story

Social commentators are alarmed about the level of anxiety in contemporary society. In this global village of rapid mobility, mass communication, and the ever-present threat of international terrorism, people can easily lose their sense of roots and security.

Many respond to feeling adrift by dabbling in spirituality, but bits and pieces blended from various traditions may not lend the anchor needed. A spiritual smoothie is not likely to stand the test of tough times, celebrate well the high times, or provide pattern for ordinary times. It seems wise, instead, to ground oneself in a particular and life-giving spiritual tradition. From there, one can sally forth to be enriched by other traditions, knowing that one has a spiritual "home."

In chapter 4, I suggested belonging to a local faith community—a place to sink roots. Here I propose a style of study for steeping oneself in the *spiritual wisdom* of Catholic Christianity, if that is one's chosen home.

Too many Christians experience religious education as a boring experience or, even worse, a negative one. Look at the stereotype of Sunday school in popular culture. Moreover, we still tend to think of catechesis as learning "about" religion, receiving knowledge in the sense of information. Religious knowledge, of course, is important but it is not enough. It stops short of spiritual wisdom. The most life-giving way to study any great religion is to approach it as a *treasury of spiritual wisdom for life*. This means not only *learning about* a tradition but *learning from* it and learning *to become wise* as it proposes. Such is the biblical approach to study.

The Hebrews placed great value on scholarship. Their aim, however, was not knowledge for knowledge's sake—as the Greeks might favor—but the pursuit of spiritual wisdom. All study was directed toward *living the covenant with God*. Biblically, the wise are those who keep the covenant; the foolish, those who break it. Thus, the old rabbis saw study of the sacred texts as a form of prayer—a way to come closer to God.

From their Hebrew/Jewish roots, the first Christians learned the value of studying for spiritual wisdom. In fact, wisdom was the primary purpose of Christian scholarship up until about the year 1100. Take, for example, the theological method of *lectio divina* (my third suggestion below); it was study for spiritual wisdom, for what would help in living as a people of God.

Beginning about the twelfth century, the formal study of Christian faith relocated to the emerging universities. Now the focus of theology shifted from a prayerful quest for spiritual wisdom to a scientific study seeking rational knowledge about God. The latter has remained theology's prime intent ever since, encouraged by the Enlightenment emphasis on "sure and certain ideas" (Descartes). Thus a rift developed between religious knowledge and spiritual wisdom, between theology and spirituality.

There are hopeful signs that, without losing the assets of critical reason, theology is once again turning toward spiritual wisdom. It is reaching beyond "faith seeking understanding"—the time-honored definition of scholastic theology—toward the intent of *faith that is lived wisely in the world*. This shift is reflected especially in the various theologies of liberation; each shares the passion that Christian faith be *for life for all*.

Christian Story is a great treasury of spiritual wisdom; it can lend the resources to live wisely as a disciple of Jesus. If we study the Story with the conscious intent of learning wisdom for life, we are most likely to find it. And to sound a familiar refrain, when we consciously bring our own lives—our everyday experiences, the issues that matter to us, the questions that perplex us, our personal insights—to the study of Scripture and Tradition, we are more likely to glean spiritual wisdom to bring back to life again.

For some reason, wisdom and becoming wise conjure up images of a premodern village; can we aspire to as much in our postmodern world? I'm convinced that the very future of the planet and of the human family depends on how we grow in spiritual wisdom. Our scientific knowledge, and especially our technical knowledge, if not accompanied by spiritual wisdom, is likely to destroy us.

It's amazing how well versed people can be in areas that are not their professional expertise. On a treadmill in a gym, I've overheard neighbors confidently discussing exercise, nutrition, and diet as if they were medical doctors. Walk along the aisles of a Home Depot and you'll find hundreds of do-it-yourself carpenters, plumbers, and painters. In areas that matter to their lives, modern people have become proactive in seeking out what they need in order to make informed decisions or to do what needs to be done. Surely this should be true in matters of faith as well. All it takes is a bit of effort; the resources are readily available.

Protestants have done far better than Catholics in continuing education, taking it for granted that Bible study is a permanent part of Christian life. In Kansas, I once met an eighty-four-year-old Methodist man who has been in the same adult Bible study group since he was a teenager, and has rarely missed a meeting. The idea that religious education is not just for children is gradually sinking in for Catholics, too. A recent Roman document calls for "permanent catechesis" across the life span, recognizing that faith development is a lifelong affair.[16]

Most parishes now have opportunities for adult faith formation, including small groups in which people can share and study their faith together. Such conversation is likely to be a hotbed of spiritual wisdom. Modern communication media, beginning with the availability of good books, ensure that all Christians now have easy access to the legacy of their Faith. That Christians study their Story for its spiritual wisdom is a worthy and rewarding spiritual practice.

3. *Practice* Lectio Divina

Lectio divina (literally, "divine reading") is an ancient style of prayerful reflection to nurture spiritual wisdom. I also recommend it as a spiritual practice here because its style of contemplation can be an experience of holistic time. Developed in the early Christian monasteries, *lectio* is now making a big comeback as a gentling practice, effective for recentering busy lives. It engages the whole person, all faculties and feelings, in personal encounter with some "text" of faith.

The typical candidates, as the *Catechism* enumerates, are "the Sacred Scriptures, particularly the Gospels, holy icons, liturgical texts of the day or season, writings of the spiritual fathers [and mothers]." The *Catechism* ends its list by also recommending "the great book of creation, and of history—the page on which the 'today' of God is written."[17] What a lovely way of describing the Spirit's present revelation, within this time—also worthy of *lectio*.

There are many approaches to *lectio divina,* but all entail a process of going down deeper into one's own heart to encounter God's word and to discern how to respond with living faith. It can be done alone or with others, with the possibility of conversation after any one of its movements. It can take a few minutes or run for hours. The sequence unfolds as follows (I'm using the old Latin titles):

Lectio (reading). Read the text slowly, prayerfully, being alert for God's word that might be here for your life now. Pause to notice whatever stands out.

Meditatio (meditating). Read again with a similar style, but now pause to meditate on the text or scene, enter into it imaginatively, and talk with God about the spiritual wisdom it might hold for your own and others' lives.

Contemplatio (contemplating). Read again with a listening heart, and now move to contemplation. Here you are more receiver than initiator, allowing the text to speak to your deep heart's core. Enhance your receptivity by focusing on a word, phrase, or image and recentering on it when distractions arise.

Oratio (praying). Come gently out of contemplation; recognize the deep desires of your heart and pray them to God.

Actio (acting). This moment is not in the traditional *lectio*, but I've experienced it in "base Christian communities" among the poor church. It helps nurture faith that is lived wisely—spiritual wisdom. The pause here is to discern what *action* God may be inviting and, by grace, choosing how to respond.

FOR REFLECTION AND CONVERSATION

- What other practices do you imagine for sanctifying time? For appreciating tradition?

- Are there any decisions emerging about your own attitude toward Scripture and Tradition?

SIX

"IN WHAT WILL WE INVEST?"—RISKING THE LEAP OF FAITH

IT SAVED OUR LIVES

*Birute was one of my translators for a two-week series of presenta-
tions throughout Lithuania in June 1992. The Soviets were not long
gone, and Lithuanians were still in the euphoria of liberation. Birute
was a graceful woman with a deep peace about her. Her long auburn
hair was beginning to gray, and her sad eyes reflected much suffering.
She spoke perfect English and was clearly an effective translator.*

*Working with a translator is like running a three-legged race;
both partners need to find a rhythm. After a stumbling start—and
my learning to speak in complete sentences—Birute and I hit our
stride. As we traveled the country, we had time to swap stories and
we became friends.*

*Birute told about the Soviet invasion of Lithuania in 1940 and the
terrible persecutions that ensued. She described the particular cruelty
toward people who practiced their faith. The Communists executed
thousands of church leaders and sent almost a million Lithuanians
into exile and likely death in Siberia. And yet the deep Catholic faith
of the Lithuanian people not only survived but thrived, as if strength-
ened by suffering and resistance to state-sponsored atheism.*

About six miles north of Siauliai, on the road to Meskuciai, I visited the revered Hill of Crosses. For hundreds of years Lithuanians have come here to "plant a cross" and ask God's blessing, making the hill into a forest of crosses of every size and design. After annexation, the Soviet government made numerous attempts to remove them but to no avail!

At one point they stationed a small army to guard the hill, but crosses would reappear overnight. People literally risked their lives to raise them. Eventually, the Soviets were forced to relent, and the Hill of Crosses became a symbol of Lithuanian faith and resistance to tyranny, truly "a sign of contradiction."

In one of my sessions, a participant shared her childhood memory of parents pushing her through a back bedroom window when that ominous knock on the door was heard. She told of running through the fields in the dark to a neighbor's house and returning next morning to find her homestead razed and her parents gone, never to be seen again. Years later, she learned they had died in Siberia. Lithuania is full of such stories.

I asked Birute how she and the Lithuanian people endured it all. Without hesitating she said, "Our faith saved us."

I probed, "But did you not feel abandoned by God?" She said, "Never! Instead, we came to understand what the cross really means for Christian faith—not that God sends suffering, but that God suffers alongside us when it comes."

Today, Birute is a sister in the first Carmelite abbey founded in Lithuania since the country's liberation—they are an order of cloistered nuns of strict observance. And I continue to marvel at her faith, at the faith of her people, and at the risks they took with their investment.

A MYSTERY BEYOND WORDS

The word *creed,* from the Latin *credere,* means "to invest one's heart." How fitting! For the question of *faith* comes down to *life* investments—so well described as a "leap"—and much is riding on if and how we take the risk. Our faith is the defining *apriori* of our lives—the fundamental priorities we choose—shaping who we become and how we live.

Since the dawn of history, people have been willing to stake everything on faith. Martyrs have embraced death thanking God for their noble cause; missionaries have left home for the ends of the earth; mendicants have chosen poverty, chastity, and obedience; and Lithuanian mothers and fathers have risked imprisonment and death to instruct their children—all for faith's sake.

Tragically, people have also killed each other in the name of faith. Religion has fueled the worst of wars. Even today, it is a festering point in many violent conflicts, or at least opportunist politicians use religious symbols to legitimate their cause. Caution is in order by way of this investment.

Faith is a human universal, a phenomenon common to all. To be human is to invest in more than ourselves, to believe that there is meaning and purpose beyond our own making, albeit grounded in Mystery. People have in-built antennae for signs of Transcendence and can recognize them in everyday life. Yet we find it difficult to name this most human phenomenon, and no wonder! It faces us with the mutual mysteries of God and ourselves.

Most people express their human faith through an instance of religion, a word that comes from the Latin *religare,* meaning "to anchor well." Some religions do not profess a personal God, but all are convinced that a Transcendent realm impinges upon this one and that the person is profoundly spiritual. All religions find their centers of value—the stuff that matters most—in some sense of Ultimate Mystery. And every religious faith expresses itself in three ways: (1) in a confession of *beliefs* that summarizes its convictions; (2) in spiritual practices and ways of *worship* that reflect relationship with the Transcendent; and (3) in a code of *ethics* that guides and evaluates life choices.

Most people imbibe religious faith from their caregivers of childhood. Yet, all traditions recognize that faith is a divine gift. Saint Paul taught Christians that faith is never "produced" by human efforts; "it is always God's gift" (Ephesians 2:8). We might say that the grace of faith typically "works" through the relationships, mentors, and communities of primary socialization.

Expressed through *creed, cult,* and *code,* yet religious faith is more than its expressions. In fact, the same faith can grow deeper in quality but change in its outward manifestation. Also, people can share a similar *faith* but express it through different *beliefs*. I think of two friends, both of whom have faith in God as Loving Creator. One believes quite literally in the biblical story of creation—all taking place in six days—whereas the other views the biblical account as a myth that teaches great truths but is not literally true. They have similar *faith* but different *beliefs*.

All this is to say that *people's faith is more than their particular religion*. This is important to remember, especially when our institutional religion disappoints us. I have a friend, Sarah, who likes to say in response to church sinfulness, "But God is greater." How wise and faith-filled! And it encourages ecumenism to remember that people with diverse religions can have much unity in faith. Often when not of one mind, we can yet be of one heart.

FOR REFLECTION AND CONVERSATION

• What do you imagine, what do you express, with the word *faith?*

• Let your imagination go to work around the metaphor "faith as an investment." What are the likely profits? The possible losses? The risks involved?

JESUS IMAGES CHRISTIAN FAITH: A GIFT FOR LIFE

The defining feature of Christian faith is Jesus Christ. In Jesus, Christians believe that God came among us as one of ourselves, revealing who God is and how we are to live as a people of God. The "heart" of Christian faith is not the Bible, not the creed, not the sacraments, not a code of ethics, but a person, Jesus of Nazareth, whom Christians believe to be the Christ and Messiah— the Anointed One of God.

The Gospels paint a general picture of Jesus recruiting follow- ers, calling them into a bonded community, and showing them how to live as people of God in their everyday lives. The first ones to respond to Jesus' invitation "Come follow me" were called *mathetes. Mathete* is usually translated as "disciple," but it also meant an "apprentice"—a term I prefer as a little more lenient;

one expects apprentices to make mistakes. So, an initial description of Christian faith might be *living as a person of God after the way of Jesus among a community of his apprentices in the midst of the world.*

For more than two hundred years, critical scripture scholars have attempted to describe "the historical Jesus"—the kind of person he was, how he lived, what he preached. From this scholarship we can now glean a reliable picture of the faith that Jesus modeled for disciples.

The scholars are nigh unanimous that the reign of God was the defining passion of Jesus' life. For Jesus, God's reign symbolized God's *involvement* in history for the well-being of humankind and the integrity of creation, God's *judgment* against whatever enslaves or diminishes people, God's *compassion* for all in need and forgiveness for sinners. No matter which "hat" Jesus wore—wisdom *teacher* of love and happiness, *prophet* of peace and justice, *miracle worker* restoring health and feeding the hungry, *liberator* from sin and oppression—they all had this defining purpose: that God's rule of peace and justice, love and freedom might come and God's will of fullness of life for all be realized on earth as in heaven. This was the core of Jesus' own faith: *living for the reign of God.*

When asked about the "greatest commandment" of God's reign, Jesus, drawing upon his Hebrew faith, offered three precepts but spoke of them as one. He quoted Deuteronomy 6:5, love God, and then united this with Leviticus 19:8, love neighbor as yourself. He was the only prophet to explicitly unite these precepts, and throughout his life he taught the three loves as ever intertwined. So, we love God *by* loving neighbor and ourselves. At the great judgment, God will not say, "People were hungry, and you fed them," but "*I* was hungry, and you fed *me*" (see Matthew 25:31–46).

Since the love command is the touchstone of Jesus' *way* for the reign of God, let's use it as a schema for outlining lived Christian faith. Deuteronomy 6:5 says, "Love the Lord your God with all your heart, soul, and strength." To the Hebrew mentality, this listing would symbolize the whole person; it's like saying, "with everything you've got." In the New Testament, however, we find four slightly varying formulations—and none of them exactly as found in Deuteronomy; remember, Christian faith began as an oral tradition.

In Mark, a scribe inquires of Jesus, "Which is the first of all the commandments?" (Note, the scribe wants only *one.*) Jesus responds, "You shall love the Lord your God with all your heart, with all your soul, with all your mind, and with all your strength . . . and you shall love your neighbor as yourself. There is no other commandment greater than these." (Note, Jesus cites three but refers to them as a *singular* commandment.) Then the scribe summarizes Jesus' response but with a slightly different naming of the whole person—with all one's "heart, mind, and strength" (Mark 12:28–33).

The other two Synoptics have the same teaching—the whole person must love God, neighbor, and self—only varying in how they describe human totality. Matthew has "with all your heart, with all your soul, and with all your mind" (Matthew 22:37). In Luke, the prompting question is slightly different; a lawyer asks, "What must I do to inherit eternal life?" Jesus turns the question back to him, and the lawyer's formulation—precise as we might expect—lists all four terms: love with "heart, soul, strength, and mind." Jesus affirms his response, "You have answered correctly; do this and you will *live*" (Luke 10:25–28). Remember, the lawyer had asked about "eternal *life.*"

Whatever else, these texts reflect that Christian faith should engage people's *heads* (all one's mind), *hearts* (all one's heart and soul), and *hands* (all one's strength). In more formal language, Christian faith has three aspects: cognitive, affective, and behavioral. Or faith entails *believing, trusting,* and *doing.* A question in the old Baltimore Catechism asked, "Why did God make you?" and the answer was "to *know,* to *love,* and to *serve*" God in this life and to be happy forever in the next. It was a fine response reflecting the *wholeness* of Christian faith—head, heart, and hands.

We can imagine them separately for due emphasis, of course, but in the life of a Christian person and community they always overlap and intertwine. The commitments of the hands won't last long without the heart and head to sustain them—the passions and reasons for acting. Beliefs that go only to people's heads won't amount to much either; they must also go to their hearts and hands. And having one's heart in the right place is crucial but needs to be expressed by the "walk and talk" of Christian faith.

So, let us review Christian faith as a *Way of the Hands,* a *Way of the Heart,* and a *Way of the Head.* All are essential to *the way of life* for God's reign that Jesus modeled for disciples. Although the three intertwine, we do well to explicate each and the several instances within them.

If there is a particular Catholic spin on Christian faith, it is to include "good works"—the hands—as integral to the life of a faithful person. Although official Catholicism often seems more concerned about right belief—orthodoxa—its spirituality would tilt more toward "right action," orthopraxis. In that tradition, then, let us begin with *the hands.*

In describing his *way,* Jesus taught that it is not the person who confesses "Lord, Lord" who enters the reign of God, but "the one who does the will of my Father" (Matthew 7:21). When John's Gospel has Jesus put all three aspects in one statement, he places "doing" first. "If you live according to my teachings, you are truly my disciples. Then, you will know the truth, and the truth will set you free" (John 8:31–32) Note the sequence—from *doing* as he taught, to a *trusting* relationship as disciples, to *knowledge* that sets one free.

CHRISTIAN FAITH AS A WAY OF THE HANDS

Let *hands* represent the lived commitments of Christian faith, the everyday "doings" required of disciples. The Epistle of Saint James states that "faith without works is dead" (James 2:26). The reverse must also be true: "by good works, faith comes alive." I can think of eight *ways* that Jesus models for apprentices to make their faith come alive: ways of *love, justice, peace and reconciliation, simplicity, integrity, compassion, repentance,* and *healing.* You will likely think of others.

A Way of Love. To state the obvious, Jesus modeled that *the* way of life for disciples is love. Beyond uniting love of God, neighbor, and self as one great commandment, Jesus made clear that "neighbor" includes everyone, even enemies. What an amazing message to preach: "love your enemies, do good to those who hate you" (Luke 6:27). It sounds a bit crazy, and yet, how will Sarajevo, or Jerusalem, or Belfast ever know peace unless enemies learn to love each other? And Jesus went even further in radicalizing the love command.

Of itself, Jesus' preaching of love was not such a new commandment; as we have seen, he was combining laws stated clearly in the Hebrew scriptures. However, in the farewell discourse of John's Gospel we hear Jesus saying, "A *new* commandment I give you; *love one another as I have loved you*" (John 13:34). And he elaborated: "As the Father loves me, so I have loved you," repeating, "This is my commandment: love one another as I have loved you" (John 15:9, 12). In other words, the *new* commandment is to love the way Jesus modeled God's love—to approximate divine love in the world. There could be no higher ideal for human living.

A *Way of Justice.* From his Hebrew faith, Jesus knew well that the reign of God means to bring about *shalom* with the justice and peace it entails. At the beginning of his public ministry, Jesus came on a sabbath day into the synagogue at Nazareth, his hometown. When he stood up to read, he searched in the Book of Isaiah for one of the great messianic promises, found it, and then read from chapter 61, verses 1–2, "The Spirit of the Lord is upon me, and . . . has anointed me . . . to bring good news to the poor . . . liberty to captives . . . sight to the blind, to let the oppressed go free, and to proclaim a year of favor from the Lord." Jesus then announced, "Today, this scripture passage is fulfilled in your hearing" (Luke 4:18–21).

Scholars say that this was the defining moment of Jesus' ministry—at least in Luke's Gospel. In political jargon, here Jesus declared his "platform." He could not have searched out a more *shalom* text to favor human liberation. Jesus lived and preached this platform throughout his public ministry. Note especially the respect with which he treated people disparaged and marginalized in the culture—tax collectors, lepers, public sinners, prostitutes,

Samaritans. For what else is injustice but a refusal to recognize the victims as full persons?

A Way of Peace and Reconciliation. The Gospels describe Jesus as possessing a deep peace about him, an inner tranquillity rooted in his relationship with God. Whether facing a storm at sea, critics of his table fellowship, opposition to his healing on the sabbath, or accusers at his trial, Jesus' whole being bespoke peace.

At Jesus' birth, the angels announced, "Peace on earth" (Luke 2:14). Echoing the prophets before him, a precondition of true worship of God is to reconcile broken relationships (Matthew 5:23–24). As a final legacy to disciples: "My peace I leave you, my peace I give you" (John 14:27). And the greeting of the Risen Christ was "Peace be with you" (Luke 24:36).

Afterward, Saint Paul offered a summary of Jesus' mission to the world: that in Jesus, God was reconciling the world to Godself and giving disciples this same ministry of reconciliation (2 Corinthians 5:18–19). Christians are to live and make peace after the way of Jesus.

A Way of Simplicity. We can hear "simple" as "unsophisticated." As modeled by Jesus, however, simplicity means freedom from false attachments and knowing what matters most—God's reign. Jesus did not condemn the goods of life; he simply said that disciples must put God first: "No one can serve two masters . . . you cannot serve God and money" (Matthew 6:24). To choose for God's reign brings true happiness, as in the Beatitudes: "Happy are . . . the poor in spirit . . . those who hunger and thirst for justice . . . the merciful . . . the pure in heart [i.e., those who put God first] . . . the peacemakers" (Matthew 5:3–12). Simplicity is to know and choose what matters most; its fruit is happiness.

A Way of Integrity. Of all the complaints Jesus' detractors made against him, they never accused him of hypocrisy. This is amazing, given the radical demands of the "good news" he preached. Apparently, Jesus' lifestyle was his most credible message. From the beginning, "the people were astonished at his teaching, for Jesus taught them as one having authority and not as the scribes" (Mark 1:22). But what authority did Jesus have? He had no official standing within the power structures. It must have been the integrity of his life.

And it was Jesus' lived commitment to the reign of God—his integrity—that led him to Calvary and death on a cross. Then, God raised up Jesus from the dead, the ultimate affirmation of his life. Clearly, Jesus both talked the talk and walked the walk. Apprentices are to "do likewise" (John 13:15).

A Way of Compassion. The Gospels tell of Jesus being "moved with compassion" by people's suffering—the sorrowing, the sick, the scared, the searching. All his miracles, in one way or another, were prompted by compassion. We should highlight his feeding the hungry. The four Gospels contain six accounts of Jesus looking upon hungry people with compassion and miraculously feeding them. That all four Gospels report this miracle is unusual—John's Gospel was drawn from very different sources than the other three. Then, there are two accounts in Mark and Matthew—apparently of two different incidents. Only the Resurrection is reported on more often. Jesus' compassion for the hungry must have been a central memory for the first Christians.

Recognizing that compassion means to "suffer along with," Jesus' greatest act of compassion for humankind was his suffering and death on the cross. Christians should be careful never to sound as if God *needed* Jesus to die, as if the suffering of "the Son" would *please* God—a perverse notion. Jesus was put to death because of his commitment to God's reign; the powers of evil are wont to destroy such goodness. Jesus died out of compassion for the human condition, "carrying the cross" in solidarity with us. As my friends in Lithuania discovered during their own crucifixion, Jesus' cross is the ultimate symbol of God's compassion for humankind—suffering alongside us.

A Way of Repentance. Let us note well that Jesus was no pushover who affirmed everyone as he found them, regardless of their lifestyle. On the contrary, out of commitment to God's reign, Jesus preached *metanoia*, a total change of life and heart. He called sinners to repentance, and hypocrites to integrity; he "upset" the money changers in the Temple and summoned religious leaders to practice what they preached. His challenge to all: "The reign of God is at hand. Change your lives and believe the good news" (Mark 1:15).

A Way of Healing. Even skeptical scripture scholars agree that the life of Jesus was marked by extraordinary acts of healing the sick— physically, spiritually, and psychologically. "He cured many who were sick with various diseases, and he drove out many demons" (Mark 1:34). Jesus' healings call disciples today to care for every kind of human brokenness: to be menders of minds, hearts, souls, and, when possible, bodies.

Note again the dire urgency in our time to be healers of creation. Jesus called attention to the beauty of "the lilies of the field," that "not even Solomon in all his glory was arrayed as one of these" (Luke 12:27). But if the present pace of destroying the environment continues, we will soon have a world without lilies. Were

Jesus directly addressing people today—and knowing what we know—he would surely make healing creation a priority for apprentices.

CHRISTIAN FAITH AS A WAY OF THE HEART

"Heart" reminds us that Christian faith engages the human emotions; it has a deep feeling aspect to it. In everyday life, there are many issues and commitments about which Jesus would expect apprentices to be passionate. And don't we know lots of Christians who seem a bit short on beliefs but are long on the right passions and actions, and vice versa.

Love, of course, is the defining passion of Christian faith; so we could place it here under *heart* as readily as under *hands*. As I noted already, all these categories intertwine. In fact, none of the commitments of the hands will stay the course unless the heart sustains them. Christians need a passion for justice, for peace, for integrity, and so on. But here I highlight that such passions are nurtured by our relationship with God and the support of other Christians. Christian faith is a profoundly relational affair—of the *heart*. This is another way of saying that the whole *way* of Christian faith requires a spirituality and a community to sustain it.

I can think of two *ways of the heart* pertaining to our relationship with God, and two apropos the communality of Christian faith. For Jesus taught disciples a *way of trusting* in God and a *way of reverencing* God through worship and prayer; likewise, he modeled a *way of becoming community* and a *way of including all* in our horizon of concern.

A Way of Trusting in God. The word *faith* comes from the Latin *fidere,* meaning "to trust." At its core, Christian faith is a trusting relationship with God in Jesus Christ. The leaders of the Protestant Reformation returned this to a central emphasis—thankfully. Faith is trust, and we can trust God because of God's unconditional love for each of us. That *God loves all people* was at the heart of Jesus' good news—the meaning of "gospel." And this divine love is not earned but is by "grace alone." In emphasizing this trusting aspect of faith, the Reformers gave a great gift to the whole Church.

The story of the Prodigal epitomizes the gratuity of God's love (read Luke 15:11–32). The people who first heard the parable must have gasped at the parent's generosity. The son had forfeited his birthright and was not entitled to family restoration. Not only did the father welcome the prodigal, but he was on the lookout for him, longing for his return. Upon seeing his son, the father "was filled with compassion . . . ran, embraced and kissed him" (v. 20). Note that this was *before* the son apologized. What a risk of unconditional love. For all the father knew, the prodigal could have been coming home to ask for more money. Not only did the father welcome the prodigal, he also promoted him within the family—the symbols of the robe, ring, and sandals (v. 22). What a graphic portrayal of God's unconditional love! Every person can trust in such divine love for them.

A Way of Reverencing God Through Worship and Prayer. Jesus taught that the divine-human partnership includes personal prayer and communal worship. Mary and Joseph reared Jesus in the prayer and worship traditions of their Jewish faith, and he drew heavily upon those rich resources. Frequently, the Gospels tell of

Jesus' "going apart" for prayer. Likewise, he urged disciples to pray often and with confidence (see Matthew 7:7–11).

Once, having seen Jesus in prayer, the disciples requested, "Lord, teach us to pray." Jesus taught them first to address God like a Loving Parent;[1] then to reverence God's holy name, to pray that God's reign might be realized as God's loving will on earth as in heaven; to pray for daily sustenance, for mercy in return for mercy, for protection from all that threatens relationship with God or human well-being (Matthew 6:9–13). The "Our Father" reflects the classic sentiments of Christian prayer, at least implicitly: *praise* and *thanksgiving, petition* and *repentance,* and the *resolution* to do God's will.

It was Jesus' "custom" to participate in sabbath worship at his home synagogue of Nazareth (Luke 4:16). When he taught his gospel to the Samaritan woman, Jesus explained that "the hour is coming" when the location where people praise God will not matter but only that they worship "in Spirit and truth" (John 4:20–25). Then, the night before he died, Jesus left Christians the sacred ritual that would forever form the core of their communal worship. At the Last Supper, Jesus identified bread and wine in a very explicit way with his own body and blood, associating this action with his immanent death the next day (Matthew 26:28). He urged disciples to "do this in memory of me" (Luke 22:19).

From the first days after Pentecost, the disciples began to meet regularly to share the gospel, to pray and build up the community, *and* for "the breaking of the bread" (see Acts 2:42). They named their "breaking of bread" as Eucharist (from *eucharistia,* "thanksgiving"). At Eucharist, the disciples remembered and thanked God for the life, death, and resurrection of Jesus, encountered again the saving presence of the Risen Christ, and anticipated the heavenly banquet.

In time, the celebration of Eucharist took on a kind of nick-name—the Mass. This was suggested by its closing words of commission, *ite, missa est,* "Go, you are sent." It's still a fine name, for in this grand celebration, a Christian people bring their lives to God, encounter God's life coming to meet them through Word and Sacrament, and then are *sent* "for the life of the world" (John 6:51).

A Way of Becoming Community. Throughout his public ministry, Jesus gathered disciples into a bonded community of faith. Starting out by the Sea of Galilee, he saw Simon and Andrew "casting their nets" and invited them, "Come, follow me, and I will make you fishers of people" (Mark 1:16–18). They did! Early on, Jesus chose twelve from among the disciples and commissioned them for communal leadership (Mark 3:13–19). On many occasions Jesus seemed to favor Simon Peter as first among these "apostles" (Matthew 16:13–20). He also chose "seventy others" and "sent them out two by two" to participate in heralding the gospel (Luke 10:1–2). Jesus promised to send God's "Spirit of truth" upon his faith community. The Paraclete—the Holy Spirit—would empower them in continuing Jesus' mission to the world (John 15:26).

Before ascending into heaven, the Risen Christ gathered the disciples "on a mountain in Galilee" and gave them this commission: "Go, make disciples of all nations," baptizing and teaching them to live *the way* of Jesus, with the promise "I will be with you always, until the end of time" (Matthew 28:16–20). Then, on the day of Pentecost, the Holy Spirit descended on the first Christian community. There were "about one hundred and twenty persons in the one place" (Acts 1:15), when "tongues of fire came to rest on each one of them, and they were all filled with the Holy Spirit" (Acts 2:3–4).

Now, empowered by the Spirit, the young Church came out preaching fearlessly, adding thousands of new members through baptism. Before long, Paul was teaching Christians that they make up "the body of Christ" (1 Corinthians 12:13, 27). The Christian community has been struggling along since then, far from perfect and often falling short of Jesus' mission, and yet, by the power of the Spirit, functioning as a sacrament of God's reign in the world.

Note the spirit of equality in the first Christian community. A great scripture scholar of our time, Elisabeth Schussler Fiorenza, argues that a defining aspect of Jesus' ministry was his attempt to forge "an inclusive discipleship of equals." Jesus' community should be totally inclusive, with a radical equality among the members. Indeed, there are roles of leadership, but all Christians are equal before God. Remember that at Pentecost the Spirit descended "on all present," and Paul insisted "we were all given to drink of the same Spirit" (1 Corinthians 12:13).

The Catholic church has yet to function as an "inclusive discipleship of equals." In fact, it has looked more like the Roman Empire (its first structural context), with top-down chains of command and severe inequalities. Its leaders often forget Jesus' admonition that "the greatest among you should serve the rest" (Luke 22:26). The kind of community that Jesus proposed is more what we are called to *become* than who we can claim to be already.

Even with lots of *becoming* to do, Catholic Christianity cherishes the call to community and insists that the Church has a crucial function in God's work of salvation (see chapter 3). When the Protestant Reformers rightly challenged the corruptions of the Church and—as a poor solution—downplayed its importance, Catholicism continued to insist that Christian faith is "a way of community." For all its sins and shortcomings, the Church is still the *typical* way that God comes looking for Christians and that they go looking for God—in other words, together.

A Way of Including All. A major mark of Jesus' public ministry was his inclusion of those excluded by society. Both friends and enemies noted this; he must have made a special effort to reach out to the marginalized.

For first-century Palestine, nothing bespoke the inclusivity of Jesus' ministry more than his table fellowship. The symbolism is a bit lost on us, but we still have an inkling that eating together can create a bond between people. The New Testament scholar John Dominic Crossan explains that in Jesus' world, "Open [table fellowship] profoundly negated distinctions and hierarchies between female and male, poor and rich, Gentile and Jew."[2] Jesus welcomed *all* to the table—total inclusion!

Worthy of special note is how Jesus welcomed women into the community of disciples, and as full participating members. This was unusual in the culture; women were excluded from the discourse of the rabbis, from studying and teaching, from bearing witness. When the disciples found Jesus sharing his gospel with the Samaritan woman, they were "amazed to find him talking to a woman" (John 4:27). It's clear that Jesus had women disciples throughout his public ministry, women "who had followed him from Galilee" (Luke 23:49).

Women stood by the foot of the cross—when the men had run away. The Risen Christ made women the first witnesses to the Resurrection. An old tradition named Mary Magdalene "the apostle to the apostles." It is clear that women carried on functions of ministry in the first Christian communities that would now be associated with priesthood.³ Disciples and their communities of faith should be as fully inclusive.

Beyond an inclusive community of disciples, Jesus modeled a *way of including all* in his care and concern, whether they belonged to his community or not. His love was not just for disciples but knew no boundaries; he helped Jew and Gentile, men and women, rich and poor. The synagogue official Jairus, the Samaritan woman, the Roman centurion, the Phoenician woman, and more, all received his ministry. Jesus' disciples should have such "catholicity" of heart, including all in their love and care.

CHRISTIAN FAITH AS ENGAGING THE HEAD

"Head" represents our capacity for knowing and becoming wise. It could be heard to exclude the body, but I certainly don't intend this. As the body is reflected in *heart* and *hands,* we must include it in *head* as well. The body has its own way of knowing. Christians—indeed all of Western culture—need to relearn to listen to their body wisdom. Often, the body *knows* more than the mind, if we would but listen to our "tummy talk." The body can *remember* long after the mind has forgotten. It seems that everything we learn along the way is "written in the body"—the literal sense of biography *(bios graphia).* And when our minds are content to compromise with a status quo, our bodies often protest, prompting *imagination* for change.

The Incarnation is at the core of Christian faith: that "the Word *became flesh*" in Jesus (John 1:14). Surely we can't know an incarnational faith by mind alone. Owning its spiritual wisdom must engage the whole person as a body-soul unity. To "know" Christian faith, we must listen to our bodies and to our lives in the world—our own incarnation.

Then, faith-knowing should be as reflective as any form of human cognition, engaging all capacities of the mind—reason, memory, and imagination. Although the mind alone will not bring a person to faith, one's faith should not seem unreasonable. In fact, Christian faith can be seen to be true on its own merits; it is eminently coherent. For this reason, it can welcome the most rigorous of critical thinking and investigation. To discourage questioning and critical reflection bespeaks a lack of faith—in people and in the Faith itself. To comprehend our faith and "see for ourselves" what it means for life should surely help us to live it.

There is a stereotype that Catholics are not allowed to think for themselves but must submit blindly to whatever the Church teaches. We have already challenged this cliché in the preceding chapter; remember that the "sense of the faithful" is integral to the Church's teaching authority. Here we can add that Catholicism, when at its best, has taught the necessity of the mind to faith, insisting that reason and revelation are necessary partners.

The Scholastic theologians championed the partnership of intellect and faith, a conviction that reached a high point with Saint Thomas Aquinas (1225–1274). Sometime when you're in a library, take a look at Thomas's *Summa Theologica*. It is a mammoth tome of relentless reasoning about faith. In it, Thomas states explicitly, "Just as grace does not destroy nature but perfects it, so sacred doctrine presupposes, uses and perfects natural reason."[4]

Later, against people recommending blind faith, the First Vatican Council (1869–70) declared: "Faith and reason . . . are . . .

mutually advantageous . . . right reason demonstrates the foundations of faith, and *faith sets reason free.*"⁵ Langdon Gilkey summarized this long Catholic tradition of partnership between faith and reason: "There has been throughout Catholic history a drive toward rationality, the insistence that the divine mystery . . . be insofar as possible penetrated, defended, and explicated by the most acute rational reflection."⁶

Although Christians should think for themselves about their faith, two cautions are in order. First, much of faith lies beyond full comprehension. Mystery always remains; human reason can never fully "grasp" God. We encounter our rational limits when facing the paradoxes of faith, for example, reconciling a loving God with human suffering. But just because we can't explain it all, should not deter us from the leap of faith. The great mathematician Blaise Pascal (1623–1662) recommended faith as a worthy "gamble" precisely because "The heart has its reasons that reason knows nothing of."

Second, the primary purpose of the mind in faith is not only to clarify ideas, but to empower a *lived* and *living* faith. The old joke that theologians can spend time debating "how many angels fit on the head of a pin" is not entirely off the mark. Even the most rigorous scholarship about faith should help people to live it. This is to say that the way of the head in Christian faith should reach beyond knowledge—without leaving it behind—toward spiritual wisdom. And this brings us back to our schema after *the way* of Jesus.

A Way of Wisdom. We noted in chapter 5 that the Bible recommends a holistic way of knowing, a way that unites theory and practice into wisdom for life. Here, I elaborate a little and situate *Jesus the Teacher* within this Wisdom tradition.

The Bible names the seat of human knowing as the *leb*. Although *leb* is usually translated as "heart," we don't really have an English equivalent. For *leb* includes what Western philosophy separates into three: emotions, intellect, and will. The *leb* is the center of affections (Psalm 4:8), the source of thought and reflection (Isaiah 6:10), and the seat of will and conscience (1 Samuel 24:5).

It is significant, too, that the Hebrew word for knowing, *yada*, is profoundly relational. In fact, *yada* can also mean human lovemaking, as in "Adam had knowledge of Eve" (Genesis 4:1). To a biblical perspective, then, the process of knowing is holistic and relational; it moves people toward wisdom for life.

The biblical understanding of wisdom is very broad. It stretches from a personal craft (Exodus 31:6) to personification as the Craftsperson whom God employs in the work of creation (Proverbs 8:30). Overall, however, the wise are those who choose to live the covenant in the everyday; the foolish, those who do not. But as always with keeping covenant, it's a two-way partnership. Indeed we must seek wisdom; as Solomon declares: "I loved and sought her from my youth" (Wisdom 8:2). On the other hand, the same Solomon says, "[T]he spirit of Wisdom came to me" (Wisdom 7:7). In other words, we seek wisdom only to encounter Her coming to meet us, seeking us out. And She ever "produces friends of God and prophets" (Wisdom 7:27), promising, "Whoever finds me, finds life" (Proverbs 8:35).

In New Testament scholarship now, a favorite way to understand the historical Jesus is as *a wisdom teacher*. He was often addressed as "Teacher," and the Gospels describe his ministry most often as teaching. They make clear that his teaching intent was people knowing and living their faith—wisdom for life.

Luke has Jesus present himself as wiser than Solomon; for Matthew, Jesus is Wisdom personified; for John, Jesus is wisdom—Sophia—made flesh.[7] Paul portrays Christ as "the wisdom of God" (1 Corinthians 1:24); and for James, one becomes wise in faith by doing the works of peace, mercy, kindness, and justice (see James 3:17–18). Apprentices to Jesus are to "know" their faith as a spiritual wisdom for life.

A Way of Traditioning. Jesus dearly cherished his Jewish faith. He readily cited its texts and traditions and declared that he had not come to abolish the law and the prophets but to fulfill them (Matthew 5:17). He would have known well the great Hebrew admonition "Teach it to your children, and to your children's children" (Deuteronomy 4:9). At the end, he told his own disciples to hand on "everything" he had taught (Matthew 28:20), and he promised to send the Holy Spirit to "remind" us of all his teachings (John 14:26)—lest we forget. Integral to *the way* of Jesus is to teach and hand on the sacred traditions of Christian faith.

Jesus was prophetic in his traditioning, however, in that he rejected simple repetition and often reinterpreted: "You have heard it said . . . but I say . . ." (see Matthew 5). He also taught that disciples who are wise in the reign of God will draw from the treasury of tradition "both the new and the old" (Matthew 13:52). Christians should hand on their traditions in vital and life-giving ways.

A Way of Evangelizing. During his lifetime, Jesus sent out disciples to evangelize—share the "good news" *(evangelion)* of God's love (see Luke 10:1–12). Then, on that hillside in Galilee, the Risen Christ gave all present the mandate "Go make disciples" (Matthew 28:19). By baptism, all Christians have the commission to bring the gospel into every aspect of their lives. Chapter 8 will review significant developments emerging in Catholic evangelization. Instead of "bringing them in"—converts into the Church—evangelization now emphasizes "bringing Christians out" into the world to do God's work of "liberating salvation." For now, I suggest that the style that Jesus himself employed is still a model for how Christians might share their faith.

Typically, Jesus began by turning people to look at their own lives, to think about their everyday world, though often in a whole new way. Then, into those lives, Jesus taught his gospel with authority—the integrity of his own life—and invited a lived response. We can see this style vividly at work in the parables. His whole intent was for people to put their lives and faith together, to see for themselves and choose to live as disciples. A riveting instance of this teaching dynamic is the encounter with the Risen Christ on the Road to Emmaus (read along in Luke 24:13–35).

Notice how "the stranger" enters into the company of the two despondent disciples and "walks along with them." They don't recognize him, but neither does he introduce himself. In fact, the Risen One never tells them *what* to see but waits for them to see for themselves. The stranger asks, "What are you discussing as you go upon your way?" Note how he turned them first to look at their own lives.

They tell of their experiences of Jesus, what their hopes had been, and about the women coming back from the tomb with an amazing story of resurrection. To shed light on their own story, Christ turns them to the great Story of their faith tradition. "Beginning then with Moses and all the prophets, he interpreted for them every passage of scripture which referred to himself." Still the Risen One does not tell them what to see.

The two disciples offer hospitality. When seated at table, their guest takes the bread, blesses, breaks, and distributes. With this, "their eyes were opened and they recognized him"—they came to see for themselves—whereupon the Risen One "vanished from their sight." To where? Might we say *into them*—now the Body of Christ in the world. Remembering how their "hearts were burning" during his teaching, they decide to return to Jerusalem. They take their rekindled faith back to life again.

I am a biased commentator, no doubt, but I perceive here what is proposed throughout as the dynamic of Christian spirituality, and, indeed, of theology as well—*bringing life to faith and faith to life*. When Christians share their faith with others, they might begin with people's own lives and issues and only then share Christian faith as appropriate and with sensitivity to where people "are at." Thereafter, respect whatever people come "to see for themselves," and their own choices. Apprentices do well to follow this gentle and respectful style of the Master Teacher.

CHRIST EMPOWERS CHRISTIAN LIVING

Jesus had a life-changing and lasting impact on disciples. In a unique way, they experienced God in Jesus. He inspired them by how he lived for God's reign, but they were confused by his horrendous death on a cross. Then, three days later and totally unexpectedly—as on the Emmaus road—they began to encounter their beloved Jesus as risen from the dead.

Christ's resurrection was not the bodily resuscitation that disciples witnessed with Jesus' raising of Lazarus (John 11:1–44) or the son of the widow of Nain (Luke 7:11–17). Both would have to die again. Rather, the body-person of the Risen Christ was transformed; "he appeared in another form" (Mark 16:12). Even so, Christ could show them the wounds, ask for food and eat it (Luke 24:36–43). So, the disciples recognized Christ's resurrection as very real and yet not fully describable; it belonged within God's eternal realm. Still, they were rock-solid in their conviction that "Jesus was raised on the third day" (1 Corinthians 15:4).

Added to the disciples' amazing experience of Christ's resurrection was the phenomenal event of Pentecost (see Acts 2). Here the small Christian community experienced an outpouring of God's own Spirit "upon all present." It transformed them from scaredy-cats afraid to show their faces to fearless witnesses ready to bring Jesus' mission to the world. Fully convinced of his resurrection and empowered by the Spirit, the first disciples began to proclaim their Jesus as "Lord and Messiah" (Acts 2:36), as the Anointed of God—the Christ.

It also began to dawn on disciples that Jesus' life, death, and resurrection were a catalytic event in God's "work of salvation," that he had forged a new covenant between God and humankind. They considered it a new day for human history; through the Christ event, even death had lost its sting (1 Corinthians 15:55).

The disciples' faith was that God had done something extraordinary in Christ to "save" humankind and that the Spirit now enabled them to continue Jesus' mission and to follow *the way*. But how were they to describe this turning point? They began searching for metaphors to express *the difference* that Jesus had made for all creation. Indeed, the search continues to this day, a search for language for what cannot be fully described. The challenge is to express—in ways meaningful to different times and places—what God has done in Jesus Christ and continues by the Holy Spirit.

Saint Paul got us started, offering a whole collage of images: salvation (Romans 1:16), liberation (Galatians 5:1), justification (Galatians 2:16–21), reconciliation (2 Corinthians 3:16–18), sanctification (1 Corinthians 1:30), a new creation (Galatians 6:15), expiation (Romans 3:25), new life (1 Corinthians 15:45), adoption (Galatians 4:4–6), forgiveness (Romans 3:25), and more. The variety reflects the mystery behind "why God became a person."[8] And the quest has continued since Paul, responding to different cultural settings. Three classic ways of talking about "the Christ of faith" are as Savior, Redeemer, and Divinizer.

In Christian faith, Christ is *Savior* from the powers of evil that threaten to destroy us. Christ is *Redeemer* who buys back *(redemeo)* humankind from the bondage of sin, canceling our debt and righting the scales of justice. Christ is *Divinizer* who restores to humanity the divine image that was tarnished by original sin and enables people to live into their divine potential. Again to cite the pithy summary of Athanasius, "God became human so that humans could become more like God."

As with all human language about divine mysteries, these metaphors say something profoundly true; yet they can never say it all. Like all metaphors, as well, if taken too literally they begin to say what is not true at all. For example, to push the metaphor of Jesus as Redeemer too far is to make God sound like a vindictive parent who is pleased by the suffering of God's own Son—what a horrible image of God.

A contemporary metaphor gaining ground is Jesus as *Liberator.* It reflects that Jesus' life, death, and resurrection are a catalyst to *free people from* all that enslaves, personal and social, and to *free them for* realizing God's will of fullness of life for all—the reign of God. We might also imagine Jesus as *Humanizing One,* enabling Christians to live into fullness of life as reflections of God. Or Jesus as *Caregiver,* encouraging people to be responsible for and to "the other." Or?

Whatever metaphors we use, the central conviction of Christian faith is that Jesus both models how to live *and* enables people by grace to follow *the way.* Jesus was such a catalyst of liberating salvation precisely because he was both one of ourselves in humanity and "one in being" with God. Here we encounter the transcendent mystery that this one and same person, Jesus of Nazareth, was truly human and truly divine, the Second Person of the Blessed Trinity.

The Christological doctrine of "two natures in one person" was hammered out over the first four centuries, accompanied by lots of controversy and accusations of heresy. The arguments seesawed back and forth. One side would emphasize Jesus' humanity, because he had to be human to represent us; then the other would highlight his divinity, because we needed someone of God to be effective on our behalf. The Church was searching for a middle ground of both/and instead of either/or. Finally it reached its classic articulation at the great Council of Chalcedon (451). This is not to say that Chalcedon gave a final explanation, but at least it set the parameters of the conversation.

Thereafter, orthodox Christian faith would affirm that Our Lord Jesus Christ, quoting Chalcedon, "is complete in his deity and complete in his humanity, truly God and truly a human being ... coessential *(homoousios)* with the Father as to his deity and coessential with us as to his humanity, a being like us in every respect apart from sin. . . ."[9] Whatever else, such faith means that the whole human condition has been "raised up" through its solidarity with Jesus, and that disciples can now follow *the way*.

FOR REFLECTION AND CONVERSATION

- What else would you add as foundational to *the way* of Jesus?

- What spiritual practices might enrich your own faith investment?

SPIRITUAL PRACTICES TO GROW THE INVESTMENT

Many practices suggested in previous and subsequent chapters can be echoed here. I suggest three specific to investing faith in Jesus Christ. As usual, two are fairly generic, and the third practice more precise.

1. Deepen the Friendship with Jesus

Like every friendship, the one with Jesus needs tending. Here are three suggestions; imagine others yourself.

Talk to Jesus as a Friend. I had a first-grade teacher who would often tell us, "No matter what, Jesus is your best friend." And she would add, "You can tell Jesus whatever is in your heart." Those sentiments have stayed with me. In the worst of times, even when

I don't want to approach God, the Creator, I can talk to Jesus and feel that he understands and cares for me. Why? Because he was one of ourselves. He knew the human condition from the inside, and loved us "unto death." There is nothing that we can't bring to Jesus for help and support, for mercy and healing.

After receiving Eucharist can be an ideal time for a heart-to-heart with Jesus. There is also an old practice of "visiting" with Jesus before the Blessed Sacrament—the Eucharist reserved in the tabernacle of every Catholic church. As a best friend, we can turn to Jesus in every time and place, even the most unlikely.

Pray the New Testament. No doubt, the Church has benefited greatly from critical scholarship of its scriptures. But more spiritually fruitful is to approach the scriptures, especially the Gospels, in a meditative way, with the interest of getting to know Jesus—personally. This means allowing Gospel readings to prompt a conversation with Jesus, talking with him as you bring your life to the text and the text to your life, listening with the heart.

You may want to read a Gospel right through—a little each day—pausing as the Spirit moves you to chat with Jesus. Or you may choose the Gospel excerpt assigned daily in the common lectionary.[10] Almost every Gospel text describes an event. It can help to enter imaginatively into the scene, to picture yourself being there as an observer or participant, talking with and listening to Jesus. Share with him your feelings as well as your thoughts. Such a meditative approach to scripture can help you get to know Jesus—and yourself—better, both from the inside.

Encounter Christ in the Poor. A rich tradition in Christian spirituality is that helping the poor is a privileged place to encounter Jesus. His "face" seems to be more evident among them. I have seen this happen many times for young people from Boston College who participate in service programs or volunteer after graduation in a third-world context. So often it awakens their Christian faith, as if they personally meet Jesus in the poor and needy.

There is no greater human pain or indignity than to be hungry for lack of food. Given their affluence, Western Christians—whose societies consume eighty percent of the world's resources with only twenty percent of the population—have an urgent responsibility to the hungry of the world. Some social strategists claim that we now have the resources and know-how to solve the problem of world hunger; what we lack is the will. Christians must be in the forefront of such efforts, locally and internationally, or else worry about this dire judgment: "Depart from me you accursed into eternal fire . . . for I was hungry and you gave me no food . . ." (Matthew 25:41–42).

And there are other kinds of poverty besides lack of food. Most of us encounter some instance of it every day. Look out for it. Let your faith prompt you to favor it with care and compassion. Outreach to the "poor" can grow a friendship with Jesus.

2. Craft a Foundation Prayer

Catholic Christians have a long tradition of saying a "morning offering." This is a pause upon rising to offer God "all the prayers, works, joys, and sufferings of this day." Building upon this old practice, I have experienced a powerful asset in having a *foundation prayer* with which to begin each day.

The intent of a foundation prayer is to refocus the core commitments in faith that you desire to live daily. It summarizes your "investment" choices. It should explicitly state your commitments and ask God for the grace to so live. The key to crafting your own foundation prayer is to recognize your deepest desires by way of living faith, to express these hopes to God, and to ask the Spirit's help to live them throughout the day.

My own expression follows a Trinitarian pattern and has been hewn over many years. Although I carefully crafted a version some twenty years ago, it proved to be only a first draft. I have made many adjustments and additions since then—a reminder that God is never finished with us until our hearts rest in God. And I rarely pray it the same way two days in a row, digressing for a special intention or pausing to dwell on a phrase as needed. To stimulate your own crafting of a foundation prayer, I share mine here—italicized—with a brief comment on each stanza.

Loving God, thank you for the gift of this new day; help us to live it as a gift.

I pray as "us" because I ask for the same graces for my spouse as for myself; on occasion, we pray it together. I learned years ago that one can approach the day as a gift or as a problem—and how foolish the latter approach; it can warp a whole day. Wiser, by far, to embrace each day as a gift, and precisely because God grants each one and a limited number.

Give us the grace to live our faith that You Are, that you are Our God, present with us and for us, loving us with unconditional love, and giving us this gift of life.

I ask first and foremost for the grace to practice our faith, beginning with the bedrock conviction that God Is, and is ever present with us in total favor and gracious love.

> *Grace us to live these gifts of life and love by loving You, loving ourselves, loving each other, loving all others—letting you be the God of our lives.*

We need grace to let God be God—instead of ourselves—and to love God, self, and every other, beginning with those nearest. This must be our response to God who first loves us, making love the greatest commandment of divine convenant in our lives.

> *Our Friend Jesus, help us to follow your way of life and love, of justice and compassion; free us from all that holds us bound; help us to live into the new life that you make possible in the Spirit.*

My fondest experience of Jesus is as Friend who invites us to live *the way* into "fullness of life" for ourselves and others. I also know him as Liberator—from all slaveries, within and without. And he makes new life possible every day as the Spirit continues Jesus' liberating mission in the world.

> *Holy Spirit, inspire, guide, and sustain us in living our faith this day; help us to grow in wisdom and holiness, to become fully alive people, with deep joy and peace in our hearts, being ever true to our faith and to ourselves.*

It is by the Spirit that we can live our faith in the day-to-day.

Christians traditionally associate the Spirit with inspiration and guidance, with helping us to "stay the course" into wisdom and holiness of life. Believing that the Spirit has many gifts for each of us, I name the ones that I need most.

> *Loving God, may our lives praise you this day and contribute to the coming of your reign. Amen.*

I conclude with these lines to remind us of our ultimate purpose in life—to give praise to God and to be instruments of grace in realizing God's dream for the world.

Why not craft your own foundation prayer? It will become a lifelong resource for putting your spirituality to work every day.

3. End the Day with an Examen of Consciousness

Spirituality amounts to consciously allowing one's faith to permeate daily life—faith at work. So consciousness is key to spirituality. A foundation prayer in the morning can start us on the right foot. Then, at day's end it can be very helpful to do a review, using what spiritual writers call an examen of consciousness (the old *examination of conscience* dressed up a bit). The intent is to look over the day with God as partner, recognizing how and where God's Spirit was moving, what was or was not of God's reign.

It helps to divide the examen into five moments:

- Quiet down and get comfortable; breathe deeply, becoming aware of your breathing.

- Become consciously aware that you are in God's presence; thank God for the gift of the day.

- Ask for the grace to see the day as God saw it, especially to discern where God was present or absent.

- Review the day slowly, with God as partner, recognizing the God-moments, what was or was not of God's reign.

- End with a prayer of repentance as needed, and always a prayer of hope. The Lord's Prayer expresses both sentiments.

FOR REFLECTION AND CONVERSATION

- How else might you grow in friendship with Jesus—if that is your heart's desire?

- What faith investment are you invited to make or renew at this time?

SEVEN

"WHAT ARE OUR POLITICS?"— WORKING FOR JUSTICE FOR ALL

A SCHOOL FOR JUSTICE'S SAKE

They hoped for rain soon in Duran, sometime in January. Then the dust—burned from the soil by the equator sun in this well-named country, Ecuador—would become like molasses. Meanwhile, we bumped along a dirt road on the way to Arbolito, with dust clouds rising behind our jeep as well as the oncoming vehicles, clogging nostrils and searing eyes.

Arbolito is a barrio within the shantytown of Duran on the outskirts of Guayaquil. It is among the poorest in all of Latin America.

Fr. John Drury made me welcome in Arbolito and so did its lovely people. We visited homes together, small bamboo huts perched on stilts against the rainy season, with as many as ten people sharing one room. Living on the verge of starvation and with no public services, few have a chance of employment and even fewer at a fair wage. And yet, the people of Arbolito maintain their dignity with a defiant joy that is rare among the well-to-do.

I loved their insistence on handshakes all around upon meeting and departing. Their offers of food and drink as hospitality—in spite of their poverty—touched me deeply. At church on Sunday, their clothes were spotlessly clean—remember the dust; I wondered how they manage it.

Many times in Arbolito, I saw pictures or statues of Dismas, the "Good Thief," the one who turned his life around and repented to Jesus on Calvary. Fr. John explained that Dismas is the patron saint of Arbolito. For a bit of fun, I poked, "The Good Thief—I didn't think he'd ever been canonized." With equal whimsy John replied, "'Round here he has!" Ah, how perspectival are all our takings on faith!

We ended a long day of visiting families in Arbolito, including three newly born babies and their mothers, all birthed at home that day without any medical attention. As we bumped our way back through the cloud of dust to the parish house of Nuestra Señora de los Angeles, I asked John, "What would bring social justice for these people, give them a chance of a decent life?"

Without hesitating, John said, "Education. They must get an education to have any chance at all. The best hope for justice here is to build a school. It's a slow strategy, but over the long haul, education can turn things around."

I was a bit surprised at his response, yet it seemed so obvious. Sure, Arbolito would benefit from honest government and an end to first-world exploitation, and no one knew this better than John. Meanwhile, build a school!

John was ready to roll. I promised to help raise funds among family and friends. Before leaving Arbolito, we reviewed a possible site; a few weeks later, John purchased it. So, as we go to press, a new school is rising in Arbolito, as a strategy for social justice! Dismas is helping with another turnaround.

POLITICS: DIRTY OR DIGNIFIED?

"What are my politics?" Everyone should ask and decide this question, so crucial to our human vocation. Our dignity as human beings requires us to be politically responsible. And Christians should ask the political question from a faith perspective. Slowly, we are realizing that faith must permeate our politics as much as our prayers. In fact, bringing faith to politics may be the most challenging instance of spirituality at work.

There is much cynicism—and with cause—about "dirty politics." But I've always resisted this too popular sentiment. My father was a politician, and I've never known anyone with more integrity. Whatever commitment I have to a faith that does justice is much indebted to him. And it was his Catholic faith that gave him a passionate concern for the downtrodden.

As communal beings, people need to participate actively in the *polis,* the community of citizens, and in its *politia,* public life. Catholicism recognizes that we are political by nature and not simply for expedience or convenience, as John Locke and company would have it. Politics arises from how God made us. Denying people their rights and responsibilities in the public realm violates God-given human dignity.

This being said, the question remains, What *should* be our politics? Thinking beyond party preference, what are the everyday values and commitments that ought to mark our society together? And what does being an apprentice to Jesus suggest for participation in the political realm?

There are Christian traditions whose negative outlook on the person and on life in the world lead them to conclude that nothing can be done to improve society—it's going to hell in a handbasket, anyway! Though Catholic Christians fail as much as any in their political responsibilities, and often are accomplices in unjust social structures, their faith teaches and demands otherwise.

As preceding chapters reflect, Catholicism positively appreciates both the person and society. It claims that by divine grace, people can work through social structures to realize the values of God's reign. In chapter 4, I proposed that Christian faith demands commitment to the *common good* of society. Here, I elaborate and propose the defining political commitment for disciples of Jesus as *justice for all—justice that builds on compassion and promotes peace.*

An old and sensible definition of justice is "everyone their due." This begs the question, however, What is a person's "due"? Aristotle favored arithmetic calculation, with each citizen receiving from society exactly in proportion to what each contributes, and lawbreakers being punished in proportion to the harm they've done to the public welfare. This precision is symbolized by the blindfolded Lady Justice—in front of many U.S. law courts—weighing her scales without bias and according to deserts.

Constitutional democracy, however, stretches social justice beyond "what's due" based on contribution, to caring for people's needs regardless of what they contribute. John Rawls, for example, proposes that the strong and wealthy have responsibilities in justice to the weak and poor, that a true democracy should help sustain members who cannot meet their own needs. A severe handicap might prevent certain people from contributing much to society, but they are entitled to what they need for quality of life, and the state must see to it.

Christian faith likewise goes beyond "everyone their due" to *justice with compassion*. It calls for generous favor toward those most in need. This is because Christianity combines justice with the great commandment of love—and as Jesus modeled God's love. From a faith perspective, the mandate of justice arises from our covenant with God. The largess of God's relationship with humankind should be the model for our relationships in society. Note, too, that all the great religions urge their adherents to reach beyond equity to compassion for the poor and needy.

Of late, many Catholics may feel surprised by the plenitude of justice rhetoric from their church leaders. A friend joked to me, "Looks like we'll become as guilt-ridden about justice as we've been about sex." But maybe it's a more worthy cause?

A now-classic summary was offered by the World Synod Of Bishops of 1971: "Action on behalf of justice and participation in the transformation of the world fully appear to us as a *constitutive dimension of the preaching of the Gospel*, or, in other words, of the Church's mission for the redemption of the human race and its *liberation from every oppressive situation*."[1] In other words, working for social justice is integral to living the gospel and to the mission of the Church in the world.

Even the most conservative bishops on church discipline can sound like leftists on social justice. Clearly, justice is now the party line of the Catholic church. Its own rhetoric, however, would seem to indict some of the church's structures as well as the economics of many conservative Catholics. In fact, how many Catholics are ready to embrace Pope John Paul II's entire body of social teachings: his opposition to communism *and* his scathing critique of free-market capitalism, his condemnation of abortion *and* all instances of the death penalty. Very few—left or right—are consistent in our commitment to justice in society and Church, all across the board.

Catholics, like other mainline Christians, hesitate wisely about the Church's interfering directly in politics. The era of Christendom—when Church and society were as one—is not a happy memory for either. Better by far to insist that the Church's first and only business is spiritual—"care of souls." It forgets this to its demise. At the same time, it's precisely the Church's spirituality that demands commitment to justice. Christian spirituality can never be apart from life but must be *put to work* at every level of human existence—personal, interpersonal, and sociopolitical. So, it's precisely their spirituality that compels Christians to a faith that does justice.

FOR REFLECTION AND CONVERSATION

- What is your own understanding of justice? Is it influenced by Christian faith? If so, how? If not, why not?

- Reflect on some of the experiences and influences that shape your current politics. Do you want to—need to—consider any adjustments?

JUSTICE TO A CHRISTIAN IMAGINATION:
A GIFT FOR LIFE

Christians of all stripes need to deepen their understanding of God's justice. In the past, Christianity tended to limit divine justice to punishment for personal sins; God's justice was sinners getting their comeuppance. Although it is true that God's justice holds people responsible for how they live, a punitive understanding alone is a caricature.

From a biblical perspective, God's concern is not to wreak vengeance on individual sinners but to bring about the reign of justice in the world. Indeed, God absolutely condemns injustice and judges against all that cheats people, diminishes their dignity, or violates their rights. But God's positive passion is to see justice realized within human history, for every person and at every level. God's justice is radical favor for human well-being and the integrity of creation; God is totally *for life for all.* God's people should live likewise.

A contemporary Catholic imagination regarding justice has biblical and theological foundations, and it reflects a philosophical tradition of natural-law ethics. It has also been enriched by awareness of how societies function, the linkages within and between them, and how social structures can hinder or enhance justice for all. What follows are but some highlights.

WHAT GOD ASKS OF US: THE BIBLE ON JUSTICE

The Hebrew scriptures make justice an absolute mandate of the divine-human covenant. They reflect the rock-solid conviction that God desires complete human well-being, favoring the best of everything for all. As noted earlier, God's dream of *shalom* requires justice and compassion, favor for the poor of all kinds, holiness as wholeness of life, and peace as human harmony and the well-being of creation.

God takes the Hebrew people into covenant, and they must allow this partnership to permeate their whole life. "I will be your God, and you will be my people" (Leviticus 26:12) means that what God wills all people to enjoy, is also the will by which God's people must live—the law. Yahweh "is a God of justice" (Isaiah 30:18) who "secures justice and the rights of all the oppressed" (Psalm 130:6), delights in its realization (Jeremiah 9:24), and hates injustice of every kind (Isaiah 61:8). Hebrew scripture scholar Walter Brueggemann summarizes, "In biblical faith, the doing of justice is the primary expectation of God."[2]

Another scripture scholar, John R. Donahue, describes the biblical notion of justice as "right relationship"—right relationship with God, self, others, and creation.[3] What, then, would make relationships "right" for justice's sake? In the Hebrew scriptures, *the model of rightness is God's relationship with humankind.* The loving-kindness *(hesed)* by which God relates with us is the ideal by which we are to relate with others and creation. And what an ideal! For God relates with humankind not as some blindfolded judge balancing the scales but as a tender, munificent, and compassionate mother.

It is surely no coincidence that the Hebrew word for compassion is *racham* and for a mother's womb *rachum.* When the Bible describes God as compassionate, it portrays God relating with us as a mother with her child. And even if a mother could forget and have no compassion "for the child of her womb . . . I will never forget you," says Yahweh (Isaiah 49:15).

This mothering God of loving-kindness and compassion has bonded with the people "in right and in justice, in love and in mercy" (Hosea 2:21). Even when God must judge against injustice, it is not for the sake of vengeance: "Behold, I am a merciful and gracious God, slow to anger, rich in kindness and fidelity" (Exodus 34:6). God's covenanted people are to imitate the divine largess in their everyday relationships. Far beyond giving everyone their due, God's justice overflows from the heavens and springs up in abundance (Isaiah 45:8).

Justice with compassion should be manifest especially in relating with "the poor." The Bible's defining sense of poverty is economic; then it repeatedly adds "the widow, the alien, and the orphan." To a contemporary reading, this includes with the economically poor the victims of sexism, racism, and child abuse. The intent, surely, is to urge compassionate justice in response to every form of poverty. For God hears the cry of the poor and oppressed (Exodus 22:22) and comes to their aid (Psalm 113:7). God's people must do likewise!

How God's people treat the poor and powerless measures their faithfulness to the covenant. The prophets continually remind the Israelites that true worship of God requires justice toward all and favor for those to whom life is most denied. Offering sacrifices while committing injustice and neglecting the needy is "loathsome" to God, or, as the old King James Version translated, "an abomination" (Isaiah 1:13).

The Hebrew scriptures have the recurring hope of a promised Messiah. In the messianic age, people "shall beat their swords into plowshares . . . nation shall not lift up sword against nation, neither shall they learn war any more" (Isaiah 2:4). Then "God will make justice and praise spring up from all the nations" (Isaiah 61: 11); then "kindness and truth shall meet, justice and peace shall kiss" (Psalm 85:11). To recognize Jesus as Messiah surely mandates Christians to help realize the messianic promises.

We find the greatest statement of what Yahweh asks of humankind in Micah 6:8, a text that summarizes the core preaching of the prophets. Micah 6:1–7 portrays a dramatic scene in which Yahweh puts Israel on trial for forgetting its divine liberation from slavery in Egypt (6:4) and forgetting what such emancipation requires of God's people. Israel tries to plea-bargain, even to buy off the Prosecutor by increasing its sacrificial offerings. Maybe God can be appeased if they sacrifice a better quality of calves, or up the number of rams, or the volume of oil. Israel even offers God the unspeakable—its own firstborn.

In the face of this pathetic bribery, Yahweh looks out beyond Israel and addresses all humankind as well: "This, O humankind, is what Yahweh asks of you, only this: that you *act justly, love tenderly,* and *walk humbly* with your God" (Micah 6:8). These are not three separate mandates. They are a unity; *justice, love,* and *faith* are integral to the covenant of "right relationship." To summarize another way, God expects *faith that does justice with love.*

The New Testament affirms and builds upon this rich Hebrew tradition. It is hard to credit, but Christians often allow the great commandment to distract from the mandate of justice, reducing love of neighbor to one-on-one charity—a handout to the beggar on the corner. But in both personal and social relations, surely love must be built on justice. How could love be true unless also just? "Christian love of neighbor and justice cannot be separated. For *love implies an absolute demand for justice*—namely, a recognition of the dignity and rights of one's neighbor."[4] We might say that love is the icing on the cake of justice and the yeast that makes it rise.

According to Luke's Gospel, before Jesus was born, Mary praised God for doing "great things" in her conceiving: deposing the mighty from their thrones, raising up the lowly, and feeding the hungry as promised. The God of Mary favors those who need the favor most (see Luke 1:46–55—the Magnificat).

At Jesus' birth, a "heavenly host" proclaimed "peace on earth" (Luke 2:13–14). At the end, Jesus left disciples with the "new commandment" to love as he had modeled divine love, along with the legacy of his peace (John 13:34, 14:27). And "Peace be with you" was the greeting of the Risen Christ (Luke 24:36).

Between his birth and rising, Jesus' whole life was one of right and loving relationship with God, self, others, and creation, with added outreach to the poor, oppressed, and marginalized. By rejecting all types of discrimination, Jesus' ministry was a countersign to the sexism, racism, and every other instance of injustice in his culture. Let us return to one text, Luke 4:16–21, because it is so central, Jesus in the synagogue at Nazareth. First, the context.

In chapter 3, Luke recounts that Jesus was baptized by John at the Jordan, at which time "the heavens were opened, and the Holy Spirit descended upon Jesus in bodily form, as a dove. And a voice from heaven said, 'This is my beloved Son in whom I am well pleased'" (3:22). Then chapter 4 begins, "Filled with the Holy Spirit, Jesus returned from the Jordan, and was led by the Spirit into the desert for forty days" (4:1–2).

There follows the account of Jesus fasting in the desert and the devil tempting him to pride, power, and presumption. But Jesus resisted, in each case reiterating that God comes first in his life— the fundamental "right relationship." The transition line reads, "Jesus returned to Galilee in the power of the Spirit" (4:14).

The dramatic scene on a sabbath day in Nazareth, his home town, now follows. Jesus went "as was his custom" to the synagogue for worship. Obviously a regular in his local faith community, Jesus was invited to read. He took the scroll of Isaiah the prophet, searched out its great messianic text (Isaiah 61:1–2), and read: "The Spirit of the Lord is upon me, and has anointed me to bring good news to the poor, to proclaim liberty to captives, recovery of sight to the blind, to set free the oppressed, and to proclaim God's year of favor." Then, after a pause, Jesus made the astonishing announcement, "Today this scripture passage is fulfilled in your hearing" (4:18–21).

Scholars have described this text from Isaiah as the most radical social-justice statement to be found in the Hebrew scriptures. Jesus chose it deliberately to launch his ministry—he *searched* it out. First, note that the Spirit empowered Jesus for his mission, and particularly for the work of justice.

Remember, at his baptism Jesus was "filled with the Holy Spirit" and then "led by the Spirit" into the desert. After his temptations, he returned to Galilee, again "in the power of the Spirit." Now, Jesus recognized himself as "anointed" by God's Spirit to fulfill Isaiah's prophecy. The Spirit empowered him for the messianic work of establishing right and loving relationship among humankind and throughout creation. Christians must look to the Spirit to empower their work for justice.

For we have forged a false divide between our prayers and politics, between the spiritual quest for *holiness* and promoting *justice*. Both are the work of God's Spirit in the world. In fact, the biblical understanding of holiness and of justice are the same—"right relationship" with God, self, others, and creation. Justice and spirituality are two sides of the same coin, and the Holy Spirit empowers both!

"Good news to the poor." "Liberty to captives." "Sight to the blind." "To set free the oppressed." What a social program! And then, to issue in "God's year of favor" (Luke 4:18–19). Scholars agree that this verse refers to the Jubilee year as described in Leviticus 25 and 27. Jubilee came each fiftieth year as the crowning of seven cycles of seventh year sabbaticals; it amounted to a radical social proposal to recognize that everything belongs to God and to give it back. The three defining stipulations of Jubilee were that the land be left fallow, that all debts be forgiven, and that all slaves be set free. By associating his mission with Jubilee, Jesus signaled that his justice includes care for the environment, economic reform, and opposing every instance of oppression.

The first disciples recognized that to live for God's reign in Jesus required them to work for justice and peace (Romans 14:17), to "put on justice" in order to preach Jesus' "gospel of peace" (Ephesians 6:15). The disciples committed themselves to Jesus Christ as the catalyst of right relationships among humankind and with God (Ephesians 2:14–18). They were convinced that God had reconciled the world in Jesus and had given disciples the ministry of reconciliation (2 Corinthians 5:18). The New Testament's distinct perspective on justice as right relationship is to add a spirit of altruistic love.

Agape is the principal term used for *love* in the New Testament, and this is a bit unusual. At the time, *agape* was the least common term for love. Two others were favored: *eros* for sexual love and *philos* for friendship. But the New Testament favors *agape* to describe God's munificent love for humankind and thus the norm for Christians. In the classic statement of "God so loved the world as to send the only Son" (John 3:16), the verb used of God is *agapao*.

Agape asks disciples to adopt a lifestyle of empathic and lavish love, one not contingent on response or results—no quid pro quo—but to love as Jesus modeled divine love.

This spirit of agapaic love should permeate the justice that Christian faith promotes. Perhaps this is another way of combining justice with compassion as the Hebrew scriptures do. Christians should be keenly aware that justice is a call to "right *and loving* relationship"—with God, self, others, and creation.

THEOLOGY OLD AND NEW

The early Christian communities became renowned for their social services to people in need, the sick and hungry, widows and orphans. In addition to the example of Jesus, they had the *imago Dei* tenet—that all are made in God's image—as their rationale for promoting justice. After Christianity emerged as the official religion of the Roman Empire (early fourth century), it had new opportunities to work for social reform. The Church was instrumental in passing laws that protected widows and orphans, curtailed slavery, reduced abortions, defended children, and secured humane treatment for criminals and prisoners of war.

Many early Church documents have a note of radical pacifism; Christians were forbidden to bear arms, and soldiers who desired baptism were required to resign from the army. This early pacifism was later overshadowed by the "just war" theory of Augustine (writing circa 400). Note, however, that Augustine began with the premise that Christian faith forbids war and then imagined conditions for making an exception to the pacifist rule of faith. (For

Augustine, going to war may be justified: as a last resort, for a just cause, if there is reasonable hope of success, and if the good intended would outweigh the evil done.)

The medieval monasteries became beacons of social service, providing hospitals for the sick, shelter for orphans and widows, food for the poor, ministry to prisoners, and hospitality to travelers. Their greatest and most effective strategy of social reform, of course, was education. The monasteries provided schools, books, and libraries that began the formal education of the Western world. Likewise, they prepared wasteland for cultivation, tutored peasants in farming methods, and apprenticed people in the trades and professions.

The Industrial Revolution of the mid-seventeen hundreds and its factory workforce, would slowly turn the Church's attention to social-justice issues such as fair wages and decent working conditions. Likewise, the new social sciences lent the tools to analyze how systems work. The Church began to recognize the linkages between politics and the conditions of everyday life, and how social structures and cultural mores can cause poverty and injustice. Gradually, the Church became conscious that the social responsibilities of Christian faith indeed demand personal honesty and private charity but also participation in political struggles to change what causes people to be hungry or homeless, oppressed or victimized in the first place. The social responsibilities of Christian faith reach beyond treating symptoms to treating the disease as well.

Developments in theology have supported this deepening social consciousness. Old symbols are being reinterpreted for their social implications. For example, the Church had interpreted the reign of

God as referring solely to a place for souls after death—heaven—but reinterprets it now to include doing God's will of *shalom* on earth as well. Scholars are looking again to the symbol of the Blessed Trinity—so long sidelined as an arcane mystery—as a warrant for social justice. For if the inner life of the Godhead is "right and loving relationship," then people made in God's image are to live likewise. Most significant, perhaps, has been *a redefining of sin and salvation.*

For a variety of reasons, Christians had come to imagine sin as something very personal—entirely between oneself and God. Forgotten was the biblical wisdom that sin hurts the life of the whole community, that it has a social detriment. Because of a deepening sense of justice, Christians are slowly becoming aware that our personal sins have social consequences and that the two are reciprocal. Personal sins lead to sinful social structures, and sinful social structures encourage personal sins. For example, people's individual greed gives rise to greedy social structures, and the latter encourage people in their greed.

If sin is both personal and social, then repentance and salvation must be likewise. The old catechisms always listed "a firm purpose of amendment" as integral to repentance. So, changing one's life away from sin must include resistance to sinful social structures. And the salvation effected by Jesus' life, death, and resurrection must surely apply to the social as well as the personal levels of human existence. Otherwise, the whole public realm of life is excluded from God's work of salvation.

The theologies of liberation have done the most to help Christians recognize that both sin and salvation are social as well as personal matters. These theologies arise from historical struggles for justice—against economic exploitation, gender, racial, and ethnic inequality, and so on. This makes them more keenly aware of sinful structures and mores, and that God's salvation should include social as well as personal liberation. Besides liberation theologies, however, the Church's official teachings have become increasingly clear about the social responsibilities of Christian faith.

The first papal encyclical on social justice was *Rerum Novarum* (Of *New Things*), issued by Pope Leo XIII in 1891. There followed—down to the present day—a huge corpus of church documents deepening and expanding the social responsibilities of Christian faith. Mainline Protestantism's Social Gospel movement[5] echoes a strong resonant note. The papal documents initially focused on the rights and responsibilities of workers, then shifted with the two world wars to relations among nations. In the 1960s and 1970s the threat of nuclear warfare became a focus, and current themes include responsibility to the environment, caution regarding globalization and postmodernity, and the promotion of solidarity among all peoples.

What follows are four summary features of Catholic social teaching.

1. "Basic Justice" Has Three Aspects: Commutative, Distributive, and Social

Commutative justice *demands honesty and fairness in all exchanges between persons or private groups.* This justice binds people to be honest and truthful in their day-to-day dealings; it condemns stealing, cheating, and lying. It requires employers to pay employees a just wage with decent working conditions, and employees to render good work. Failure to fulfill commutative justice requires restitution—insofar as possible—restoring whatever was taken to its rightful owner.

Distributive justice *requires society to ensure that its social goods are fairly distributed.* Society must ensure that all its members have the resources to meet their human needs, to enjoy their rights, and to fulfill their responsibilities. Distributive justice requires fair apportioning of burdens and benefits according to people's bounty and wants. Though not a popular example, *income tax* arises out of distributive justice—taking in proportion to people's ability to pay and distributing in proportion to people's need to receive.

Social justice *is the responsibility of society to create structures that protect the dignity of all and allow each member to participate in the public life.* Social justice condemns every kind of discrimination on any basis—sex, race, ethnicity, class, sexual orientation, religion, or condition—and every structure that exploits or excludes any group's full participation in society. Stated positively, social justice requires that society arrange itself to welcome the participation of all according to their needs and talents.

Although these distinctions are helpful, church documents often collapse all three under the umbrella of "social justice." And isn't it true that all justice pertains to life in society?

2. Justice Requires Both Subsidiarity and Government Intervention

Subsidiarity means addressing social needs at the local level instead of expecting everything to be done by the state. In other words, let local organizations and groups do what they can for the common good, retaining as much freedom and initiative as possible at the grassroots. On the other hand, the state is responsible to step in and provide whatever is beyond local initiative. To U. S. readers, subsidiarity may sound like a Republican sentiment, whereas government intervention sounds more Democratic. Note that Catholic social teaching affirms both principles.

3. Justice and Peace Are Symbiotic

As evident already, justice and peace go hand in hand. Both are integral to God's vision of *shalom;* "the fruits of justice are peace" (Isaiah 32:17). A radical Christian pacifism has existed from the beginning, enduring as a subtradition to the more dominant "just war" theory. Yet, even the latter begins with the biblical presumption that war is evil and then tries to balance this with the principle of self-defense. Both traditions—pacifism and just war—reflect that a people of God should always favor peace; for Christians, war is never "holy."

We recognize the unity of peace and justice when we name injustice as a form of violence, what the Church now calls institutional violence. Debates about major warfare can overlook violence that is more local. In their pastoral letter *The Challenge of Peace,* the American Catholic bishops state: "Violence has many faces: oppression of the poor, deprivation of basic human rights, economic exploitation, sexual exploitation and pornography, neglect or abuse of the aged and the helpless, and innumerable other acts of inhumanity. Abortion in particular blunts a sense of the sacredness of human life."[6]

Here let me draw attention to domestic violence, most often perpetrated by men against women and children. Statistics suggest that it is on the rise in modern societies and is yet to be challenged in many traditional ones. Might we not consider domestic violence the most pernicious injustice of all in that it terrorizes people physically and emotionally in the sanctuary of their own homes? People of Christian faith must eschew domestic violence in their lives and help eradicate it from church and society.

4. The Church Must Practice the Justice It Preaches

The pages of history are strewn with evidence that the Catholic church has failed—often miserably—to live by a faith that does justice. It has waged violent and sectarian crusades in the name of Christ, quoted the "curse of Canaan" from Genesis 9 to justify slavery, and encouraged rabid anti-Semitism, even referring in its liturgy to "the perfidious Jews." It has executed countless people for dissent by its Inquisition, and conducted witch-hunts, using horrible misogynist rhetoric to justify destroying millions of innocent women.

One could say defensively that the Church in each era was the product of its time, but it should have known better. In fact, the traces of its past injustices are yet to be erased; much remains, albeit in more sophisticated form. It is imperative that the Church practice the justice it preaches; this goes to the very heart of its mission as a sacrament of God's salvation. Without credibility, the Church cannot be an effective sign of the reign of God.

The Bishops Synod of 1971 declared: "While the Church is

bound to give witness to justice . . . anyone who ventures to speak to people about justice must first be just in their eyes."[7] Pope John Paul II has led the way for Catholics, convinced that a new millennium requires "repentance of past errors and instances of infidelity."[8] And likewise to eradicate present ones!

FOR REFLECTION AND CONVERSATION

- Imagine that you must argue that working for social justice is a mandate of Christian faith. What points would you be sure to make?

- What can help Christians to sustain a commitment to justice?

PRACTICES TO "KEEP ON" IN A FAITH
THAT DOES JUSTICE

I find it very challenging to "keep on" in a faith that does justice. Two of my difficulties are feeling overwhelmed by the size of the problems and becoming discouraged with my lack of evident success. I'm ever tempted to keep my faith a private matter, not to get involved in the messiness and time-consuming causes of the public arena. But that would not be a faith that places God at the center of my life nor apprentices me to Jesus.

The challenge to live justly underscores the absolute necessity of a spirituality to sustain it. Without a spiritual grounding, efforts for justice are likely to be short-lived. I know. I've tried it both ways.

I have a friend who has dedicated his life to the struggle of the poor of Latin America for economic liberation. I've heard him say that what distinguishes Christians in the struggle is their ability to "keep on," even in the face of insurmountable odds, whereas non-believers are more likely to lose heart. Christian faith should sustain the effort precisely because realizing justice does not depend entirely on human efforts, crucial though they be. As with everything else about the covenant, justice is a partnership of God's grace and human effort.

To stimulate your own imagining, I suggest five spiritual practices that might help persons and communities to "keep on" in a faith that does justice with love.

1. Ask the Spirit for the Grace of Justice

Living one's faith always requires God's help, and this is eminently true in living justly. Ask for the grace—every day—and be confident that the Spirit will respond. Justice has a way of tempting people into either of two heresies: the Catholic favorite of "good works" or the Protestant one of "cheap grace." Praying often for the grace to live justly helps us recognize that while justice does not depend only on human efforts, neither will God create justice without us. Instead, we must ask the Spirit's help to make our own best efforts for justice sake.

2. Invest Time and Energy in a Favorite Social Cause

No one can take on all the worthy social causes. Better to choose one with personal appeal, a cause that ignites fire in the belly or for which you have a talent, and invest time and energy in it. Even within a given issue, one may need to focus. Suppose that you choose to actively oppose discrimination. Vatican II taught that "every type of discrimination, whether social or cultural, whether based on sex, race, color, social condition, language, or religion, is to be overcome and eradicated as contrary to God's intent."[9] Fine, but just looking at this listing reminds that there are many forms of discrimination. For "keeping on," it may be wisest to choose one for your focused efforts, while supporting other people's work to eradicate every instance of discrimination.

A focus of my social commitment is life-giving education and the struggle that everyone may have ready access to as much. I refer to this not to draw personal attention but to make the point that we need to broaden our horizons about what is political and what might promote social justice. Although education is a long-term strategy and the situation in Arbolito requires more immediate remedies, its people will have a better chance of justice with a new school.

3. Sharpen Your Social Consciousness in Personal Life

Christian faith has always taught people to be honest and truthful in their personal dealings; that it is sinful to lie, steal, or cheat. Such character formation is imperative for commutative justice.

But home and personal lifestyle should reflect commitment to *social* justice as well.

I once commented to a pacifist friend how much I admired the courage of his convictions—he had just been arrested for the umpteenth time, on this occasion for protesting U. S. complicity with Latin American oligarchies through the School of the Americas. His response was, "Ah, this civil disobedience stuff is easy compared to being a pacifist at home every day." He went on to explain that he had three teenage children, and "Every day, I need to choose peace all over again." The personal is always political!

"Political correctness" has become a joke, and I don't want to add to the caricature. It's nigh impossible in personal life to avoid all complicity with injustice. But we can scrutinize our lifestyle for the ways we may be accomplices in structures of injustice and imagine how to resist such collusion. We can review everything in our personal world for right relationship with God, self, others, and creation: the values that permeate our home and work, how we spend leisure time, the products we buy and consume, how we make, hold, and spend money, the causes we support or neglect, and the list goes on.

4. Redefine Success and See Every Effort as Worthwhile

The modern mentality is that "success" with a problem means its complete solution; anything less is considered a failure. If we perceive that the whole problem cannot be solved soon (e.g., world hunger), we are tempted not even to try. But this false consciousness prompts passivity instead of agency. We need to redefine suc-

cess and become convinced that the smallest efforts are worthwhile, that everyone *can do something*. Some plant the seeds, others
water, still others reap the harvest, and it is God who gives the
increase (1 Corinthians 3:6)

5. Avoid Elitism and Debilitating Guilt

Faith that does justice is a lifetime conversion for everyone; there
is no room for self-righteousness here. As Jesus said to the accusers
of the woman caught committing adultery, "Let the one who is
without sin among you be the first to cast a stone" (John 8:8). At
least, they had the integrity—beginning with the eldest—to walk
away.

Christians must walk away from a better-than-thou attitude on
social justice; we have too many sins of our own. But we must
confront them rather than complying. Nor are guilt trips an effective way to motivate lasting commitment. Oh, there is a kind of
guilt that everyone should have about their sins, personal and
social, but let it be a healthy one that prompts us to repent and
change our ways and world.

FOR REFLECTION AND CONVERSATION

- From your conversation with this chapter, how has your own
  consciousness about justice clarified, shifted, or changed?

- How do you imagine sustaining your commitment to a faith
  that does justice with love?

EIGHT

"WHO IS OUR NEIGHBOR?"— LOVING BEYOND BORDERS

TRACES OF CATHOLICITY

From the bottom of the Via della Conciliazione, it towers in breath-taking array—Saint Peter's Basilica, the oldest and largest church in the world. The emperor Constantine built the first basilica here over the tomb of Saint Peter, completing it in 319. The present church is a reconstruction. Begun in 1506 and taking 120 years to complete, it reflects the genius of the greatest artists of the time: Bramante, Raphael, Michelangelo.

You walk forward into a great semicircular colonnade, which embraces you like outstretched arms of welcome. Its four rows of huge columns are topped by a choir of 140 statues of saints, or so my guidebook counted, all designed by Bernini himself. Two massive statues of Peter and Paul stand as sentinels, left and right of the front steps. On either side of the portico are two other dramatic statues, the emperors Constantine and Charlemagne, each astride a rearing horse as if still sallying forth for Christendom. As influential on the life of the Church as any pope, their commanding presence reflects the fuzzy line between secular and salvation history.

I visited on the Feast of Epiphany, January 6, 2000, and so I could enter through the privileged Holy Door, one of five massive porticos and open only during Jubilee years. I was instantly swept up by the grandeur of the space, with its breathtaking collage of marble, bronze, and gold. Its architectural lines and focal points weave into a centripetal force that elevates eye, mind, and heart—surely the intent. Down the two-hundred-yard nave, Bernini's bronze bal-dacchino towers as a great imperial canopy over the high altar and tomb of Saint Peter. In the backdrop behind stands the Chair of Peter—symbol of the Petrine office—supported by four "fathers" of the Church. Above the chair hovers a dove, symbol of the Holy Spirit.

The vast throng of people that morning was a rainbow of humanity, many arrayed in ethnic costumes and whispering in a babel of tongues. Here in living color was the breadth universal *of the Church. When one stands on the tomb of the first among the apostles—archaeologists are now convinced that this is Peter's rest-ing place—the whole environment appears steeped in antiquity, reminding of the* length *over* time *of this faith tradition. The panoply of mosaics, statues, and adornments, with their aesthetic refinement and great beauty climaxed by the Pietà, expresses the* spiritual depth *of humanity and the human reach for God. And the sacred seems palpable; the whole magnificent edifice, crowned by Michelangelo's 435-foot grand dome, bespeaks the divine initiative toward the human, the* height *that reaches into our hearts. The* breadth, length, depth, *and* height *of Christian faith are all here; truly a* catholic *place!*

Or is it? After a while, I began to notice signs of contradiction to catholicity. Most of the papal statues reflect a pompous pride, as if these popes desired only to perpetuate their own importance. Triumphal power seems more the sentiment than "servant of the servants"—an old title for the pope. To anyone who remembers a little church history, many of these monuments are a whitewash. The massive memorial to a pious-looking Urban VIII never hints at the truth about him: a corrupt nepotist who used the papacy to enrich himself and his family. And the place reeks of patriarchy. Many of the papal statues (including Urban's) have women lying at their feet. The guidebook says these feminine figures represent "the virtues." I wondered which ones.

Indeed, apart from decoration at the feet of popes, Saint Peter's has scant representation of women. Even images of Mary seem sparser than in other traditional churches. And I found no representation at all of people of color or of the poor. To wonder if this religion were exclusive to white and wealthy males would be only to notice the obvious about Saint Peter's.

I was present for the papal mass on that Epiphany morning, and the liturgy reflected the same exclusivity—no women or people of color in the sanctuary, only white men and none of them looked poor. Now I found myself wondering if Jesus, who founded a radically inclusive community of disciples—catholic at its best—would recognize any of this as his legacy.

But as often happens with Catholicism and its contradictions, a sign of hope emerged to offset the temptation to lose heart. I found the simple bronze relief of the big-hearted and saintly Pope John XXIII (1881–1963). He is depicted with prison bars separating him from a group of prisoners, though which side is incarcerated is ambiguous. Each of the 262 popes has some memorial in Saint Peter's. The much-loved John, catalyst and guiding spirit of Vatican II, requested to be remembered for visiting prisoners in Rome's municipal jail. Typical of him!

Then, descending to the crypt (some 130 popes are buried at Saint Peter's), I discovered that the tomb of John XXIII is clearly the favored place of pilgrimage for people—where they stop with reverence to pray. It seems that the sensus fidelium remains a reliable trustee of the true spirit of Catholicism. So though he might have to search a bit, the Carpenter of Nazareth could find some traces here of what he intended. For the hope endures and springs eternal: this church may yet become catholic.

BECOMING CATHOLIC—AND MILES TO TRAVEL

To ask "What makes us *catholic?*"—with a small *c*—really comes down to "Who is our neighbor?" In other words, how open is our hearts, how wide our concern, whom will we welcome and include? The opposite to sectarianism, *catholicity* invites me and my community of faith into solidarity with all humankind. At its best, *catholicity* means to welcome and love every "other."

Jesus championed *catholicity.* Scholars say that in the context of his time, "neighbor" meant fellow Jew. But Jesus preached the great law of love with no exceptions—even of enemies. He said that people will come from "the east and west, from the north and south to recline at table in the reign of God" (Luke 13:29), and everyone will be welcome. He taught that God will hold all people accountable for their lives and by the same criterion of how they treated their neighbors in need (Matthew 25:31–46). Jesus sent his disciples to bring the good news of God's love to the ends of the earth (Matthew 28:16–20). And he taught that "in my Father's house, there are many mansions" (John 14:2); heaven will be *catholic*—welcoming all.

The Catholic church often sins egregiously against *catholicity.* Both insiders and outsiders can experience it as a hierarchical club, marked by inhospitable signs of sexism, racism, classism, and homophobia. Its dominant culture—patterns of thought, symbols and rituals, structures and laws—all are distinctly Western, or even European parochial. A visitor to the Vatican and its art galleries could readily conclude that God, Jesus, Mary, the saints and sinners of this religion are mostly Florentine. For all its claims to *catholicity,* Catholicism is struggling to become an inclusive church.

While Catholicism has intertwined well with the old Western cultures, it has been reluctant to embrace the cultures of its mission lands. We will return to this point later under the challenge of *inculturation*. For now, I only point out that Christian evangelization and Western colonization have often worked hand in glove, with missionaries imposing aspects of their culture as if integral to Christian faith.

I've met a Chinese Catholic with the name Colleen who celebrates Saint Patrick's Day with more enthusiasm than I do. In response to my inquiry, she explained that her pastor in China was a priest from Ireland (as I had suspected) and catechized her to rank March 17 just a shade below Christmas and Easter. The pages of mission history are strewn with less-benign examples of cultural imperialism disguised as Christian evangelization.

Happily, the Holy Spirit is not finished with the Catholic church yet; major renovations are afoot. Many cradle Catholics were shocked in the aftermath of Vatican II to discover that the ground had shifted seismically regarding what is and is not "Catholic"—in both the capital *C* and the small *c* senses. My father told a story of his mother scolding him for saying "Lord, have mercy on her soul" when a Protestant neighbor died; she said that Catholics could not pray for Protestants. Although reflecting Irish politics more than Catholic faith, my grandmother's sentiment was not that unusual.

What a shock, then, when Vatican II taught that baptism forges "a sacramental bond of unity" among all Christians,[1] urging Catholics and Protestants to function as one Body of Christ in the world. In this spirit, Vatican II avoided the term *Roman Catholic,* wanting to honor the *catholicity* of the whole Church of Christ—Protestant, Orthodox, and Catholic.[2]

I'm convinced that *catholicity* is an aspiration of humanity at its best, calling us to oppose sectarianism and chauvinism of every kind and to practice solidarity and interdependence instead. Surely, a Christian community that explicitly names itself "Catholic" should patently reflect this value.

My friend Mike was going to a fund-raiser sponsored by an ultraconservative Catholic group. "It's just the politics of my job," he explained. "I'm not *that* kind of Catholic." So I asked, "Well, what kind are you?" His response was inspiring and echoed much of what I propose in this book as core to what makes us Catholic. But Mike never mentioned *catholicity* itself in his description, and that's typical. It may seem a bit ironic, but Catholics and our church need to heighten our consciousness and renew commitment to becoming *catholic.* And we have miles to travel!

FOR REFLECTION AND CONVERSATION

- When you think about being *catholic,* what images and associations emerge?

- What are some ways in which your faith community is already *catholic?* In what ways is it not—yet? Reflect on why and how it might become more consistently *catholic.*

THE CHURCH AS "CATHOLIC": HISTORICAL NOTES

I mentioned in the preface that the word *catholic* comes from combining two Greek terms, *kata* and *holos. Holos,* the root of our word *whole,* suggests different elements uniting and working together. *Kata* has various meanings (every, according to, as if, including). Combining it with *holos* to form *katholos,* we can translate the word literally as "including everyone to work together." The implication is that all people are welcome, bonding as a united community amid great diversity. James Joyce said it well in *Finnegans Wake:* "Catholic means here comes everybody."

Throughout his public ministry, Jesus taught by word and example that everyone would be welcome in his community, and that his community should care about everyone—whether disciple or not. So inclusive was his table fellowship that it scandalized traditional piety and was the first criticism raised against him: "Some scribes asked, 'Why does he eat with tax collectors and sinners?'" (Mark 2:16).

Beyond *diversity, welcome,* and *care* for all, Jesus emphasized *unity* among his community of faith. The classic instance was his prayer for disciples at the Last Supper. In it, Jesus asked God "that they may be one, just as we are one," and proposed unity among disciples as a sign to the world of their credibility (John 17:11, 20–23).

Saint Paul described the Church as a diverse but united community that should work together like a body—becoming "the *body* of Christ" in the world. Paul knew that unity without diversity would be uniformity, whereas diversity without unity would be fragmentation. "The body is not a single part, but many," so "the eye cannot say to the hand, 'I do not need you.'" All must work together. As "the body is one though it has many parts," then "so also Christ's body" the Church (1 Corinthians 12:12–26).

Thereafter, the first Christian communities reflected both *diversity* and *unity* in faith. Even something as obvious as having four

Gospels instead of one reflects diversity from the beginning. In the years of preaching after the resurrection and before written texts, Jesus' Good News spread out from Jerusalem to people of different cultures and varied social contexts. In response to local needs and issues, each community had its own "spin"—scholars call it "redaction principle"—in teaching about Jesus and teaching what he taught. So, when the first Christian writings emerged, they already reflected diversity in perspective. Matthew, for example, emphasized that Jesus was the fulfillment of Old Testament prophecy—his context was a Jewish audience—whereas John presented Jesus as the preexistent eternal *Logos* (word) of God, reflecting the Greek philosophical ethos of his community.

And yet, those first Christians were committed to uniting around "the Gospel" of Jesus—as one. Although honoring diversity, they were determined to hold to "one Lord, one faith, one baptism" (Ephesians 4:5). And down through history, the Church has struggled to balance *unity* and *diversity* as coessential aspects of its *catholicity*—with varying degrees of success.

Saint Ignatius of Antioch (d. 107), a bishop and martyr of the early Church, was the first to use the word *catholic* to describe the Christian community. Ignatius was arrested for being a Christian and brought to Rome to be thrown to the wild animals in the Colosseum. As he traveled, he wrote a kind of thank-you letter back to Christian communities who had offered him hospitality along the journey to martyrdom. In his letter to the Smyrnaeans we find this statement: "Where Jesus is, there is the catholic Church."[3]

The surrounding text indicates Ignatius's meaning, namely, that when the spirit of Jesus prevails in a community, it is complete, the "whole" Church is present. In other words, each Christian community constitutes its own unique expression of Church, and the completeness of the local community is an instance of Christian *catholicity.*

After Ignatius, attributing *catholicity* to the Church caught on; it must have struck a chord. Christians described both the universal and the local Church as *catholic.* Clearly their intent was to honor diversity both within and between the local communities, and yet to emphasize their communion as one Body of Christ. The *catholicity* of each local community required it to welcome and care for everyone of every race and station—in the spirit of Jesus—and likewise to be bonded in communion with all the other churches.

Saint Cyril of Jerusalem (d. 386) explained that the Church is *catholic* because it is confined to no one place or nation, teaches everything needed for salvation, welcomes to "right worship" people of every class—"rulers and subjects, learned and ignorant"—forgives every kind of sin, and mediates the grace needed for living every virtue.[4]

The Apostles' Creed, whose formulations of faith date back to the first centuries, has Christians profess, "I believe . . . in the holy *catholic* Church." The Nicene Creed, first drafted at the Council of Nicea in 325, has the confession "We believe in *one, holy, catholic,* and *apostolic* Church." And though all four "marks" were counted as essential to the Church, it chose to name itself "Catholic."

Saint Augustine used *catholicity* as an argument against the Donatists. These were a group of overly ardent Christians in North Africa who claimed that they alone were the *true Church* and that only saints could belong. Augustine—knowing a little of both sin and sanctity—argued that the true Church of Christ must welcome saints and sinners alike. Further, the Donatists could not be the true Church because they were limited to one geographic area, having severed communion with the universal Church. Augustine also added the fascinating note that *catholicity* requires Christians to be *open to the truth* wherever it can be found. In other words, to be *catholic* includes having open minds as well as open hearts and hands.[5]

Echoing scholastic philosophy, Aquinas saw the *catholicity* of the Church instanced in each particular community, all of which then unite into a universal communion, without limit of place or time, rank or station. After the Reformation, however, few Protestants used *catholic* to describe the Church, except when reciting the creeds. The Reformers associated *catholic* with the hegemony they were rejecting. By contrast, Western and Eastern Catholics began to claim that they were fully *catholic* and that this proved their credential as the Church of Jesus Christ.

Vatican II avoided such polemics and proposed *catholicity* as a challenge for the whole Christian Church. *Catholic* is not an accomplishment of any denomination but a vision for what Christians—Protestant and Catholic—should become together. The *Catechism* echoed this sentiment, saying that the Church is ever "called to realize"[6] its *catholicity*.

Avery Dulles, a senior theologian and cardinal, offers a rich description of the challenge of *catholicity* for the whole Church. He uses the spatial terms breadth, length, depth, and height. *Breadth* challenges the Church to welcome and care for all, avoiding sectarianism or favoritism for any one place or people. *Length* calls for dynamic faithfulness over time, ever drawing old and new wisdom from its original roots. *Depth* requires that the Christian gospel be preached in ways that find resonance in the human heart. And *height* reminds the Church of its divine dimension; it is not an end in itself but an instrument of God's saving work in Jesus that continues through the Holy Spirit.[7]

Vatican II was a watershed for the *catholicity* of the Church. It revivified the dual emphases that the Church is both universal and particular, worldwide and local. First, Catholicism had long boasted of universality, and with some good reason. But its dominant culture was narrowly European, with unity purchased at the price of uniformity and Roman centralization. The late, great Karl Rahner recognized Vatican II as pushing Catholicism out of Western "confinement" to become a truly "world church." The Council urged the Church to welcome multiple cultural expressions of Christian faith—to look like a universal community rather than a "Roman" church in different parts of the world.

Second, Vatican II renewed emphasis on the local church, that it also is whole within itself and in its communion with other churches. On the defensive after the Protestant Reformation, the Catholic church moved to massive centralization of its structural power. Then more than ever, Catholicism functioned as a pyramid with authority concentrated at the top—the pope—and trickling down by papal delegation to local bishops. This made them the pope's factotums rather than—as in the first thousand years of the Church—brother bishops with whom to exercise collegial leadership.

By contrast, Vatican II reclaimed that "the Church of Christ is truly present in all legitimate local congregations of the faithful"; in every local diocese, "the one, holy, catholic, and apostolic church of Christ is truly present."[8] In other words, local dioceses are not administrative units of Rome but whole and living churches, each charged to reflect the distinctive character of its culture and to unite with diversity as Church universal. As Walter Kasper, renowned theologian and cardinal archbishop of Stuttgart, summarizes, "Just as the local churches are not mere extensions or provinces of the universal church, so the universal church is not the mere sum of the local churches. The local churches and the universal church are intimately united."[9] Such sentiments renewed hope for the Church becoming *catholic.*

From these historical roots, let us summarize the *catholicity* to which the whole Christian Church should aspire. I discern three overlapping features. Christian communities are called to be catholic in that they (1) *welcome and extend their care to all people;* (2) *affirm the integrity of each local church and the communion of all particular churches into a universal whole;* and (3) *maintain unity as reconciled diversity—not through uniformity.*

FOR REFLECTION AND CONVERSATION

- What are some of your experiences and reflections around the *catholicity* of the Church?

- What might *catholicity* presently demand of you? Of your community of faith?

IMAGINE THE HORIZON OF *CATHOLICITY*:
A GIFT FOR LIFE

For all Catholics—myself included—*catholicity* remains a tremendous challenge, a horizon to imagine. For all our talk, we harbor deep vestiges of *noncatholicity*. Racism and sexism, sectarianism and parochialism still flourish in our hearts and church institutions. On the other hand, and happily, the Spirit continues to work and there are signs of a new moment for our becoming *catholic*.

Much of what I proposed in chapter 4 on the Church as community would help to realize *catholicity*, and likewise the proposals of chapter 7 on justice. Here, I highlight some horizons specific to *catholicity*. I suggest three, and likely you will imagine others. The Catholic Christian community must grow as (1) *a truly "world church" and faith* and as (2) *an indigenous "local church" and faith,* and it must ever renew its (3) *imagination for paradox.*

1. A World Church and Faith

From the beginning, Christianity took its *catholicity* to mean welcome and care for all peoples, transcending borders of place and race. One of the charisms of Catholicism has been its ability to reach across history and into every culture while maintaining a deep bond in faith. My first impression of *catholicity* at Saint Peter's was not without warrant. Most Catholics are conscious of themselves as belonging to a great worldwide community of common Christian identity, sharing core patterns of belief, ethics, and worship. At the same time, Karl Rahner was perceptive to recognize

Vatican II as a watershed for becoming a truly *world* Church, one reaching far beyond the confines of Western culture.

Rahner imagined "a world Church, in which the churches of Africa, South America and Asia will really be autonomous elements with their own specific character and their own importance in the whole Church." He even wondered "whether the seat of primacy in the Church will have to remain in Rome in the future, when the real centers of power and authority will no longer lie in the older Europe."[10] Such sentiments may sound revolutionary to Catholic ears, but they are worth discussing as we move toward a "world church."

Besides becoming a "world church," *catholicity* invites Christians to embrace a *world* faith. By this I mean *to experience a deep spiritual bond with all humankind* while cherishing our own identity in faith.

Chapter 1 reminded that every effort to state "what makes us Catholic" must appreciate the spiritual solidarity of humanity. From a Christian perspective, we are all God's family; that's our "world faith." It's fitting to echo this sentiment again here; it surely bears repeating.

The vision of Vatican II was that the *catholicity* of Christians should prompt them to promote solidarity among all humankind. We should nurture a sense of unity and interdependence among all peoples with the goal of universal peace. For though the Church "may . . . look like a small flock," nevertheless it should be "a lasting and sure seed of unity . . . for the whole human race." Indeed, "all people are called to be part of this *catholic* unity of the People of God, a unity which is harbinger of the universal peace it promotes."[11]

We must say, then, that *catholicity* calls Christians to a world consciousness and faith, to recognize themselves as citizens of a global village with profound responsibilities to every person. Concretely, what might this mean? I make five suggestions.

- Foster solidarity and interdependence with all people;

- Render care and compassion for all people;

- Respect the "other" in all people;

- Be open to share with and learn from all people;

- Welcome and appreciate God's saving work among all people.

Foster solidarity and interdependence with all people. The universality of God's love ranks as a dogma of Christian faith. Thus, divine love is the foundation of Christian solidarity with every person. Christian faith couples the Genesis stories of creation—in God's image (Genesis 1:27) and alive by God's life (Genesis 2:7)—with the climactic statement near the end of the Bible that "God is love" (1 John 4:8). So, the very lifeblood coursing though all human veins is God's love in us, for us, and through us to each other and creation. This is true of every person, bar none.

Beyond our common genesis, all humanity shares in the Incarnation of Jesus Christ—God among us as one of ourselves. As Vatican II reiterated, "[B]y his incarnation, the Son of God united himself with all [humankind]."[12] And the Council reminded Christians that "God's providence . . . manifestation of goodness, and . . . saving designs extend to all people."[13] God's love and work of salvation bonds Christians with all humanity. In Christian spirituality, there should never be an "us and them" but only a "we."

I'm sure it's true of other cultures, but the Irish love to sit around at weddings and wakes and figure out how we are "connected"—who and how people are related by birth or marriage. Truth is that we're all "connected"—the one human family of God. That's *catholicity!*

Render care and compassion for all people. Here we need only reiterate that Christian love of neighbors must know no limits; we should be "Christians without borders." People who are suffering on the far side of the world and are a different religion from us, must be equally included in our care and compassion. There are religions that place great emphasis on caring for fellow members and have elaborate networks of inner support—the Mormons, for example. The *catholicity* of Christians, however, demands care and compassion for all people. Our neighbor is everyone.

Further, we must be proactive, taking initiative toward those in need rather than waiting to stumble over them. Remember the Good Samaritan parable; the priest and Levite pass by "on the opposite side" of the person waylaid by robbers, but the Samaritan goes out of his way to help (Luke 10:29–37). Christians should go out of their way with care and compassion for all.

Respect the "other" in all people. Christian faith requires unqualified respect for every "other," including people not like ourselves at all. To paraphrase the postmodern philosopher Emmanuel Levinas, respect means not trying to remake "the other" into "the same" as ourselves but accepting and appreciating them precisely in their difference. Such respect amid difference is based on *reverence* for every person because all reflect the divine image. As

Levinas reminds us, in every "other" we can encounter "the face of the Other."

Be open to share with and learn from all people. Since the Risen Christ gave the great commission, "Go make disciples of all nations" (Matthew 28:19), evangelization has been a defining mission of the Christian community. Of late, however, two far-reaching developments have emerged around Christian evangelization.

First, for a long time Catholics thought of evangelization as "bringing them in"—converting into their church anyone who was not already a member. Now the church itself has redefined the focus of evangelization away from "bringing converts in" to "bringing Christians out"—out into the world with their faith alive. Evangelization is to take God's word of "liberating salvation" into "every strata of society . . . transforming humanity from within."[14] In sum, evangelization means Christians living their faith in the world with enthusiasm and the credibility that comes from practicing what we preach. Pope John Paul II has championed this "new evangelization" both for non-Christian contexts and amid tired old cultural faith, vivifying the latter again.

The second development is that evangelization calls for real dialogue with people of other religious traditions. Again, Vatican II proposed such openness as an aspect of *catholicity.* The Council urged Christians to engage in "truly human conversation" with all peoples of good will and "to learn by sincere and patient dialogue what treasures a bountiful God has distributed among the nations of the earth."[15] And though the Church "must ever proclaim Christ, 'the way, the truth, and the life,'" their very faith in Jesus should lead Christians into "dialogue and cooperation with the followers of other religions."[16] A *catholic* perspective, then, is the opposite to being closed-minded. Echoing Augustine, *catholicity* means being open to truth wherever it can be found because all truth has the one divine Source.

Welcome and appreciate God's saving work among all people. Every Christian community is mandated to welcome into full and equal membership anyone who desires to belong; otherwise it is not *catholic.* We noted already that Jesus practiced such inclusion; he welcomed all into the community of disciples, with special out-reach to the socially marginalized—women, people of foreign races, public sinners, tax collectors, lepers and others considered unclean. Jesus went out of his way to make the point of inclusion.

The first Christian communities considered hospitality central to discipleship (see Romans 12:13); one of the conditions for becoming a bishop was to be hospitable (Titus 1:8). The story of Pentecost—considered the official launching of the Church—tells that there were people in Jerusalem "from every nation under heaven" (Acts 2:5), that all miraculously heard Peter's inaugural sermon "in their own tongue" (Acts 2:6) and "about three thousand persons were added" (Acts 2:41) on that opening Sunday. So, the first miracle of the young Church was to make people of every race feel included and welcome.

The first great controversy to beset the Christian community was whether male converts could become Christian without first being circumcised according to the law of Moses. So, "the apostles and the elders" assembled in Jerusalem for what would be the first general council of the Church (read the whole story in Acts 15:1–35). There was "much debate." Peter gave a great speech arguing that God makes "no distinction between them and us," so neither should the Christian community. After what must have been a mighty struggle of letting go—comparable to any change in church policy we might imagine in our time—they decided that "those Gentiles who are turning to God" (15:19) would be welcome without circumcision. Thereafter, open enrollment has been the official policy of the Church.

Let us now face the obvious question: what of people who see the welcome sign of Christian community and decline the invitation, or who have never heard of Jesus Christ and follow another or no religion? Here we confront a vexing theological issue for Christians, and it deserves much more attention than we can give it. Christian theologians who appreciate the religious diversity of humankind are proposing cutting-edge responses, recognizing that all salvation is from God and surely God can save in diverse ways.[17] Here I only summarize a traditional response, but one well worth noting, for there is an age-old Catholic conviction that all people can be saved—without being Christian.

Christians have long struggled to affirm the universality of God's love and saving will and, at the same time, their faith that "there is one mediator between God and the human race, Christ Jesus" (1 Timothy 2:5–6). The balance of holding to both convictions was threatened by the famous and too often cited declaration by Pope Boniface VIII in 1302, "Outside of the Church there is no salvation." This dictum, however, was originally aimed at apostate Christians—not people outside of Christendom—and specifically to force a recalcitrant French king, Philip IV, to obey the pope. Later the church condemned its literal interpretation as heresy.[18]

The persistent Catholic proposal for affirming both the primacy of Christ and the universality of salvation has been "baptism of desire." This is the notion that all people who do God's will—as best they know it—have a virtual desire for baptism and thus are saved by their *implicit faith* in Jesus. Essentially, Vatican II took this position: "Those also can attain to everlasting salvation who through no fault of their own do not know the gospel of Christ or His Church, yet sincerely seek God and, moved by grace, strive by their deeds to do His will as it is known to them through the dictates of conscience."[19]

Although other religions might hear a note of imperialism, this time-honored response has allowed Catholic Christians to get around a theological conundrum. It also affirms with some coherence the *catholicity* of God's saving grace. Again to quote Vatican II: "For since Christ died for all [people] . . . we ought to believe that the Holy Spirit *in a manner known only to God,* offers to every person the possibility of being associated with this paschal mystery."[20] So, we don't have a ready answer to how all people can be saved—"a manner known only to God"—but the Council echoes the sentiment of Jesus: "In my Father's house, there are many mansions" (John 14:2).

2. A Local Church and Faith

Each local Christian community should be a church and faith that is truly *catholic*. This means being universal in that it welcomes all and is in communion with other churches, and yet reflects its own unique identity, being spiritually complete within itself. For *catholicity,* each church must be faithful to the core of Christian faith *and* truly indigenous to its local context. This means that it lives its faith with the style and symbols of its locale rather than looking like a foreign import.

With Vatican II, the Catholic church became aware that its evangelization often imposed a foreign culture on people—invariably a Western one—in the name of the gospel. The church also realized that there is *never a cultureless Christianity.* In other words, Christian faith is always expressed through a particular culture, the customs of life and patterns of meaning that distinguish a people. By the same token, there is *never a God-less culture.* In other words, every culture has the seeds of faith within it and is capable of bringing its own unique expression to Christianity. In fact, Christian faith is far more authentic when realized through people's native culture. A new term has emerged to describe this give-and-take between Christianity and culture—*inculturation.*

Much progress on inculturation has been made since the 1960s, and Vatican II paved the way. The Council said that Christian faith and each native culture should be placed in a "living exchange" that enriches the culture and likewise the universal Christian community.[21] Today inculturation can be understood as *an exchange of gifts whereby Christian faith, remaining true to its core, becomes native within each culture, thereby enhancing both the local culture and the mosaic of Christian faith with a unique expression.* At its heart, inculturation means people realizing the Christian Story through their own culture so that they express and live it as their local church and faith.

For inculturation to occur, the exchange between faith and culture must be a two-way street; imagine both sides being enriched. So, upon encountering a culture, Christian faith will affirm and celebrate those aspects that already reflect God's saving presence;

other aspects it will challenge and change to become more life-giving, advancing God's work of salvation. Likewise, each culture should appropriate the truths, worship, and commitments of Christian faith in ways native to this particular people, making its own singular contribution to the universal Church. In a sense, each people will decline the cultural medium of the Christianity they receive and replace it with their own. What emerges will be a unique expression of Christian faith, enhancing the Church's *catholicity.*

That Christianity should be inculturated—become a local church and faith—is the logic of the Incarnation. Jesus took on the language, mores, and ethos of a particular culture. Thereafter, Christian faith should be realized and expressed in the culture native to each particular time, place, and people. My point here is that the Church becomes all the more *catholic* as it encourages diverse expressions of Christian faith through multiple local cultures. Inculturation is essential to the church becoming *catholic.*

3. An Imagination for Paradox

All people of faith are challenged to embrace paradoxes, apparent contradictions that yet both are true. But in a particular way, Christians need an imagination for paradox if they are to be *catholic.* Think about it: to welcome diversity and yet maintain unity in faith; to affirm the local church and likewise the universal Church; to confess Jesus as "the one mediator between God and the human race" and yet that all can be saved; to cherish one's own tradition while being open to learn from others; and so on—all are paradoxical.

Some strands in the braid of Christianity tend more toward an *either/or* stance. For example, the congregational model can affirm each local church as autonomous but with little communion among them. By contrast, some Romanizing sentiments within Catholicism want to unite the universal Church through uniformity. When Catholic Christianity is at its best, however, it affirms *both/and*—unity and diversity, universal and local.

An imagination for paradox has long distinguished Catholic Christianity. So, are we saved by "faith alone" or by our own "good works"? The best Catholic sentiment is that we are saved by faith, which expresses itself through good works. Does living a Christian life depend on God's grace or on our human nature? On God's grace, which works through nature. What is the norm of faith, Scripture or Tradition? Scripture, indeed, but its original revelation unfolds through Tradition. And so on, with paradoxes such as both gospel and law, both cross and resurrection, both revelation and reason, both authority and freedom of conscience, both judgment and mercy, both marriage and celibacy, and the list is long.

Although an imagination for paradox is a rich aspect of Catholic tradition, there are often elements in the church that attempt to force an *either/or* choice. Thankfully, it is often the *sensus fidelium* that holds out for *both/and*. I was once giving a conference in New Orleans on the Saturday before Lent began. Well suspecting what their response might be, I invited the participants to make a clear choice this year between Mardi Gras (literally, "fat Tuesday") and Ash Wednesday. They responded raucously that they needed *both*. I congratulated them on their *catholicity*—both feasting and fasting. A good Puritan would be scandalized!

SPIRITUAL PRACTICES FOR *CATHOLICITY*

The preceding section already moved us toward a spirituality that supports *catholicity*. To close, I suggest some specific practices to nurture *catholic* consciousness and commitment. You will imagine other possibilities.

1. Make Friends Among People Who Are Very Different

All of us feel at home among "our own kind." It may take an effort to engage with people who are distinctly different from us, and to do so with respect and appreciation. But *catholicity* invites far beyond token politeness or the reductionism of "Well, they're like us really." It encourages us to become friends and to delight in "others" precisely as they are, with appreciation more than toleration.

2. Promote Justice and Compassion for People Who Are "Far Away"

Our natural instinct is to get involved in causes close to home. But surely a *catholic* faith demands more than local or self-interest, encouraging justice and compassion for those who are "far away." Choosing a specific cause on the other side of the world and becoming involved with it will enhance one's *catholicity*. I remember my father encouraging us as children to send some of our piggy-bank money to starving children in far-off Biafra, and he helped us find their homeland in a world atlas. Whether he knew it or not, he was encouraging a *catholic* consciousness.

3. Place No Borders on Your Concern and Prayers

As a variation of the preceding practice, I have in mind our spiritual concern for the well-being of others. Notice how parochial U.S. news media can be; it's as if we were the center of the universe and whatever is happening elsewhere is of little import, unless American interests (e.g., oil supply) are directly implicated. One must listen to the BBC news on public radio to hear what is happening in East Timor, or Peru, or the Congo—or other troubled parts of the world. Every conflict and tragedy should be of concern to *catholic* Christians. If nothing else, we can pray for people who are suffering the agonies of war, natural or human-made devastation.

4. Recognize Faith as an Ultimate Mystery; Be Ever Ready to Say "I Don't Know"

A favorite routine of comedian George Carlin has Catholics saying, "It's a mystery." Much of the laughter is in recognition. And let's face it: there are all kinds of things about life and faith that no one can explain in human language. But faith as ultimate Mystery is not "what we can't explain" but that Mystery *is* often the explanation.

The ground of all is gracious Mystery that draws us ever more deeply into unfathomable Love. We can always "know" enough to get on with living as a people of God. After that, "the breadth and length and height and depth . . . surpasses all knowledge" (Ephesians 3:18).

Catholics can have an air of know-it-all, acting as if ours is the only and completely true faith, replete with all the answers. Surely, this is more the sin of pride than a truly *catholic* spirituality. Some of the hubris is encouraged by a teaching magisterium that typically sounds absolutely certain in its pronouncements, as if faith is no longer a "leap" and all can be assured. The joke rings true that when the Catholic church finally agrees to ordain women, the pronouncement will begin with, "As we have always taught . . ."

Catholicity should lend Christians a spirituality that is open to surprises, that knows well the leap of faith, that is humble before incomprehensible Mystery. We should be ever ready to say "I don't know" if such be the case, and yet cherish our faith as a piton on the mountainside of life.

FOR REFLECTION AND CONVERSATION

- What do you imagine is your next step into *catholic* consciousness and commitment?

- What spiritual practices might help to nurture *catholicity* in yourself? In your faith community? In society at large?

NINE

"WHAT IS OUR HEART'S DESIRE?"— GROWING SPIRITUALLY FOR LIFE

SPIRITUALITY: WHY ME?

Twelve of us sat in the seminar circle. Our focus was "spirituality at work"—how our faith should permeate daily life. I was anchoring the conversation and opened with the exercise below. You may want to pause and do it, too. It might surprise you as it did me. Take a few minutes with each direction.

- *Make yourself comfortable. Relax and take long, deliberate breaths.*

- *From personal acquaintances, living or dead, choose one person in whom you readily recognize "spirituality at work," someone whose faith permeates everything about their daily life.*

- *Close your eyes and imagine the person being with you. Look into their face. What are your feelings?*

- *Exchange greetings, in whatever way is comfortable. Explain why you readily recognize their spirituality in how they live or lived.*

- *Inquire about the key to their integrating life and faith so thoroughly.*

- *Ask what wisdom they can offer you about "spirituality at work."*

- *Take leave of each other. Come back to be present here.*

My friends were much engaged by the exercise and had a kaleidoscope of people to talk about—from a high-school volleyball coach to an esteemed professor, from a ten-year-old daughter to a venerable grandparent. To my surprise, I was drawn deeply into the exercise—when my first concern was to facilitate it for the rest—and had an amazing exchange with my deceased mother. A few highlights!

Mom was surprised that I recalled her on this occasion, protesting, "Spirituality? Why me?" Though happy to chat, she thought this was not the right topic. Another time, perhaps, on something she would know more about, like getting an infant to sleep through the night. She chided me for not calling up her sister, "a holy nun." I confessed that Aunt May had never occurred to me, though I agreed she likely was a saint. Now I was defending my choice of my mom to my mom. It ran along these lines:

"Well, I think you did a great job raising the nine of us (a tenth died in childhood) and of coping with all the problems we gave you—almost every imaginable one. You loved each of us in our own unique way, and let us know that we were cherished and much loved. And every child turned out okay. You held us together as a family and forged a bond that has stood the test of the years.

"You loved and supported our father through good and bad times, and ran the show by yourself when he was away so often on political business. Even in the worst of times, you never lost your sense of humor and joy about life. You were most kind to the poor in our neighborhood—and we had lots of them back then. In fact, you had great compassion for anyone in trouble.

"You steeped us in the Catholic faith, giving us a love for it, mostly by how you lived it. Everyone could tell that your faith was the anchor of your life. You seemed to have a palpable sense of God's presence in the everyday. Now that's spirituality at work!"

My mother was amazed—and a little flattered, I thought. Then she smiled and said, *"Well, if that's what you mean by spirituality, I suppose I'm entitled to be here."* We both laughed. *"Still,"* she said, *"you should talk to your aunt May, 'cause she really was very holy."* I promised I would sometime.

When I asked Mom for advice, she said, *"Well, in my time, we didn't talk about spirituality, but a lot about living our faith. So, you be fair and honest, and look out for people in need. Say your prayers every day. Enjoy your life with your family. And be sure to get to Mass on Sundays."* Ah, I knew that was coming.

SPIRITUALITY WITHOUT RELIGION—
BUT FOR HOW LONG?

This whole book is about spirituality. It draws out from the depths of Catholic Christianity how people might bring *life to faith* and *faith to life*. At its best, Catholicism doesn't *have* a spirituality, it *is* a spirituality. However, because spirituality permeates every aspect, it is another gift to *what makes us Catholic*. So, we review it and weave a summary in this closing chapter.

As the work of God's Spirit in people's lives, a comprehensive description of spirituality is impossible. The Spirit "blows where and as She will"—cannot be tied down (from John 3:8). My friend Janie grew up a devout Catholic but says she never experienced a spirituality until joining Alcoholics Anonymous. It's a wonderful sign of God's free Spirit at work that Twelve-Step programs are lending so many people a life-giving spirituality.

There are definitions of spirituality that never mention God, focusing only on the aspirations of the human spirit. For example, spirituality is "the diverse ways we answer the heart's longing to be connected with the largeness of life."[1] Or spirituality is "the experience of conscious involvement in the project of life integration through self-transcendence toward the ultimate value one perceives."[2]

Such descriptions make the valid point that spirituality is a universal of the human heart, far broader than any particular religious affiliation or confession of faith. Yet, they reflect only one side of the covenant. For the longings of our hearts are prompted and met by God, who comes to meet us in love. Spiritually, the initiative is always from God's Spirit who prompts our own.

My friend Janie says, "I wouldn't be *caught dead* in church now
. . . too much stuff I don't agree with." (I'm tempted to pull her leg
and say, "I bet you'll be buried from church—ah, 'caught dead'
there after all!" So many Christians come back to church in a
hearse.) Janie's comment reflects the strong sentiment now to set
spirituality apart from any particular religion. Whereas my mother would have thought of herself as religious but not spiritual, now
the situation is reversed. It's a cliché of the New Age to say, "Oh,
I'm spiritual but not religious." Perhaps both sentiments reflect
only half the story.

There are promising signs that lay Catholics are embracing their
call to holiness, a theme we return to below. So, people like my
mother not recognizing their spirituality is on the wane. What,
then, of spirituality apart from religion? Before dismissing the
Janies, religionists should confront what may lie beneath attempts
to wrench spirituality free of religion. The truth is that many people
find institutional religion oppressive whereas they experience spirituality as liberating. I have some sympathy for their sentiments.

Oftentimes, people need to separate spirituality from a personal
God or from organized religion, just for the sake of their souls.
Janie had a terrible time with Step Three in the Twelve Steps of
AA—"to turn my will and my life over to the care of God as I
understand him [*sic*]." Janie's problem was that her understanding
of God since childhood was of someone she would trust with
nothing. She first had to wrest her God representation away from
an abusive father. Not everyone has experienced the Transcendent
as a God of loving-kindness.

People can encounter the Church as stymieing their spiritual
lives, as controlling rather than facilitating their access to God. My

friend Barbara says she was reared to think that the priests were entirely in charge of God's presence and the Church the sole mediator of God's grace—all conditioned on its own rules and regulations. "But then, through my practice of yoga and transcendental meditation, I experienced the divine presence *within me.* Now, I didn't need the Church any longer. And what a liberation!"

As echoed throughout this work, each person is alive by God's Spirit and has constant access into the heart of the Divine. These are core convictions of Catholic Christianity, yet the Church that Barbara encountered gave her the opposite impression. So, when someone like her, conscious of deep spiritual hunger, turns away from the institutional church, it is reaping what it sowed.

So often, I find, it is *clericalism* that alienates people from the Church. This is the attitude that clergy are entitled to unquestioned authority in all matters of faith, that they control people's access to the divine and the divine mediation to people. Of course, clericalism is the antithesis of priesthood. A good priest companions people like a soul friend and serves the community's spiritual hungers through Word and Sacrament. Instead of "lording it over," the priest fosters the gifts of all to work well together—in "holy order."

Whatever the reason, the Church should feel confronted by people who leave it to find spiritual sustenance elsewhere. Surely their departure signals a failure in the Church's very reason for being. For what else is the purpose of organized religion, and certainly of Christianity, but to provide people with a community and a tradition of faith to nurture their spirituality? The whole Christian movement is first and foremost about bringing life to faith and faith to life.

Since ancient times, the work of the Church has been described as *cura animarum,* "the care of souls." I believe this still describes the Church's defining task in the world—fundamentally spiritual. Of course, we should understand "soul" as *the life of the whole person* (chapter 2), so "care of souls" is concerned for the social as well as the personal, for here as well as hereafter. Yet, the Church is not the Red Cross or another good social agency; its reason and way of caring for people is always by a spiritual path.

This book reflects the conviction that contemporary people can draw great spiritual nurture from an old religion like Catholic Christianity and by associating with its community of faith. I also resist the popular sentiment that is so favorable to spirituality but gives religion a bit of a bum rap. Although I have sympathy for people who turn away from institutional religion for their spiritual needs, I think their move is unwise and unlikely to stand the test of time. For religion and spirituality are two sides of the same coin, and they badly need each other.

Spirituality without deep roots in a religious tradition may not weather the storms of life. Trying to go it alone spiritually, without a faith community, seems foolhardy, even a bit of a contradiction. Life-giving spirituality is surely relational; remember, we are "made for each other." On the other hand, religion that does not nurture people's spirituality is as dead as a doornail.

FOR REFLECTION AND CONVERSATION

- What are your thoughts on the current divide between institutional religion and spirituality?

- Reflecting on your own "care of soul" over the years, how would you describe spirituality?

FROM THE STORY OF CHRISTIAN SPIRITUALITY: GIFTS FOR LIFE

A Trinitarian Description

Christian faith can foster a life-giving spirituality, and for sure, a relational one. Its conviction is that our very life shares in the relational life of God, which is why we're spiritual beings in the first place. When Christians say "God" we mean a Trinity of Loving Relationships, both within God's own self and always toward humankind. Let us reflect on what God as Triune might suggest for a description of Christian spirituality. At the outset we can make a summary point: *God as Trinity of Loving Relationships points to a spirituality of right and loving relationships for God's people.*

God as Creator is at least "personal" toward humankind. I say "at least" because God is more than a person like you or me, and yet is surely *as* personal as we—then infinitely more. So I can relate with God in the same way that I would relate with a person, and then as the grounding Presence in my life who ever regards me with unconditional love. I can converse with God by direct address and a listening heart. I can share my joys and sorrows, hopes and fears with God as with my most intimate Friend.

My personal God is present to me through life in the world and in the depths of my own heart—closer than my own heartbeat. I can express my *praise* and *thanksgiving* for God's creation and daily gifts, my *petition* for God's provident care and grace, *repentance* for my sins, asking mercy, and my *resolve,* by divine grace, to live as a faithful partner with God.

To echo the Bible's understanding, a spirituality involves *con-*

sciously living in right and loving relationship with God. This means recognizing God as the center of my life, making God the mooring that anchors everything else. It means allowing my God-consciousness to permeate every nook and cranny of daily living, being alert to God's presence in the world and within my own person, discerning and responding according to God's reign of love and freedom, peace and justice, holiness and wholeness of life for all.

God desires us to place God at the center of our lives, not because the divine ego craves human attention—ludicrous—but for our own good. We live most humanly by obeying that First Commandment. Note its biblical setting: "I am the Lord your God who brought you out of Egypt, that place of slavery. You shall not have others gods besides me" (Exodus 20:2–3). In effect, God is saying, I'm a God of freedom; I've set you free; now, to remain free, put me at the center of your life. This commandment, then, so fittingly placed first, is the clue to human freedom. Giving our lives over to God sets us free, whereas making anything else our god—fame or fortune, power or pleasure—will enslave us. God at the center keeps us free from every "place of slavery."

Then, our *right and loving relationship with God* must permeate all other relationships—*with self, others, and creation.* The measure of Christian spirituality will always be the life-giving quality of our relationships. There are spiritual traditions that focus exclusively on the individual's interior life. And Christian spirituality also aspires to a deep interiority—to intimacy with God and peace with oneself in the depths of the soul. But given the relationality of God, Christian spirituality demands right and loving relationships with all others as well.

This relational emphasis is writ even larger for Christians, because they try to imitate the spirituality of Jesus. The *way* of Jesus constitutes the Christian spiritual *path*. Here we need only summarize from previous chapters.

Jesus Christ is the ultimate divine outreach toward humankind and of us toward God; Jesus made flesh the loving relationship between God and humanity. As such, the historical Jesus models *the way* that Christians are to live their covenant. His living for God's reign and by its greatest commandment of radical love is ever the paradigm of Christian spirituality. The Beatitudes and subsequent Sermon on the Mount (see Matthew 5:1–7:29) epitomize the *pervading spirit* of Jesus' way of holiness.

In the Beatitudes, Jesus proposed holiness as trusting in God, opposing evil, living with compassion, doing justice, making peace, and putting God first at all costs. Then, in the Sermon on the Mount, Jesus called disciples to be light to the world and salt to the earth by obeying and teaching God's commandments, avoiding sin, being reconciled as needed, living faithful lives, turning the other cheek, going the extra mile, loving even enemies, caring for the needy, praying and fasting regularly, depending on providence instead of money, judging with kindness, and doing unto others as we would have them do to ourselves (the Golden Rule).

Beyond exemplar of human relationality, Jesus is also the Risen Christ, God's Anointed One. Through his life, death, and resurrection, Jesus Christ has irrevocably bonded God and humankind in right and loving relationship. For Christian faith, Jesus is the ultimate catalyst in history of God's grace, the One who both models *the way* and mediates the grace to follow it.

In gathering a community of disciples, Jesus also emphasized the relational core of Christian spirituality. We have already high-lighted the communal nature of Christian faith (chapters 4 and 6). How could it be otherwise, then, for Christian spirituality—the conscious living out of such faith?

For all the Church's sins and shortcomings, God usually works through it to sustain the spiritual journey of Christians. Here we find a home within God's family, a community of support and a life-giving tradition of spiritual wisdom. Christian spirituality is sustained through the relationships, word and sacrament of Christian community, a "body" of saints and sinners that stretches from Peter, Paul, and Mary to here, and into eternity.

The Church should never appear as a cozy members-only salva-tion club whose sole goal is to get individual souls to heaven. It must also be a sacrament of God's reign in the world. Christian spirituality calls the whole Church to help realize God's reign now. It is surely significant that the biblical understanding of *holiness* and of *justice* are the same: *right relationship with God, self, others, and creation.* Catholicism, at its best, encourages such relational holi-ness and the whole Church to exist "for the life of the world" (John 6:51).

And what of God's Spirit in spirituality, the Third Person of the Blessed Trinity? Since Augustine, a favorite old way of imagining the Trinity is as the Lover, the Beloved, and the Loving between them. The Spirit *is* the Loving Relationship within the Godhead, and thus God's loving relationship with and among people. In other words, the Spirit is God's Love at work in the world now. All right and loving relationships are empowered by the Spirit.

This is why Christian tradition understands the Spirit as the sanctifier of humankind, the One who actively inspires, sustains, and draws us into holiness of life. Spirituality as conscious relationship with God comes by divine initiative rather than by our own. And God's perennial outreach through our own hearts and everyday lives in the world is the work of God's Spirit. So, too, is the grace for us to respond.

How does this partnership between ourselves and God's Spirit work? We could simply refer to the relationship between grace and nature proposed in chapter 2—for grace is the Spirit at work in the world. However, let us recast it here in terms of spirituality.

God's Spirit is the abiding desire in God's heart for each and every person. This is why we have a natural affinity to respond to the Spirit's outreach. By divine design, God's desire for us finds a resonant desire in us for God, a grand simpatico between the divine and human. So, the *spirit* in *spirit*uality is both God's and our own; the Holy Spirit functions as God's desire for us and as our desire for God.

Although this perspective is very Christian, and my emphasis on desire has an Ignatian ring,[3] it describes the spiritual disposition of all humankind. God desires to draw every person into God's love, and every person is equally desired by God. The same is true from the human side. The desire that God's Spirit implants in every "deep heart's core" (Yeats) lends a yearning that only God can satisfy. Blaise Pascal described this inspiringly: "There is a God shaped hollow in the human heart that nothing else can fill." It would appear that the converse is also true—analogously: there is a human-shaped hollow in God's heart that nothing else can fill.

So, a Trinitarian description of spirituality might be: *consciously living in right and loving relationship with God, self, others, and creation after the way of Jesus Christ, empowered by the Spirit, in solidarity with*

278

a Christian community, and for the coming of God's reign in the world. When in a hurry, a more pithy description would be *faith at work.*

BAPTIZED TO BE HOLY

Jesus' promise to send the Holy Spirit was fulfilled at Pentecost, literally "fifty days" after the Resurrection. The small Christian community was gathered in an upper room in Jerusalem, about 120 women and men (Acts 1:15), including Mary, the mother of Jesus. Suddenly, "tongues as of fire came to rest on each one of them, and they were all filled with the Holy Spirit" (Acts 2:3–4). Note well that the Spirit descended upon and "filled" every disciple present, not just the leaders.

Then Peter preached the opening sermon of the young Church, urging listeners, "Change your lives and be baptized, every one of you, in the name of Jesus Christ for the forgiveness of your sins; and you, too, will receive the gift of the Holy Spirit" (Acts 2:38).

From that time onward, the first Christians viewed baptism as a call to transformation of life by the power of the Holy Spirit. They believed they were baptized into the "Body of Christ" to live as disciples of Jesus, to continue his mission in the world, and to be ever rising with the Risen One into new life. Those first disciples were convinced that baptism calls every Christian to holiness after *the way* of Jesus.

This inclusive sentiment continued throughout the first three centuries—that all Christians are equally called to bring *life to faith and faith to life.* There is no evidence that the vocation to holiness was exclusive to a few or to be ranked hierarchically, though both attitudes would emerge later. *All* Christians have this spiritual vocation by their baptism.

The profound care that the early Church took to prepare new converts through the Order of Catechumens reflected this radical understanding of baptism. The catechumenate was a rigorous process of intense socialization into Christian identity, often lasting as long as three years. Its emphasis was on *forming* and *transforming* people to become Christians, encouraging catechumens to abandon old sinful ways and readying them to embrace the full Christian life. Only after a makeover in lifestyle was there an intense period of *informing*—usually during Holy Week—in the creeds and core beliefs of Christian faith.

That the Roman Empire actively persecuted Christians and martyred thousands for their faith meant that would-be catechumens did not take the step lightly. Oftentimes, they were literally putting their lives on the line. Then, along came the emperor Constantine (d. 337), who granted toleration to Christians with the Edict of Milan (circa 313). Though not baptized until his deathbed, Constantine effectively made Christianity the official state religion. What a turnabout—from a persecuted minority to the driver's seat of the Roman Empire.

As one might expect, this change of fortune brought a huge influx of new Christians. The careful catechumenal process of conversion began to break down. When Constantine decreed that only Christians could become officers in the Roman army, guess what? Thousands of Roman soldiers suddenly became converts. Baptism shifted from a transformation of life to a cultural expectation.

There were more radical Christians who resisted the dangers they saw in the Church's new social privileges of compromising the life-transforming demands of the gospel. They insisted on living the full spiritual vocation of baptism. Out of this resistance, Christian monasticism was born. At first, it was not a distinctive or elite spirituality but simply a lay-led movement determined to take baptism seriously.

Saint Anthony of Egypt (d. 356) is considered the founder of Christian monasticism in that he wrote its first "rule" of life. So determined were the early monks and nuns to resist compromise, they reached beyond the normal demands of Christian faith to a life of heroic virtue. Monasticism became a severe asceticism, demanding that its men and women forgo spouse, family, and all worldly possessions. At first they lived as hermits. Then, as they formed into communities, *obedience* was added to *poverty* and *chastity* as the three *evangelical virtues* of Christian spirituality.

The Rule of Saint Benedict (written circa 530) regularized monastic life into communities of strict enclosure away from the world. According to the Benedictine charism, the monastic life is to worship together, to pray for God's reign in the world, and to labor in communal support. Later, the emperor Charlemagne decreed (circa 800) that monasteries should run schools for the whole citizenry, not just for their own recruits. This marked the beginning of universal education in the West.

The thirteenth century saw the emergence of the first great *mendicant* orders (literally, "licensed to beg"), the Franciscans and the Dominicans. They were modeled on their monastic predecessors and continued to live the three vows within communal life. However, they set aside strict cloister. Mendicants could move out into the world to take on public apostolates such as teaching, preaching, and caring for the poor.

In response to social and ecclesial upheavals, the sixteenth century brought forth more "modern" orders (like the Jesuits), possessed with even greater flexibility for ministry in the world and inspired more by active than by contemplative spiritualities. In the seventeenth and eighteenth centuries, and with an explosion in the nineteenth, myriad new religious orders and congregations of both men and women were founded.[4] These were all communal, vowed, and officially approved by some ecclesial authority to carry on the church's public apostolates.

An old Catholic joke has it that not even God knows exactly how many religious orders there are and certainly cannot remember all their identifying initials. Yet, the spirituality of each order had its own distinctive emphasis, its "charism." Thus, there are literally hundreds of Catholic spiritualities, differing however slightly. What an array of options for people to choose from, all of them thoroughly Christian and varying according to emphasis of virtue, or style of prayer, or form of service! And many can readily be combined according to preference.

So, the Rule of Benedict can help busy people to maintain perspective and sanctify their time.[5] The Exercises of Ignatius of Loyola can provide a prayerful approach to discernment and decision making. Mary Ward's counsels can encourage teachers to treat students with gentleness and respect. Catherine McCauley and her charism of mercy motivate care for the needy and hospitality toward all. Besides diverse charisms, the vowed orders provide myriad models of holiness for people to emulate. Who would not be inspired by Francis of Assisi (d. 1226) and his care for the poor or by Thérèse of Lisieux (d. 1897) and her efforts to do small things well.

In spite of this rich legacy, that the vowed life became *the* paradigm of Catholic spirituality had at least two drawbacks. First, it gave the impression that to really grow in Christian holiness requires renouncing all possessions, forgoing marriage and children, and relinquishing personal autonomy, when, in fact, a Jesus-like handling of possessions, intimacy, and freedom is also an eminent path to holiness of life.

Second, because the vast majority do not have a vocation to the vowed life, the attitude grew up among ordinary Catholics that they don't need to take seriously their baptismal call to holiness. They came to presume that spirituality is something for "the religious" (even the name is loaded!). And there was little encouragement of a "lay" spirituality—by and for laypeople. They could say a few prayers of petition to Mary or the saints and should "attend" Mass, though not as active participants. Beyond that, though, the spirituality business belonged to the elite. In effect, the vowed life made the "merely" baptized seem second class. This is why my mother was surprised to be called upon, readily deferring to her sister, the nun.

It was a spiritual watershed, then, when Vatican II roundly refuted both of these notions as false. Though it reaffirmed the legacy of the vowed life, as was most fitting, it called the Church back to a more inclusive spirituality—for everyone, everywhere, and all the time. Of course, this was less a development than a return to the sentiments of the first Christian communities. Essentially, the Council reclaimed a radical theology of baptism, and thus a spirituality that includes every Christian.

Vatican II also called Christians into partnership with modern society, declaring that "the Church and the World are mutually related."[6] For "the joys and the hopes, the griefs and the anxieties of the people of this age, especially those who are poor or in any way afflicted, these too are the joys and hopes, the griefs and anxieties of the followers of Christ."[7] Christian spirituality can and should be lived in the marketplace of life.

The Council made clear that baptism is the foundation of all Christian spirituality. Nothing more is needed. Even the title of chapter 5 of its Constitution on the Church, "The Call of the Whole Church to Holiness," summarized this growth in consciousness. Everyone is called because "[t]he Lord Jesus ... preached holiness of life to each and every one of His disciples, regardless of their situation."[8] In sum, the Council heralded a new day for an inclusive and life-centered spirituality.

DUSTING OFF SOME OLD CATEGORIES

In the history of Christian spirituality, there are a number of old couplets that often have been posed as rivals. With a bit of dusting off, a contemporary spirituality may find wisdom in a free-flow between them. They are: (1) kataphatic and apophatic; (2) contemplative and active; (3) vowed and lay.

Kataphatic and Apophatic. These strange-sounding old terms can still identify two distinctive approaches to spirituality and, perhaps, spiritual "types" of people. *Kataphatic* (literally, "with images") is a spirituality that readily sees signs of God's activity in creation and the everyday, in the midst of ordinary human experiences. There are people—maybe yourself among them—who have a keen sense of God's presence within and without, who have an aptitude for a spiritual consciousness in daily life. Ignatius of Loyola's "to see God in all things" is the epitome of a *kataphatic* spirituality.

Apophatic (literally, "without images"), sometimes called the negative way *(via negativa)*, refers to a spirituality that more keenly experiences the "absence" of God. Its prevailing sentiment is God's total transcendence and "otherness." In times of tragedy, many people have this experience—of feeling overwhelmed by the suffering and abandoned by God. For some, it can last for a significant period; the spiritual writers describe this as a "dark night of the soul." Even so, the apophatic sentiment is not a loss of faith but belief in spite of feeling the absence of God. Luther, who leaned toward the apophatic, called it hoping against hope.

Although Christian tradition in general has emphasized the transcendence of God, thus favoring the apophatic way, it seems that the more positive approach has lately come into favor. Contemporary spirituality seems more aware of the nearness of God, finding God in one's own heart and enmeshed in daily life. Certainly, New Age spirituality emphasizes experience as the locus of encounter with God.

Given the principle of sacramentality (chapter 3), Catholics can find the kataphatic way very congenial. On the other hand, the apophatic is needed to remind that God is ultimate Mystery and to help us hold the dividing line between faith and magic—the latter presumes that God can be placed at our beck and call. Better, then, to see the two approaches (kataphatic and apophatic) as partners rather than competitors, as varying from one experience to another, or as being dominant during different times in our lives. This side of eternity, most often we feel an absence in God's presence and a presence in God's absence.

Contemplative and Active. Although these approaches are often viewed as opposites, our own time needs wisdom from both. Given the dominance of monasticism in Christian spirituality, the Church presumed that the contemplative life of prayer and praising God was superior to an active life of service. But with the emergence of more active spiritual charisms, and the awareness that every Christian is called to holiness in the world, we can see that they are complementary and that both are much needed.

Contemplative and mystical practices can lend people a deep inner peace and encourage them to become pray-ers, reaching beyond saying prayers to be heart-to-heart with God. Contrary to an old stereotype, one's prayer life is not synonymous with spirituality. As reiterated many times, spirituality is *a person's whole way of life lived with a faith perspective;* spirituality is *faith at work.* Yet, a regular prayer life, both personal practices and communal worship, is an essential provision for the spiritual journey. Like any loving relationship, ours with God is deepened by good communication.

The old catechism defined prayer as "raising *the mind and heart* to God." It's still a good definition, but let's explicitly add *the body.* Many people spend time in some body-engaging prayer each day and find it beneficial for physical as well as spiritual health. With the rediscovery of traditional Christian approaches to prayer (e.g., *lectio divina,* prayer of the breath, centering prayer), coupled with openness to rich practices from other traditions (e.g., mindfulness, yoga as "prayer in motion"), every Christian can find styles to their liking.

Christian communal prayer is the liturgy of the Church, with its high point in sabbath worship of word and sacrament. For Catholic Christians, the Mass symbolically gathers up the divine-human partnership of the everyday and creates a heightened experience of "our lives to God, and God's life to us, for the life of the world."[9] When celebrated prayerfully and participatively by a faith community, Eucharist can be an apex of the divine-human partnership. In sum, every Christian needs meaningful ways of personal prayer and communal worship.

Having said this, we must then recognize that the vast majority of people lead busy lives in the world. Most need an active spirituality, one that permeates everything they do in the marketplace of life. This includes works of service motivated by Christian faith, and then putting one's spirituality to work in daily affairs—bringing a faith perspective to rearing children, daily work, making ends meet, negotiating relationships, doing business, reaching into every nook and cranny of life. So, while some people are more contemplative and others are more active, most need to unite both as "contemplatives in action."

Vowed and Lay. Lay Catholics have tended to place people in the vowed life on a pedestal. Although this needed a bit of debunking, the Church should always cherish the vowed religious life, encouraging it as a powerful symbol of God's reign in the world. At the same time, we must rejoice that a lay spirituality is emerging, warranted by no more than "the vows" of baptism. Previously, most writings on spirituality were by vowed religious and often did not engage the daily issues of laypeople. Now, a contemporary spiritual literature is emerging by and for the laity. It will advance the holiness of the whole Church.

Instead of forgoing sexual intimacy, laypeople are required to integrate it into their spirituality, often leading into the vocation of parenthood. There is little help in the traditional literature.

Written by celibates, much of it poses sexuality and spirituality as antagonists, whereas the laity must make them partners. And when approached from a faith perspective, no spiritual practice outranks child rearing as a means of holiness—for both parent and child.

Instead of eschewing possessions, laypeople face the task of acquiring, utilizing, and holding them responsibly, without undue attachment and using them to promote the values of God's reign. For example, the task of monitoring where retirement funds are invested takes a lot of time and vigilance, but this is an aspect of the layperson's commitment to justice.

Instead of obedience to a religious authority, the lay task is to bring one's faith to bear on every choice and decision. I have a friend who recently turned down a big job promotion because it would have meant uprooting his kids from school. This was a layperson's "obedience" in faith—spirituality at work.

"CATHOLIC" GIFTS FOR ALL

Some abiding aspects of Catholic spirituality have much to contribute to the present spiritual ferment. Six of the themes that echo throughout this book can help counterbalance some misleading New Age trends. For easy remembering, I describe each with a c word: I'm thinking of Catholicism's emphasis on *commitment,* on *community,* on *conversation,* on *compassion,* on *celebration,* and on lifelong *conversion.*

Commitment. Catholic Christianity emphasizes that spirituality ld permeate one's whole lifestyle, that it must be *lived* in and through the everyday. Reaching far beyond a pious sentiment or a good feeling between ourselves and God, Christian spirituality is realized through our lived commitments—the things we do. Again, it's our way of life in the world, our faith at work.

Of course, Catholics should beware of their favorite old heresy of "work's righteousness," as if we can save ourselves by our own good efforts. But remembering that we depend on God's grace, we can say that the core of Catholic spirituality is the commitment to integrate *faith* and *life* as *living faith*.

Community. Christian spirituality is relational through and through. So, its home base is a faith community. This contrasts with the go-it-alone and do-it-yourself attitudes of New Age spirituality. The Catholic sentiment is that we need a faith community to help us stay the course, partnership to nurture our holiness of life, and people to pray with us when we can and for us when we can't.

A vibrant faith community gives us past saints as inspiring models and present companions—*companis,* "to break bread with"—along the way. The community can provide guidance and encouragement, challenge and correction, and conversation to test discernment. A Christian faith community offers the resources of God's word through Scripture and Tradition, the sacraments as deepened experiences of God's presence and grace, and a rich legacy of spiritual wisdom. Why would anyone want to go it alone?

Conversation. Correlating with community, Catholic spirituality reflects a strong tradition of sharing the affairs of one's soul with other pilgrims. Such conversation is epitomized in the practice of having a soul friend, a spiritual companion with whom to reflect on the journey. A dialogue partner is particularly helpful for discerning the movements of the Spirit in everyday life and how to respond in faith. There is a great revival of "spiritual direction" in our time, marked by its extension among laypeople. Beyond this, there are many efforts now to invite people into "faith-sharing" conversations, nurturing a "base Christian community" of immediate and mutual support. The conviction is that people reflecting on their lives in the light of Christian faith and sharing this in conversation—real talking and real listening in mutual exchange—is a rich resource for the spiritual journey.

Compassion. The Hebrew scriptures use two most heartening terms to describe God: *hesed,* often translated as "loving-kindness," and *rachum,* meaning "compassion." Both words carry a sense of largess—that God goes the extra mile for everyone, with added favor toward those who need it most. God relates to us with great compassion. The spirituality of God's people should prompt them to do likewise.

Jesus described the forgiving father as "filled with compassion" for the returning prodigal (Luke 15:20). Even the most critical of scripture scholars agree that a defining commitment of Jesus' public life was compassion toward all.[10] Compassion, then, must be a central commitment of Christian spirituality. By contrast, the New Age literature contains little about care for the other in need; again, its focus is the self.

Remember, too, that Christian compassion cannot be limited to one-on-one charity; it demands social justice as well. Compassion as justice requires challenging the social structures that oppress or make people poor in the first place and helping to forge more liberating and just alternatives. The spirituality of Jesus' disciples should prompt compassion and liberation on every level—personal, interpersonal, and sociopolitical.

Celebration. It's not an accident that Catholics throw better parties than most; they have a theology and spirituality that encourage celebrating life. Catholics can joke about what they hold most sacred—what they would die for—presuming that God, too, has a sense of humor. One of the earliest childhood jokes I remember was about the terrible hangover Saint Joseph had the morning after the wedding feast of Cana. He called into the kitchen, "Jesus, please bring me a drink of water—but not the same again."

Catholic celebration includes a spirit of hope and optimism, of joy and good humor, of élan about life. It is encouraged by *a positive outlook* on the person (chapter 2), on life in the world (chapter 3), and on community (chapter 4). A recent conversation also brought home to me how a Catholic theology of grace—that we can rely on God's help to make our own best efforts—encourages celebration.

A neighbor on a plane ride was describing all the spiritual practices she follows daily, deep breathing, yoga, journaling, tai chi, and more. At first, I was in awe of her discipline, but I became uncomfortable because it seemed as if everything hung on her own efforts, making her spirituality terribly onerous. There was no note of celebration at all. When I inquired, "Do you ever ask for God's help in your efforts?" she was mystified by my question. As we talked on, I shared how I need God's help to have any good fun at all. Otherwise, too much would depend on me!

Catholic spirituality encourages celebration because *the spiritual journey is sustained by the Spirit.* Of course, it demands discipline and our own good efforts, but even these we muster by God's grace. If we thought everything depended on ourselves, we couldn't afford to celebrate; we'd be too busy pulling ourselves up by our bootstraps. But even in the midst of our sins and shortcomings, God's love endures, God's Spirit ever allures our hearts and graces us to respond. We can afford to celebrate.

Conversion as a Lifelong Journey into Holiness. For many people, "holiness" has had a bad press, stereotyped as nerdy, wimpy, or running-to-church-to-say-prayers. In contrast, recall again that the biblical image of holiness is interchangeable with justice—both being "right relationship" with God, self, others, and creation. So, the classic *holiness code* of the Hebrew scriptures, Leviticus 19, begins with "Be holy, for I, the Lord, your God, am holy" (19:2). Then, it summarizes holiness as works of justice and compassion, including the mandates "You shall love your neighbor as yourself" (v. 18) *and* "You shall love the stranger as yourself" (v. 34).

In presenting himself as the Good Shepherd, Jesus instructed disciples, "I came that you might have life, and have it to the full" (John 10:10). Christian *holiness is wholeness*—an invitation into fullness of life.[11] Holiness means integrity and life-integration, making one's whole way of life consistent with *the way* of Jesus. Such holiness takes a lifetime.

I once met someone who asked me, "Are you saved?" After recovering, I said, "Well, some days more than others! Are you?" The unhesitating response was, "Yes, in Kansas City on June 9, 1983, at a revival meeting." The person could tell me exactly when and where. Without judging her spirituality, I simply note that I found her question and claims very strange.

In Catholic tradition, conversion to Jesus is both personal and communal; I am responsible for my own soul-care and for my companions as well. And though Catholicism recognizes the possibility of a catalytic conversion experience—figuratively, being knocked off one's horse on the way to Damascus—the dominant tradition sees conversion as a lifelong process of fits and starts, needing daily renewal and reaching into eternity.

Life is like a great spiritual journey, coming forth from God at birth to return to God's eternal presence when "life is changed, not ended."[12] For Christians, the way to travel is *the way* of Jesus. The journey's horizon amounts to our fullest potential as human beings—to become more like our God. Thus, holiness is a journey into both humanization and divinization as the same affair.

Most of us experience spiritual highways and byways, free-wheeling downhill and backbreaking mountain ascents, swamp-lands and dry ground. But the old Catholic tradition is that we do it by small increments. Gradually and by God's grace we become converted, enlightened, and move toward perfection—though never complete this side of eternity. Even the greatest of saints were keenly aware of their sins. But God never gives up on any of us until we rest in God. How consoling for sinners like myself, Catholic and otherwise. Holiness as wholeness takes a lifetime, and God works with us all along the way.

FOR REFLECTION AND CONVERSATION

- What other gifts might Catholic Christianity contribute to a contemporary spirituality?

- What are your own reflections on the baptismal call to holiness?

SPIRITUAL PRACTICES:
SOME MORE FOR THE ROAD

All the practices suggested throughout *What Makes Us Catholic* can help nurture a spirituality for life. Now, I offer a few more to sustain the spiritual journey.

1. Recommit to Care of Soul

The empirical evidence is now beyond question: people who invest time and energy in their spirituality have a better chance of physical good health than those who don't. It's amazing to hear medical doctors encouraging soul care as an aspect of health care. Many encourage centering prayer to reduce stress and its related illnesses, meditation to aid recovery, focusing against deadly disease, and more.

This popular development reflects the conviction that runs throughout this book: that people are essentially spiritual beings. Thus, we live more humanly by tending to our spirituality. If we remember that the person is a unity and that "soul" means *the whole life of the whole person,* then old phrases about "losing" and "saving" one's soul might still reflect much wisdom.

The surest way to lose soul is to forget our spiritual nature— that we belong to God—and to allow any *thing* else to define who we are. In other words, loss of soul is typically to an idol. Of course, our modern idols seem more sophisticated, but they are nonetheless oppressive and destructive of soul. So, we commit idolatry to power or pleasure, fame or fortune, the company or collective; even the church can become an idol if we make it an end in itself. On the other hand, to keep God at the center of our lives is likely to save our souls.

I find that I need to commit to care of soul over and over again, at every turn and twist of the journey. By way of staying the course, this book has made some rather conservative proposals, drawn out from old traditions of Catholic Christianity. We can also be greatly enriched by contemporary spiritual consciousness.

For example, many authors urge ecological awareness as a spiritual discipline—both encountering God in nature and being its responsible stewards. Likewise, much life-giving spiritual literature draws explicitly upon women's experience; this seems "new" only because largely overlooked heretofore with the predominance of male authors. What a blessing that this lacuna is being filled. Not only women's but men's spirituality limps badly if it is unduly masculine in tone.

In a spirit of *catholicity* (chapter 8), the spiritual realm is ideal for Christians to appropriate the resources of other religious traditions. Our age is fortunate to have ready access to the treasuries of Buddhism, Hinduism, Islam, Judaism, the traditions of aboriginal peoples, and more. For example, many in the West are being greatly enriched by the spiritual practices of breath awareness and mindfulness from Buddhism.[13] Christians should be well grounded in their own spiritual traditions, thus having guidelines for what to borrow or pass by from others; that said, we are blessed to have the spiritual resources of humankind so readily available in our time.

2. Develop a Prayer Style to Your Liking

Ancient Christian wisdom advises that a pattern of daily prayer is essential to maintaining a God-consciousness about life and a commitment to live after *the way* of Jesus. Within Christian spiritualities, one finds myriad styles of prayer, from centered contemplation to chatty conversation, from formulas to free-for-alls, from the stations of the cross to making pilgrimage, from penance to festivals, and a thousand other possibilities.

Prayer can be done morning, noon, or night, for extended periods or in a passing moment, in an urban setting or amid the glories of nature, alone or with others, in every conceivable time and place. Jesus modeled this diversity in his prayer life, advising disciples to "pray always" (Luke 21:36).

I struggled for years with the direction of Ignatius of Loyola to set aside at least an hour a day for personal prayer and to follow a fairly set pattern. The problem was that oftentimes I couldn't do a full hour or just didn't find the Ignatian style conducive on a particular day. Then I would feel like a failure.

To my relief, I came upon the spiritual writings of Saint Alphonsus Liguori (d. 1787); his greatest reputation was as a moral theologian. In effect, Alphonsus advised praying *whenever* you find it convenient and *however* you find most conducive. That's what I've tried to do ever since—occasionally for an hour! The key is to develop a style of prayer that you enjoy—and thus will be likely to practice—and then a pattern for prayer times throughout the day and week.

3. Practice Spiritual Discernment

I could have suggested this practice in preceding chapters. I've kept it until now because it seems a fitting suggestion with which to conclude. Discernment is deliberate reflection on the events, circumstances, and people in our lives with a view to figuring out "what's what" before God, how to interpret the daily from a faith perspective. Discernment is "reading the signs" in our lives, confident that they can help us to discern God's desire for us and how to respond.

Saint Paul in 1 Corinthians 12:10 writes of evaluating "the spirits"—discerning between good and bad. Saint John advises, "Beloved, do not trust every spirit but test the spirits to see whether they belong to God" (1 John 4:1). Both are advising that we need to evaluate carefully the movements and sentiments of our own spirit for how the Spirit invites us.

Spiritual discernment, then, is a prayerful way to listen to the promptings of the Spirit through our own spirit, of uncovering the best desires of our hearts as a clue to God's desire for us as well. Discerning the divine promptings is especially wise when making life decisions, but it's also a good regular practice. We ever need discernment to bring *life to faith and faith to life.*

The Ignatian tradition of discernment is likely the best known. It emphasizes taking note of *consolation* and *desolation* as pointers in the right or wrong direction—respectively. For moments of significant life decisions, it also recommends having a soul friend for conversation. Whether done alone, with a partner, or in dialogue with a faith community, a step-by-step method can be very helpful. For example:

- Place yourself consciously in God's presence and ask for openness to whatever is most faithful to God's will—confident that God desires what is best for us.

- Focus on the particular issue at hand; assemble whatever data may be needed to make an informed and wise decision.

- Begin to recognize the different possibilities. Then, from a faith perspective make a list of pros and cons for each way of proceeding.

- Ask God to help you weigh the pros and cons of each possible response. This is not just a rational process; it should engage feelings, emotions, and intuitions as well.

- Notice which course of action seems wisest in faith and which most appeals, probing your own desires for their authenticity and integrity (here's where a soul friend is particularly needed).

- Make a decision, at first postponing action and observing your own spirit for sentiments of consolation or desolation. This does not mean "pleasant" or "unpleasant" feelings, but more a deep-down sense of peace or hesitancy about how to proceed. (Oftentimes, the best choice may be unpleasant but consoling in faith.)

- If consolation continues and the decision seems appropriate to God's reign, act on it.

FOR REFLECTION AND CONVERSATION

- What are the deepest desires of your own heart at this time? How might you evaluate them?

- Is there a decision about your spiritual journey that you would like to make and act upon? What is it? What grace will you ask of God?
- What stands out for you as most significant in *What Makes Us Cahtolic?*

NOTES

PREFACE

1. I know—this construct is grammatically incorrect, a plural referent to a singular pronoun. I take a dispensation, however, when it helps to avoid gender-exclusive language and the awkward "he or she," "his or hers." This adjustment has been endorsed by the U.S. National Council of Teachers of English; in fact, it marks a return to the practice of Elizabethan English. As Shakespeare prayed, "May God send everyone their heart's desire." Amen!

2. Lines from Yeats's poem "The Second Coming."

3. Angelo Roncalli (1881–1963), elected Pope John XXIII in 1958, became the most beloved pope of modern times. John was considered a compromise choice, and little was expected of him. Within six months he surprised the pundits by calling for an "ecumenical council," literally, a gathering of the world church. (There have been twenty-one such general councils, approximately one for each century of Christian history.) The complete reference for the version of the Vatican II documents that I use is Walter Abbott, ed., *The Documents of Vatican II* (New York: America Press, 1966); hereafter referred to as Abbott, *Documents*.

CHAPTER ONE

1. "Declaration on Non-Christian Religions," #4, in Abbott, *Documents*, 664–65.

2. For a review of our past sins of anti-semitism and of the work that remains to be done, see Mary Boys, *Has God Only One Blessing?* (New York: Paulist Press, 2000).

3. "Decree on Ecumenism," #22, in Abbott, *Documents*, 364.

4. I take this powerful phrase describing the work of Jesus in human history from a 1975 pastoral letter of Pope Paul VI entitled *On Evangelization in the Modern World* (Washington, DC: USCC, 1976).

5. "Constitution on Divine Revelation," #12, in Abbott, *Documents*, 121. This is why I refer to Scripture and Tradition as *media* of God's word; they are not *immediate* divine communications.

6. "Decree on Ecumenism," #11, in Abbott, *Documents,* 354.

7. The English edition of the *Catechism of the Catholic Church* was first published in 1994, with a second edition in 2000. Many publishers offer the official translation; I will refer to it throughout this book simply as the *Catechism.*

8. "Constitution on Divine Revelation," #15, in Abbott, *Documents,* 116. Emphasis added.

9. The technical name for the process of interpreting texts and symbols of meaning is *hermeneutics.* This very ancient art has received much attention and development among contemporary scholars.

10. David Tracy, *Plurality and Ambiguity* (San Francisco: Harper & Row, 1987), 12.

11. "Constitution on Divine Revelation," #8, in Abbott, *Documents,* 116. Emphasis added.

12. "Constitution on Divine Revelation," #8, in Abbott, *Documents,* 116.

13. Pope John Paul II, *On the Coming of the Third Millennium* (Washington, DC: USCC, 1994), #32.

14. Andrew Greeley, "It's Fun to Be Catholic," in *I Like Being Catholic,* edited by Michael Leach and Therese J. Borchard (New York: Doubleday, 2000), 5. Greeley has developed this thesis at length beginning with *The Catholic Myth: The Behavior and Beliefs of American Catholics* (New York: Simon & Schuster, 1990).

CHAPTER TWO

1. It seems that the Hebrew word *adam* is no longer well translated as "man" since it is a gender-inclusive term that literally means "person from the earth." See Phyllis Trible, *God and the Rhetoric of Sexuality* (Philadelphia: Fortress Press, 1978), ch. 4.

2. Saint Irenaeus, *Against the Heretics,* bk. 4, ch. 20, #7.

3. *Catechism,* #1934.

4. See Pope John XXIII's encyclical *Pacem in Terris,* in *The Gospel of Peace and Justice,* edited by Joseph Gremillion (Maryknoll, NY: Orbis Books, 1976), 203–6.

5. This does not deny the fact of psychopaths who are particularly prone to destructive behavior; the point is that we recognize psychopaths as mentally ill.

6. See the *Catechism,* #1707 and #2566.

7. See "Catalogue of Errors on Grace and Original Sin," in *The Church Teaches,* compiled by John Clarkson et al. (Rockford, IL: Tan Books, 1973), 156–57.

8. From translation by Richard A. Norris, in *The Christological Controversy* (Philadelphia: Fortress Press, 1980), 159.

9. Saint Athanasius, *On the Incarnation,* chapter 54.

CHAPTER THREE

1. Richard P. McBrien, *Catholicism,* rev. ed. (San Francisco: HarperSanFrancisco, 1994), 1196.

2. Rosemary Haughton, in Leach and Borchard, *I Like Being Catholic,* 43.

3. Gerard Manley Hopkins, *Poems and Prose* (London: David Campbell, 1995), 27.

4. *Catechism,* #311.

5. Patrick Kavanagh, "The Great Hunger," in *Collected Poems* (London: Martin, Brian, & O'Keeffe, 1972), 22.

6. Elizabeth Barrett Browning, *Aurora Leigh and Other Poems* (New York: Penguin, 1995), 232.

7. *Catechism*, #2705.

8. "Constitution on the Church," #11, in Abbott, *Documents*, 28.

9. I describe this dynamic of liturgy in detail in *Sharing Faith* (San Francisco: Harper & Row, 1991), ch. 12.

10. "Constitution on the Liturgy," #14, in Abbott, *Documents*, 144.

CHAPTER FOUR

1. "Decree on Ecumenism," #3, in Abbott, *Documents*, 345.

2. See the *Catechism*, #774–76.

3. Aquinas actually used the term *sign*, but his intent was closer to today's meaning of *symbol*.

4. Pope John Paul II, *On Evangelization in the Modern World*, #9 and #18.

5. "Constitution on the Liturgy," #14, in Abbott, *Documents*, 144.

CHAPTER FIVE

1. Patrick Kavanagh, "My Birthday, October 1935," in *The Complete Poems* (Newbridge, Ireland: Goldsmith Press, 1972), 24.

2. Saint Augustine, *The Confessions* (Garden City, NY: Doubleday, 1960), bk. 11, par. 14, 287.

3. Augustine, *Confessions*, bk. 11, par. 14, 291 and 293.

4. See Hans-Georg Gadamer, *Truth and Method* (New York: Crossroad, 1989), 277–80.

5. Langdon Gilkey, *Catholicism Confronts Modernity* (New York: Seabury Press, 1975), 17.

6. See "Constitution on Divine Revelation," #8, in Abbott, *Documents*, 116. Emphasis added.

7. "Constitution on Divine Revelation," #15, in Abbott, *Documents*, 116. Emphasis added.

8. "Constitution on Divine Revelation," #13, in Abbott, *Documents*, 121.

9. "Constitution on Divine Revelation," #22, in Abbott, *Documents*, 125.

10. "Constitution on Divine Revelation," #9 and #10, in Abbott, *Documents*, 117–18.

11. Richard P. McBrien, *Catholicism* (San Francisco: HarperSanFrancisco, 1994), 1189.

12. See "Constitution on the Church," #25, in Abbott, *Documents*, 47ff.

13. For a contemporary interpretation of Aquinas, see Yves Congar, "The Magisterium and Theologians," *Theology Digest* 25 (Spring 1971): 15–20.

14. "Church in the Modern World," #16, and "Religious Freedom," #3, in Abbott, *Documents*, 213, 681.

15. It is regrettable that the Rosary skipped over the public life of Jesus, going from the "finding in the temple" (fifth Joyful mystery) to the "agony in the garden" (first of the Sorrowful). Catholic Christians might have more appreciation for the historical Jesus, his values and commitments, if some of the mysteries meditated on his public ministry.

I can imagine a reconfiguration of the mysteries of the Rosary that would delete or combine five of the old and insert five new ones such as Jesus feeds the hungry, Jesus welcomes all people, Jesus calls women disciples, Jesus preaches the Great Commandment, and Jesus forgives sinners.

16. The *General Directory for Catechesis* (Washington, DC: USCC, 1997) uses this phrase repeatedly to emphasize adult faith education.

17. *Catechism*, #2705.

CHAPTER SIX

1. The texts of the New Testament make it clear that Jesus addressed God as "Father." It is also evident, however, that Jesus' sense of father included many characteristics that, even today, would be associated culturally with a mother. It certainly is true that by referring to God as father Jesus never intended to legitimate patriarchy or male superiority.

2. John Dominic Crossan, *The Historical Jesus* (San Francisco: HarperCollins, 1991), 263.

3. See "Women and Priestly Ministry," *Task Force of Catholic Biblical Association Catholic Biblical Quarterly* 41 (Oct. 1979): 222–30.

4. Thomas Aquinas, *Summa Theologica* Ia. 1.8.–2.

5. Vatican I, "Constitution on Faith," in *The Church Teaches* (Rockford, IL: Tan Books, 1973), 34. Emphasis added.

6. Gilkey, *Catholicism Confronts Modernity.*

7. See Elizabeth Johnson, *She Who Is* (New York: Crossroad, 1992), esp. chap. 8.

8. This was how the great theologian Saint Anselm (1033–1109) posed the question of what Jesus means for us: *Cur Deus home?* (Why did God become a person?).

9. Richard N. Norris, trans. and ed., *The Christological Controversy* (Philadelphia: Fortress Press, 1980), 159.

10. You can order the daily lectionary readings, month by month, from Novalis of Toronto (telephone: 800-387-7164).

CHAPTER SEVEN

1. This statement is from a document entitled *Justice in the World* that emerged from the Second General Synod of Catholic Bishops (1971). Found in Gremillion, *Gospel of Peace and Justice*, 514, 520. Emphasis added.

2. Walter Brueggemann, "Voices of the Night," in *To Act Justly, Love Tenderly, Walk Humbly* (New York: Paulist Press, 1986), 5.

3. See John R. Donahue, "Biblical Perspectives on Justice," in *The Faith That Does Justice*, edited by John C. Haughey (New York: Paulist Press, 1977).

4. "Justice in the World," in Gremillion, *Gospel of Peace and Justice*, 520. Emphasis added.

5. The Protestant theologian Walter Rauschenbusch (1861–1918) is considered the grandfather of the Social Gospel movement. See especially his *Christianity and the Social Crisis* (first published 1907).

6. U.S. Catholic Bishops, *The Challenge of Peace* (Boston: Daughters of St. Paul, 1983), 71.

7. "Justice in the World," in Gremillion, *Gospel of Peace and Justice*, 522.

8. Pope John Paul II, *On the Coming of the Third Millennium*, #32 and #33.
9. "Church in the Modern World," #29, in Abbott, *Documents*, 227–28.

CHAPTER EIGHT

1. "Decree on Ecumenism," #22, in Abbott, *Documents, 364*.
2. See, e.g., "Constitution on the Church," #8, in Abbott, *Documents*, 22–24.
3. Ignatius of Antioch, "Letter to the Smyrnaeans," ch. 8, v. 2.
4. Saint Cyril of Jerusalem, *Catechetical Lectures* (Washington, DC: Catholic University Press, 1970), 18:23.
5. Augustine wrote, "All good and true Christians should understand that truth, wherever they may find it, belongs to their God." *Teaching Christianity* (Hyde Park, NY: New City Press, 1996), 144.
6. *Catechism*, #811.
7. See Avery Dulles, *The Catholicity of the Church* (Oxford: Clarendon Press, 1985).
8. "Constitution on the Church," #26, and "Decree on Bishops," #11, in Abbott, *Documents, 50, 403*.
9. Walter Cardinal Kasper, "On the Church," *America*, April 23–30, 2001, 12.
10. Karl Rahner, *Concern for the Church* (New York: Crossroads, 1981), 110, 126–27.
11. "Constitution on the Church," #9 and #14, in Abbott, *Documents, 26, 32*.
12. "Church in the Modern World," #22, in Abbott, *Documents*, 220–21.
13. "Declaration on Non-Christian Religions," #1, in Abbott, *Documents, 661*.
14. These phrases are from the previously cited apostolic letter of Pope Paul VI entitled *On Evangelization in the Modern World*.
15. "Decree on the Missions," #1, in Abbott, *Documents, 598*.
16. "Declaration on Non-Christian Religions," #2, in Abbott, *Documents, 662–63*.
17. For a scholarly review of this issue and a creative response, see Roger Haight, *Jesus: Symbol of God* (Maryknoll, NY: Orbis Books, 2000), esp. ch. 14.
18. The most notorious recent case of such heresy was by the Jesuit priest Leonard Feeney (1897–1978). In 1953, Feeney was excommunicated and dismissed from the Jesuits for a too literal interpretation of "Outside of the Church there is no salvation."
19. "Constitution on the Church," #16, in Abbott, *Documents, 35*.
20. "Church in the Modern World," #22, in Abbott, *Documents, 221–22*. Emphasis added.
21. "Church in the Modern World," #42 and #44, in Abbott, *Documents, 242, 246*. To emphasize that inculturation should be a two-way exchange—between gospel and culture—some authors now prefer the term *interculturation*.

CHAPTER NINE

1. Parker Palmer, *The Courage to Teach* (San Francisco: Jossey-Bass, 1998), 5.
2. Sandra M. Schneider, "Religion and Spirituality: Strangers, Rivals, or Partners?" *The Santa Clara Lectures* (Santa Clara, CA) 6 (Feb. 2000): 4.
3. This is the spiritual charism that was crafted by St. Ignatius of Loyola (1491–1556), who also founded the Jesuit Order—formally known as The Society of Jesus (SJ).
4. Although overshadowed by men in the monastic movement, vowed communities of women are evident from the middle of the fourth century onward. When the men's

orders of active apostolate emerged in the thirteenth century, the effort to found similar orders of women was suppressed, precisely on the grounds that women should not take part in the public ministry of the Church. However, a women's movement called the Beguines—mostly in Flanders, northern Germany, and northern France—resisted this exclusion and carried on a kind of unofficial ministry and communal life. In the sixteenth and seventeenth centuries, great women leaders rose up, among them Angela Merici, founder of the Ursulines, and Mary Ward, founder of the Lorettos, who insisted on women's participation in the Church's ministry. At first, the church resisted, but eventually relented and gave official approval to women's religious orders with a public apostolate. Thereafter, an avalanche of such communities emerged and continue to make an extraordinary contribution to the Church's ministries, especially to education, health care, and social justice.

5. See Joan Chittister, *The Rule of Benedict: Insights for the Ages* (New York: Crossroads, 1992).

6. "Church in the Modern World," #40, in Abbott, *Documents,* 238.

7. "Church in the Modern World," #1, in Abbott, *Documents,* 199–200.

8. "Constitution on the Church," #39 in Abbott, *Documents,* 66.

9. This is my proposal for the dynamics of liturgy; see Groome, *Sharing Faith,* ch. 12.

10. The Jesus Seminar is a group of New Testament scholars who work together to portray the historical Jesus according to the canons of critical scholarship; they highlight *compassion* as the defining characteristic of his life. See, e.g., Marcus Borg, *Meeting Jesus Again for the First Time* (San Francisco: HarperSanFrancisco, 1994).

11. I borrow this phrase from the title of a book by Josef Goldbrunner, *Holiness Is Wholeness* (Notre Dame, IN: Univ. of Notre Dame Press, 1964).

12. This reference to death is from the Preface of the Mass of the Resurrection, Roman rite.

13. For a rich resource, see Thich Nhat Hanh, *Living Buddha, Living Christ* (New York: Riverhead, 1995).

INDEX

Abortion, 213, 227

Alcohol, 101, 130

Alphonsus Liguori, Saint, 296

Anthony of Egypt, Saint, 281

Anthropology, 44; Catholic, and free will, 62, 66–67

Apocalypse, 141

Apostles' Creed, 9, 53, 246

Aquinas, Saint Thomas, 57, 58, 86, 90, 120, 144, 155, 156–57, 191

Aristotle, 88, 113

Athanasius, Saint, 65, 198

Augustine, Saint, 11, 85, 112, 137, 142, 157, 246–47, 255, 277

Aurora Leigh (Barrett Browning), 94

Baltimore Catechism, 56

Baptism, 3–4, 9, 86, 117, 129, 130–31, 194–95, 242, 279–84, 287; "of desire," 256–57; Order of Catechumens and, 280

Beatitudes, 181, 276

Bible (scripture), 9; apocrypha, 14; approaching with critical appreciation and creative appropriation, 152–55; canon, 14, 146–47; ; compassion, 216; creation myths in, 50, 55, 83; cultures of origin and, 16; God's self-disclosure to Hebrews, 145–46; fundamentalism, 13–14,

148; honor as word of God, 151–52; interpret within the whole Christian community and in dialogue with the world, 155–58; interpretation, 14, 16–17, 18, 149–58; on justice, 215–22; *leb*, 193; *lectio divina*, practice of, 166–67, 286; New Testament, 13; Old Testament (Hebrew Bible), 13, 145–46; praying the New Testament, 201; revelation through, 148, 151–52; *Scriptura sola*, 147; story of the Fall, 55–56; study and religious education, 165–66; time as *kairos*, 141; Vatican II and access, 151–52; wisdom and, 192–94

Bishops Synod, 1971, 228–29

Boniface VIII, Pope, 256

Browning, Elizabeth Barrett, 94

Brueggemann, Walter, 216

Cain, question of, 110–11, 116

Calvin, John and Calvinism, 56–57, 58, 59, 117; *massa peccati*, 56–57

Catechism of the Catholic Church, The (1994), 15, 57, 91, 247

Catholic (small "c"), 10, 34, 157; five suggestions to foster world consciousness and faith, 252–57; historical notes, 243–49; horizons to be reached, 250–60; imagination for